TOUGH FAITH

JANET & CRAIG
PARSHALL

HARVEST HOUSE PUBLISHERS
Eugene, Oregon 97402

All Scripture quotations are taken from the New American Standard Bible, © 1960, 1962, 1963, 1968, 1971, 1972, 1973, 1975, 1977 by the Lockman Foundation. Used by permission.

Cover by Koechel Peterson & Associates, Minneapolis, Minnesota

TOUGH FAITH

Copyright © 1999 by Janet and Craig Parshall
Published by Harvest House Publishers
Eugene, Oregon 97402

Library of Congress Cataloging-in-Publication Data

Parshall, Janet, 1950–
    Tough faith / Janet and Craig Parshall.
        p.   cm.
    ISBN 1-56507-997-3
    1. United States—Religion—1960–   2. Christianity and culture—United
States.   3. Christian life—United States.   I. Parshall, Craig 1950–
    II. Title
BR526.P37   1999
277.3'0829—dc21   99-21977
                                                                             CIP

Printed in the United States of America.

99 00 01 02 03 04 / BC / 10 9 8 7 6 5 4 3 2 1

DEDICATION

To Vince, Margaret, and Barbara; to John, Charlie, Richard, and Gail; and to Sarah, Rebekah, Samuel, and Joseph. You who have shared your love and faith, and are our family and our future.

We offer this book in love to the Lord, Who remains ever faithful no matter how tough the times.

CONTENTS

The Good
Ship Millennium

Have you ever wondered what it would be like to gaze into a crystal ball and see exactly what the future holds? In the midst of millennium fever, it is interesting to hear what the modern-day crystal-ball gazers are saying. There is a consistent message from the prognosticators that all will be well. The electricity of happy optimism is in the air. In the words of Ralph Waldo Emerson, the 19th-century American idealist and philosopher, "Every day, in every way, man is getting better and better."

With all of this "good karma" floating around, with all of these "positive vibes" reverberating throughout our culture, why worry? Why not simply adopt the "Don't worry—be happy" philosophy, book a ticket on the good ship *Millennium*, and enjoy the ride?

Christians are in the unique and powerful position to ask an even more critical question: What if this new age of optimism does not take us to the promised destination? What if the future holds disaster for the self-assured, for those who place unlimited confidence in human technology, for those who depend on the innate goodness of human nature, and for those counting on the triumph of the global economy? In other words, what if the voyage of the 21st century begins looking more like the *Titanic* than the *Love Boat?*

The HMS *Titanic* serves as a modern-day parable of our journey into the future. That tragic voyage offers lessons for our age of self-confidence, technological arrogance, and prosperous self-indulgence. The sinking of that great ocean liner has held a fascination for every generation. Ever since the massive hull slipped under the icy waters of the north Atlantic in the early morning hours of April 14, 1912, it has kept a mysterious hold on us. The tragic voyage sparked a congressional inquiry, spawned several major films, and helped create countless books and articles. Historian Walter Lord described its sinking as the most important news story of the 20th century. In 1985, the imagination of the world was again ignited when the ship's eerie remains were discovered on the ocean floor.

Perhaps it was the terrible loss of life that grips us—1522 people dead. Perhaps it is the human drama of hundreds of passengers scrambling frantically for refuge on their sinking world—a world that had too little safety for too many people. Or perhaps the story haunts us because this magnificent ship was the product of an age that had become too impressed with its own technological prowess. It was the longest vessel that had ever been built—four city blocks—and was considered the world's largest, movable, man-made object. It had accommodations for 3500 passengers and an 860-person crew. Most importantly, it had been constructed with the greatest technical knowledge and workmanship the world had ever known. Its state-of-the-art bulkhead design was supposed to make it safe from any imaginable risk.

The lessons of the *Titanic* may well apply to the new millennium. In the case of that tragic ship, human ingenuity failed, an immovable iceberg and human error prevailed, and a monumental test of human character—and faith—began.

In many ways, the test that confronted those passengers in the short span of time it took the *Titanic* to sink may be the same kind of challenge that will face us. We are entering a time that will test the values we hold most dear and shake and sift us to the most basic elements of our faith. The rapidly failing ship forced its passengers to reveal their true character. In the same way, the new millennium may test the fiber of our faith like no other generation in recent history.

During the congressional hearings that were later held on the *Titanic* tragedy, J. Bruce Ismay, managing director of White Star Line and a First Class passenger on the ship the night it sank, testified that the ship could have withstood a direct frontal collision with an iceberg. But the catastrophes of life sometimes evade our most careful designs. Instead of a direct hit, the iceberg struck a glancing blow along the side of the ship, puncturing a number of small holes in several of the hull's compartments. Unfortunately, eight of the compartments began to fail. Two hours and 40 minutes later, the mighty *Titanic* slipped under the icy waters.

Let's consider the passengers of the *Titanic*. They came from every strata of society. The cheap lower decks (the "steerage," travelers in Third Class) were populated by immigrants and low-income laborers. Just a few decks above them, in First Class, there were staterooms and suites housing some of the most powerful and wealthiest people in the world.

As the ship began to sink, officers struggled to keep order amid the crowds that were surging around the lifeboats as they were being lowered. Crewmen yelled at the men to stand back and allow the women and children to get into the boats first. The first lifeboats launched carried only First Class ticket holders. Though the boats were only half-full, many of the passengers refused to go back and pick up those who were foundering in the sea. John

Jacob Astor, the richest man in the world, tried to make his way into a lifeboat reserved for women and children, but was forced back by a Second Officer who probably had made less in a year than Astor did in a day. Daniel Buckley also earned his enrollment in the annals of cowardice by disguising himself as a woman and attempting to sneak into a lifeboat. But courage and character also prevailed. Charles M. Hayes, president of the Grand Trunk Railway, was there. He went down with the ship. Benjamin Guggenheim and his manservant stood on deck in their formal evening attire, ready "to go down like gentlemen."

Amid the frantic crowds scrambling for safety, the Reverend John Harper, an evangelist from Scotland, gave away his own life jacket. A Second Class passenger, he had brought no financial fortune or social prestige to the *Titanic*. Instead, Harper was on his way to America to preach the gospel at the famed Moody Memorial Church, as he had done the year before. This pastor from Glasgow calmly, resolutely, spent his last hours urging others to believe in the Lord Jesus Christ.

Harper's illustration of tough faith is a perfect picture of what is needed for these perilous times. His mission did not change with his circumstances. He had the same faith as the ship went down as he'd had during the quiet day of smooth sailing.

The question we must each ask ourselves is simple: "Had I been on board, how would I have responded?" "And if the coming millennium brings trial and tribulation for the Church, how will I react?"

Be warned: These types of questions run counter to the happy hedonism and empty optimism of our present age. In the first half of this century, two world wars and countless human atrocities seemed to have proven idealists like Emerson wrong. Human beings, and their world, seemed as greedy, power-hungry, and destructive as ever. But then things seemed to change. The Berlin Wall came down. Most of us remember the pictures of East Berliners joyously swinging sledgehammers at the crumbling wall, a symbol of tyranny since it had been erected. Then the entire communist empire collapsed. Democracy blossomed everywhere.

America's financial prosperity was on a perpetual upswing. We had finally begun to put the political nightmares of the Vietnam War and the first forced resignation of an American president (Nixon) behind us. We were told during a presidential election that "it's the economy, stupid," which revealed our emphasis on financial stability. Judging by the election results, vast numbers of Americans agreed. People were feeling more secure. We had gotten our hostages back from Iran. The United States won seemingly effortless victories in two straight military engagements—one in Grenada, the other in the Persian Gulf. By the 1990s, we could see the shining horizon of the new century stretched before us. Our politicians tell us we are building a grand "bridge to the 21st century." It is as if the coming millennium is a kind of Emerald City, and all we have to do is find the yellow-brick road.

Scientists tell us that, at long last, they have the technology to maximize longevity and health. Medical researchers announce that they are within just a few years of being able to "grow" many of the human body's most intricate and essential organs. They may even be able to regenerate damaged spinal cord nerves. Dozens of bio-medical companies have already raised about two-and-one-half billion dollars of investment capital to pursue this lucrative new industry.

According to the editors of *Life* magazine:

> We are about to enter the millennium of miracles. If a person cuts off his hand while fixing a lawnmower, doctors will be able to grow him a new one. Houses and cars will be made of materials that can fix themselves when damaged. There will be a white powdered food that is 90 percent protein and can be made to taste like almost anything. These predictions may sound bold, but in truth they're pretty conservative.[1]

Such predictions are actually based on innovations currently in place, like the day when computers can begin redesigning themselves on an ongoing basis to become smarter and more efficient, and the need for human programmers and designers will slowly become a thing of the past. We are already at the stage where supercomputers are capable of performing incredibly complex tasks with breathtaking speed. Silicon Graphics, Inc., a computer company that builds mega-computers for U.S. government nuclear weapons analysts at Los Alamos, claims that its "Blue Mountain" computer can run more than three trillion calculations per second. IBM's "Pacific Blue" computer can do nearly four trillion calculations in a single second.

Considering these innovations, together with the human urge for longer and healthier life, rebuilding the human body may become as popular and easy in the next century as restoring an antique car was in this century. And with limitless artificial intelligence of self-teaching computers at our disposal, technological breakthroughs will increase at a breathtaking pace.

Meanwhile, experts in the social sciences tell us that we are now capable of minimizing (or even eliminating) conflict through new forms of international cooperation. Paul Hoffman, former chair of Amnesty International-USA predicts: "The next century is likely to see the flowering of an even more vibrant and powerful international human rights movement. Just as the economies of the world have been affected by globalization, human rights struggles cannot be confined within national borders any longer."[2] In fact, as we approach the brink of the next century, a monumentally significant step was taken by the creation of a new "world court." The United Nations Secretary General Kofi Annan has boldly declared that this international tribunal is a "gift of hope to future generations and a giant step forward in the march toward universal human rights and the rule of law."

Financial wizards inform us that we will enjoy prosperity as a result of the opening of world markets. Many financial consultants are predicting an economic boom, including sky high jumps on Wall Street that will continue at least until the year 2009. And in the field of religion, gurus advise that we can achieve never-before-realized inner harmony through new forms of spiritual awareness. Books like *New Thought for a New Millennium* are proclaiming the creation of a new citizenry on the planet Earth: the species of the "possible human." They would have us believe that the 21st century holds the promise for the utopia we have all been hoping and dreaming for. It would seem we can achieve the perfect life by simply tapping into the limitless spiritual energy of our own human potential.

Maybe all those things will occur. Or maybe those happy pictures of the future are dangerously false, lulling us to sleep when we should be most vigilant. This book offers a different view of the future. In it, you will be exposed to the social, moral, and spiritual hurricane that the coming age may bring. It is about the dark night of the soul that could confront us, as it confronted John Harper.

How will the faith of the Christian Church be tested in the decades to come? How will each of us handle those crisis points, both personal and national, when they come crashing into our lives like the unforgiving face of some great iceberg? Will we scramble over others in an effort at simple self-preservation? Or will we boldly speak the truth, trusting God and leaving behind a legacy of faith triumphant?

This book is about the voyage of the future and the tough faith that will be needed to survive it. We hope it will cause you to pause and reflect on the perils ahead. It is our prayer that we will measure our conduct against the Word of God, then prepare, through God's empowerment, to live courageously for Him as we race into the uncertainties of tomorrow.

The Good Ship Millennium's great horn is blasting. The last passengers are scurrying up the gangplank. The voyage into the future is about to begin.

Part One

❦

Doctrine and Deception

❦

"Finding Faith in Christ only requires casting off false interpretations."
—Leo Tolstoy

"We spoke about the weather, calmness of the sea; the clearness; about the time we should be getting up toward the vicinity of the ice and how we should recognize it if we should see it...."
—Charles H. Lightoller, second officer of the *Titanic*, on his conversation with the ship's captain

"God himself couldn't sink this ship."
—A deckhand helping Mrs. Albert Caldwell onto the *Titanic*, April 10, 1912

CHAPTER ONE

The Mind of Man
and the New Altars

The 20th century has often been described in terms of several unifying themes. For instance, a popular philosophy series has labeled our century as "the age of analysis." This describes the tendency of modern society to try to evaluate with scientific precision all corners of the universe, all questions of life. On the other hand, the poet W.H. Auden has described ours as "the age of anxiety." Perhaps both are correct.

Those two labels, in fact, accurately describe our current dilemma. The human race has engaged in a great intellectual search into the depths of space and into the innermost workings of subatomic particles, yet at the end of the search there is a nagging

17

anxiety that we have missed the most important question of all: *Who are we as a human race, and why are we here?*

In the search for answers, modern men and women have erected new idols. These do not bear the images of beasts or ancient gods, as the Apostle Paul confronted in his missionary journeys, but they are idols nonetheless. If we are going to be effective missionaries to the urban and suburban tribes of the 21st century, we will have to recognize these idols. The Christian Church needs to expose them and point out that they are but images with feet of clay. These new idols cannot provide the ultimate answers to life.

At Mount Sinai when God commanded His people to "have no other gods before me" (Exodus 20:3), He did not limit His commandment just to calves made of gold. Anything that receives our absolute and total devotion has displaced the God of Abraham, Isaac, and Jacob. Yet one of the great idols of the 20th century has been the worship of the "scientific method" as the guide to all truth. This involves the idea of learning about our world through careful observation, then trying to explain what we observe by testing a hypothesis through controlled experimentation. This system of knowledge has been around in some form or another for thousands of years, but it has come into its own within the last 500 years. Within the last century, science has become the preeminent method by which civilized people view their world, attempt to answer the great questions, and try to solve the problems of everyday living.

As believers, we know the idea of science is not inconsistent with the God of the Bible. Science is possible because God gave us the ability to reason and draw certain conclusions from what we observe. Science is possible because we live in a universe that operates on the basis of certain laws of nature and physics—laws our God established when He created our world according to His orderly design. Science begins with the idea that these laws can be discovered and utilized. It is only when science asks us for our absolute trust or pretends that it can give us absolute truth that we run into problems.

If you think this issue does not involve you or your family, think again. When your child comes home from biology class and tells you about the evolutionary origins of life, when a purely biological explanation of conception, birth, and abortion are given to your child in a sex education class, and when your co-worker explains that science has proven "miracles do not happen," you'll want to know how to respond.

The Worship of Science

It is no wonder science has attracted increasing numbers of faithful worshipers. After all, it has brought us, within the space of just a few decades, both the splitting of the atom and the creation of plastics, two of the greatest achievements of the last 1000 years. But recently science has been expanded beyond its logical scope. It now lays claim to being the primary source of wisdom and knowledge. One of the best illustrations of how the scientific method has slowly evolved into an unabashed worship is the amazing statement of Sir Brian Pippard, a physicist who claims the scientist "is right to despise dogmas about God that imply a God whose grandeur does not match up to the grandeur of the universe he knows."[1]

Translated, this means that science must reject statements about who God is when those statements do not match up with what the scientific method tells us about the universe. In other words, the wisdom of mankind is greater than the wisdom of God. Science has made an objective observation about the "grandeur" of the universe, and God must be measured by that standard.

Yet science has no measurement for "grandeur." And Pippard's statement tells us nothing about science, only about the author's wholly personal (and quite emotional) feelings about what he sees through his telescope. He must feel a kind of grandeur when he studies the vast size and complexity of the universe, and he apparently feels that a God who does not measure up to his idea of beauty, vastness, and complexity is no real God at all.

Thus what Pippard has done is what much of modern intellectualism has done. Science becomes a kind of schoolyard bully, and we Christians are beaten-up with scientific rationalism if we don't share scientists' views, or if our God doesn't fit with their emotional response. Pippard, like many scientific rationalists, commits the fallacy of pretending that science is capable of addressing fully and completely what the universe tells us about God.

Psalm 19:1 tells us that "the heavens are telling of the glory of God; and their expanse is declaring the work of His hands." This means that there is a general revelation about God through His creation, but it does not mean that everyone will be able to appreciate it. Psalm 14:1 says that "the fool has said in his heart, 'There is no God.'" The hardened atheist has already excluded God from the heavens before looking through his telescope. Is it any wonder the skeptical scientist does not find God in the created grandeur of the universe?

The 20th century has erred in failing to understand the innate limits of science. Even physicist Stephen Hawkins has noted that questions raised by science about the nature of matter and the origins of the universe naturally lead to the greatest of all questions: "Why are we here?" He admits, candidly, that the issue of God's existence is obviously involved in that question.[2] But like any good bond-servant of science, Hawkins believes that science ultimately holds the potential for answering that kind of question as well. When science can answer that, he says, it will represent the ultimate triumph of human reason.

Perhaps scientists like Hawkins need to be reminded of the scandal surrounding Piltdown Man. Some 80 years ago, two British geologists discovered the jawbone of a primate and a human skull in close proximity in a quarry in Southern England. This discovery was later codified into the name *Eoanthropus dawsoni* (nicknamed Piltdown Man), and was heralded as the missing evolutionary link. Some 500 scientific papers were published about this great archaeological find. It was not until the 1950s that it was finally concluded the bone fragments had been juxta-positioned to create a hoax of enormous proportions. The bones were, in fact, what they first appeared to be—a human skull buried in the ground next to an ape's jawbone. The proevolution presup-positions of the scientists who analyzed those bone fragments had fatally obscured their objectivity.[3]

Paul Harvey is one of the world's best-known radio commen-tators, and one of Janet's earliest role models in broadcasting. Paul has kept files over his long broadcasting career of many trends, one of which is the radical vacillation of medical science. For example, his chronology of salt intake shows:

1950 — salt is determined to cause hypertension

1960 — salt is determined not to cause hypertension

1970 — salt is determined to cause hypertension

1980 — salt is determined to, in fact, relieve hypertension

1998 — the AMA *Journal* evaluated 114 studies on salt and concluded that it does not affect hypertension either way.[4]

The point of this is not to diminish true science as we enter the new millennium, but to remind us that science, like all knowl-edge, is a gift from God. Properly understood and applied within its true scope, science is a blessing from the Creator who formed the heavens and the earth from a position of perfect knowledge and understanding. When it is viewed as the "tree of all knowl-edge" however, it becomes intellectual idolatry. This in turn leads to what is soundly condemned in Romans 1:25—the worship of the creation rather than the Creator.

The split between Christianity and science is often traced back to the dispute between Galileo and the Catholic Church in the 17th century. Galileo had come to conclude that the earth was not the center of the universe—a position at odds with the flawed theology of the medieval Church. The Bible makes no astronomical claim of that sort, but the Roman Catholic Church had adopted an earth-centered cosmology. It forced Galileo to formally recant his controversial findings and placed him under house arrest.

Today, some 300 years later, we are entering a new century that promises to create a bizarre twist on the Galileo story. We are seeing the origin of the "reverse Galileo effect." Scientists and other intellectual leaders of our day are being stripped of their academic authority when their conclusions take human reason out of the center of the universe and replace it with God.

Dean Kenyon was a biology professor at San Francisco State University, a world authority on chemical evolutionary theory and on the scientific study of the origin of life, and the coauthor, in 1969, of a book that gave one of the most persuasive arguments on record for how living cells may have organized themselves out of the supposed primordial muck and mire mega-millions of years ago. But in the 1970s, Kenyon started seeing flaws in his own theorems. His lab work indicated that simple chemicals could not arrange themselves into the complicated forms of DNA molecules necessary for life without intelligent intervention from "outside" the actual experiment.

By the 1980s, Doctor Kenyon had come to conclude that DNA suggests a guiding kind of intelligence, outside the natural order of things, would have been necessary in order to adequately explain the origins of life on earth. In the fall of 1993, Kenyon started raising these kinds of possibilities in his biology classes. He began teaching classical evolutionary theory as well as the evidence that tended to disprove evolution. Soon the chairman of his department demanded that Kenyon "teach the dominant scientific view" of the origins of life. Further, he was forbidden from teaching anything resembling an argument for "special creation on a young earth." The dispute broke into a full-fledged academic battle between Kenyon and his supporters (including the American Association of University Professors) and the department chairman and the academic dean of the university, who decided that Kenyon needed reining in. The result? Kenyon was removed from teaching his introductory biology classes.[5]

Science teachers in public schools are continually pressured into placing an emphasis on evolution in their classes. The National Academy of Sciences has released a school guide that urges teachers to present the theory of evolution as the "most important concept in modern biology," and to exclude any teachings about creationism.[6] The 140-page booklet entitled "Teaching Evolution and the Nature of Science," which makes a direct attack on "creation science," is being distributed to state science supervisors and 2000 biology teachers around the country. Meanwhile, scientists are coming to the realization that science will be unable to supercede traditional religious beliefs. Thus, a new kind of merger is occurring between the two. This is the new face of the future debate between the scientific method and the theological approach to life as we approach the 21st century.

In Berkeley, California, 27 of the world's top scientists met in June 1998, at a conference dubbed "Science and the Spiritual Quest." The one-and-a-half million-dollar project was sponsored by the John Templeton Foundation, and its purpose was to discuss how these scientists (each of them at the top rung of their disciplines) reconciled science with their spiritual beliefs. The requirement for entrance to the conference was a belief in a god of some kind. If that conference is a good predictor for the coming millennial battle between faith and science, then the "reverse Galileo effect" will continue for some time. According to W. Mark Richardson, an Episcopal priest from the Graduate Theological Union that helped establish the conference, "religious fundamentalists" were specifically excluded from the conference, implying that men and women who believe in *sola scriptura* are no longer bona fide members of the faith community.

Inside the conference center, untainted by the presence of scientists who take both science and the Bible seriously, presenters discussed such things as how humanoid robots will soon be able to illuminate the mystery of Christ's resurrection. Another speaker, an Anglican priest and a biochemist, compared the Bible to scientific theories—finding it "alive" enough to be applied to the discoveries of life, but always susceptible to radical new interpretations and never presenting an unchanging truth.

The Worship of Technologies

There is an ever-increasing group of "futurists" who believe that man can, by applying his intellect to the new technologies, create his own future free of the old superstitions of religious belief. For example, Alvin Toffler (mentor of former House Speaker Newt Gingrich) in his book *The Third Wave*, predicted our ability to create a bright and bold new future. But what are the stumbling blocks? In Toffler's view, which is shared by most futurists, religious fundamentalists (he named Billy Graham) will pose the biggest threat to our future progress. Such Christians could be the new "Ayatollahs" of an American theocracy that will make us look like another Iran, according to Toffler.

Similarly, a grass-roots movement of political liberals, meeting shortly before the fall of the Iron Curtain, explored how to create world peace. They identified the *real* enemies of peace as those who held to rigid religious ideologies. The two of us had a chance to sit in on some of their conferences. The bigotry and hatred toward believers of Scripture was palpable. It was chilling to see how easily conservative Christians could be demonized. Imagine how quickly we could become the enemies of international peace when the world appears to be on the brink of nuclear war—and Bible-believing Christians are the only ones refusing to bow down to the idol of internationalism while all others are crying "peace, peace."

People of faith are viewed as kill-joys of progress. Progress, we are told, is the birthright of the thoroughly modern age of science and technology. Faith in human progress is reasonable, while faith in a "medieval" God, the argument goes, consigns us to forever stalk the stone age of ignorance, poverty, and unenlightenment. Here, the story of the *Titanic* is illustrative. One of its most telling messages is that disaster is inevitable when we place absolute faith in any human system or technology. During the congressional hearings that were held by Senator William Alden Smith, the failings of such human systems became powerfully apparent.

One sailor, Frederick Fleet, who was on lookout the night of the disaster, was called as a witness. He shocked the select subcommittee when he explained how the binoculars, with which he was equipped on the first leg of the trip, had disappeared. He did not have them during the second, fateful phase of the voyage. Here's how the follow-up questions and answers went:

> *Senator Smith:* Suppose you had the glasses…could you have seen this black object [the iceberg] at a greater distance?
>
> *Mr. Fleet:* We could have seen it a bit sooner.
>
> *Senator Smith:* How much sooner?
>
> *Mr. Fleet:* Well, enough to get out of the way….

As we read this testimony, it becomes almost unimaginable to us that such a small, routine mistake like misplacing a single pair of binoculars could have cost the lives of 1500 human beings.

In the three-quarters of a century since the *Titanic*, human ingenuity and technology have penetrated the cold void of outer space. Space travel has become commonplace, so that the reentry and landing of our space shuttles takes on the look of an airliner coming in after a short jaunt from Cleveland or Chicago. What has not changed is the lesson that the *Titanic* taught us about the failure of human systems. As a reminder, this lesson had to be learned again on January 28, 1986. The space shuttle Challenger was only into its flight for 73 seconds when it exploded in the brilliant blue of the Florida sky, killing all seven crew members. It was later learned the disaster was caused by a small O-ring that failed, permitting the escape of fuel, which was then ignited by the heat of the jet engines.

When will we learn that we should have absolute faith only in the omniscience of God? And when will we learn that no matter how refined the science and technologies of the 21st century become, there is "nothing new under the sun." Human failings, whether by ignorance, negligence, or willful sin, are inevitable. We must ensure that the Church holds to the eternal truths that endure, and not simply lend its worship to the siren-like cries of innovation and scientific advance. While we can (and should) praise God for the blessings of technology and the increasingly sophisticated and complex accomplishments of mankind, we must not stake our future on them.

Christians must speak prophetically to a lost world about the limits of human reason. We must intelligently but persistently warn fellow travelers in the next century not to look to the intellect of mankind or the promises of science to guarantee a safe, secure, and bountiful future. To bank our entire future on the promises of science is to enslave ourselves to those catastrophes that will inevitably come when the binoculars are misplaced, the O-ring fails, or the "perfectly planned" technology meets the hard, flinty face of the horrible and the unexpected.

This is not a popular message because science has racked up an impressive list of accomplishments in the last century. More importantly, scientific advances have created comfort and convenience for us all. But to avoid sharing this warning is to accommodate one of the greatest and most effective lies of Satan, the evil one: "Your eyes will be opened, and you will be like God."

The Worship of Strange New Spirits

The 21st century will present a devastating intellectual challenge to those Christians who cannot recognize the signposts of false ideas. To do so is to fall into one of two traps. Either we will fall prey to false ideas that are contrary to Scripture or we will be woefully ignorant of how to handle those concepts when they arise during our attempts to effectively share the gospel with others.

In the last section, we saw one extreme on the spectrum of ideas—the tendency that 21st century folks will have to rely on a pure form of scientific rationalism to give them the answers of life. There is an equally disastrous tendency at the other end of the spectrum as well.

So while it is a mistake to look for all answers in science, it is just as dangerous to look for all answers in mysticism. This is not an esoteric problem, but one that has seeped into every aspect of our music, art, and cinema, and has influenced the way a lot of us talk and think about Christianity.

Mysticism has a long history in the world of ideas and should raise major objections from any Christian who is able to recognize it. Suppose you are good friends with a married couple who spend their time as adventurers. They are the kind of folks who sail around the world, go deep-sea diving for buried treasure, and explore undiscovered geography in far-flung parts of the globe. You always look forward to your next gathering with them because they tell such amazing stories. They are quite articulate, and their tales are wonderfully descriptive and lively. In fact, when the night is over, you leave feeling as if you had actually been with them on their last great adventure. One day they return after having been away for a considerable period of time, but where you do not know. You drop over at their home with great anticipation, sit down across the kitchen table from them, and ask them with great excitement to tell you about their recent travels.

"Well," they begin, "we have made the most incredible discovery of our lives. In fact, it may be the most important discovery in the history of the human race." You are taken aback for a second, then press on. You begin asking a flood of questions, such as the location of their travels, what they saw, and the details about their great discovery. But they only smile. You ask more details: how long it took for them to get there, was it by boat or plane, and was it a place, a person, or a thing they discovered. But they only smile serenely and shake their heads.

They finally say, "We experienced the most important thing in the world. But, unfortunately, we cannot really describe it. In fact, it is the very greatness of the experience that so overwhelms us we cannot really tell you about it." Needless to say, your night with them is shorter than usual. You leave feeling confused about their story. They are nice people, and good friends, and they sounded sincere so you would like to believe them. But you really don't know what it is that you are supposed to believe. They have been unable to give you what the newspaper reporter calls the "five W's:" *who* did *what, where* did they do it, *when* did they do it, and *why?* In the end, you begin questioning the credibility of these folks and wonder if they had another motivation behind their silence.

You have just experienced a kind of mysticism. It is the worldview that claims to have encountered God (or some other great spiritual reality), but participants cannot describe what it means, what He is like, or what our response to Him ought to be. The first principle of mysticism is that it is based on a religious experience that defies description.

Of course, if someone tried to use mysticism in areas other than theology, the failure of that belief system would become apparent. For example, mysticism does not work as a reason why you cannot describe a certain piece of geography. We have a common core of experience with different locations and places—perhaps not the exact place, but close enough to understand what the other person is talking about when they describe a strange and remote kind of city, forest, or waterfall. Besides, matters of geography, like other tangible things in life, are capable of being described and understood in common language. It's hard to conceive of any place that would totally defy any attempt to describe it.

We would never let our explorer friends get off the hook with the excuse of mysticism. But the spiritual geography of God is something different. We might be willing to give the religious adventurer a great deal more leeway. After all, we do not all have the same kind of core of experience with God. He is infinite; we are finite. Perhaps we have to allow for a variety of expressions about the experiences human beings have with Him. God is not physical, so we may be willing to concede that He can't be adequately described, let alone explained, the same way we describe a trip abroad. In fact, we might even conclude that if we could describe Him, then He could not really be God. But if Christians follow this line of reasoning they have already fallen into the dark, murky, swirling pool of mysticism. The ultimate evil of that philosophy is the denial that anything objectively truthful can ever be said about God. As Christians, we know this is false.

First, we worship a "God who is there," as Francis Schaeffer once described it. The Lord is not merely an inexpressible divine reality, He has real existence, a real personality, and when He sent Christ to us He sent Him into real space and real time to walk the streets of Jerusalem. Second, we worship a God in truth and knowledge because He has chosen to reveal Himself to us, both in real history and in the inspired written record of that history we call the Bible. Those who appeal to an indescribable God are wooing the Church to abandon what we know about the true God in return for the false unknowns of the mystic.

The mystics always place an emphasis on a union, or oneness, between themselves and some divine or ultimate reality. They claim this experience is inaccessible to rational understanding or description. Make no mistake, this movement toward mysticism is all around us. It has so permeated American culture that we hardly detect it. Public television has popularized Hindu teacher Deepak Chopra, blurring the lines between eastern mysticism and Christianity. We've all observed the growth in popularity of eastern religions, such as Buddhism and Transcendental Meditation. The hallucinogenic subculture of the 1960s claimed that traditional Western ideas about God were passé, irrelevant, or even destructive. "God" was something to be experienced mystically; hallucinogens were simply the vehicle to get us there.

The Beatles traveled to India to become disciples of Maharishi Mahesh Yogi. Brian Williams of the Beach Boys described his experience dropping acid as an experience with God. Writer Tom Wolfe described the drug cult in the Haight-Asbury district of San Francisco as one great, confused parody on a pseudoreligious encounter. American culture, rock music, and the images we saw on television began to reflect this shift toward mysticism. Even the term "psychedelic," which was coined in the 1960s drug experience, began being applied to mainstream American culture. It gained popularity as a soft-peddled form of counterculture rebellion in prime-time television shows like Rowan and Martin's "Laugh-In." But while the love beads and bell-bottom pants of the hippie generation disappeared in the 1970s and 1980s, the underlying openness to the mystical elements of religion settled in for a long stay.

In cinema, spiritual power increasingly has been portrayed as having its source in the outer reaches of the mystical, where it is bestowed not on the faithful believer but on those who randomly blunder into it. An ordinary woman who happens to survive a near-death experience as a result of a car crash is given the supernatural power to heal in the movie *Resurrection*. Love was spiritualized in a vague world of mystical survival in *Ghost*. In *City of Angels*, the angelic beings are not messengers of God but merely spiritual beings bent on connecting with the material world.

Miracles are not portrayed as having been sent from the hand of God, but as inexplicable and magical coincidences that happen to intersect our lives. In movies like *Grand Canyon*, we are left with the impression that spiritual events are for everyone, at any time, without reference to such things as the nature of God or His ultimate sovereignty over the universe.

The world of the spirit in these films is not a world where we encounter a Creator who has ordained certain moral laws. *Doing* right is replaced with *feeling* right. The sovereignty and holiness of God is not discussed, yet the autonomy of man as an eternal being is celebrated.

Space travel has given a new twist to old notions of mysticism. In fact, a kind of outer-space mystic religion has developed. It first gained prominence in the film *2001—A Space Odyssey*, where the evolution of man is linked to an amorphous and impersonal intelligence in the universe. The religion grew with the notion of an impersonal "force" in the *Star Wars* movies. It reached its peak in *Contact*—a film which parodies traditional Christianity, turns believers into wild-eyed villains, and posits space as the ultimate expression of beauty, peace, and ambiguous spirituality. The screen play, which was written by humanistic scientist Carl Sagan, shows what happens when a scientific rationalist comes to the limits of his own reason in a search for ultimate answers. When he refuses to take the step of faith toward a Creator-God, there is only one step left—a leap into a kind of mysticism that evokes much sound and fury, but in the end signifies nothing.

Old Age Mysticism and New Age Religion

More traditional forms of religious mysticism are breaking into popular American thought and combining with New Age religions. We are quickly becoming a society that sees God entirely in terms of mystical experiences rather than in terms of His perfect and divine personality. The Bible tells us that God is a person with whom we can have a real relationship, not just a vague religious experience. His truth has real moral and spiritual content to it, and as a result, it can change our lives rather than just tickle our spiritual fancy.

This union of mysticism and the New Age has social and moral implications for America in the coming years. It has created a whole new demographic section of the nation that will view the world in a radically different way. This may impact the debate over a range of social issues as practical as free market economics or as profound as whether "morality" has become an outdated idea. In the newly published *Love, Soul and Freedom*, Denise

Breton and Christopher Largent apply the philosophy of 13th century Sufi mystic Jelaluddin Rumi to contemporary life. They have drawn praise from the likes of the Dalai Lama and New Age guru Marianne Williamson. Their work is more than a handbook for readers to become self-made, new millennium disciples of mysticism. It is also a blueprint for a radical transformation of American society. They predict the death of the traditional "corporate culture of control" over work and economics, painting a picture that seems to be a strange new form of New Age socialism. And they praise Indian mystic Pandurang Shastri Athavale, who won the 1997 Templeton Prize for Progress in Religion. This same award had previously been bestowed on evangelical Christian author Chuck Colson, whose bibliocentric worldview couldn't be further from Athavale's bizarre ramblings.

People are gravitating to these kinds of ideas with increasing gusto. Bookstores are replete with texts pandering this false worldview. The book *Conversations with God: An Uncommon Dialogue*, by Neale Donald Walsch, has been selling with extraordinary success. In this hypothetical dialogue with God, "fundamentalist" Christians are bashed and the reader is fed the feel-good bromide that the core of spirituality is not "obligation," but rather "opportunity." In this view, we are to see the great ocean of spiritual opportunity that swirls around us, free of those old-fashioned notions of "moral guilt" that supposedly burden us. This is the end-game of this view of the world: sin is out, total autonomy and personal freedom are in.

This is why mysticism is at war with the first principle of salvation: "For all have sinned and fall short of the glory of God" (Romans 3:23). We need to communicate the truth of the profound reality of sin to our generation of mystical thinkers. Such people are all around us. They no longer live only in Greenwich Village, nor are they limited to the eastern religion departments of Ivy League colleges. Today there is a good chance the cab driver, or the person in front of you at the check-out line of the grocery store, or your child's public-school teacher has been influenced by mystical thinking. We need to share with our voices and show in our lives how moral "obligation" arises because we live in a universe that was created by a God of moral order. When we seek to shed ourselves of moral obligation, we can never hope to see our duty and privilege of obeying God. And if we fail to see our duty toward God, we fail to understand sin, which is the result of our failure to live in righteousness before Him. If we fail, therefore, to understand sin, the great deceiver has tricked us into believing that we do not need a Savior.

The current trend in mysticism is at war with the idea of faith as God-oriented as opposed to being self-oriented. That's why books like Iyanla Vanzant's *In the Meantime (Finding Yourself and the Love You Want)* advises readers to "trust yourself, God, other people, and the process of life." Notice that Vanzant says, first and foremost, "trust yourself." Contrast this with the Word of God, in which the Apostle Paul says,

> For I know that nothing good dwells in me, that is, in my flesh; for the wishing is present in me, but the doing of the good is not....I find then the principle that evil is present in me, the one who wishes to do good. (Romans 7:18,21)

The problem is that both "people" and the "process of life" are held captive in the grip of sin. The creation will be set free from its slavery to sin *only* when God establishes His kingdom—and not before.

Mysticism is an ancient lie, but the new millennium will undoubtedly see a new and strange hybrid: Man's reverence for science and its power to explain the natural world may well become married to the mystic's view of the indefinable realm of the supernatural. This strange new image of mysticism in the 21st century is well illustrated by the final wishes of Timothy Leary. He expressed the desire to die while connected to thousands of people around the world by means of the Internet. After his death, his ashes were to be sent up in space in a satellite. Leary, who began his twisted dance with drugs as a Harvard scientist, was the perfect pioneer for this false religion. The witchdoctor with a Ph.D., he promised a generation of lost and searching young people a new vision of reality. But in the end, he was just peddling the same old deception.

That's the perfect picture of the new mysticism. It will embrace the worship of science and technology, while at the same time fooling us into believing that we can enter the arena of the spirit without dealing with concepts such as sin, salvation, heaven, and hell. The searching antennae of the astronomer replaces the cross of Calvary.

CHAPTER TWO

Engaging in the Battle of the Mind

During the Renaissance, the "enlightened" cultures gained a new allegiance to the ideas and achievements of man. God was no longer at the center of the universe; man was becoming the measure of all things. Faith was no longer the chief means by which we obtained answers; human reason became the new source for ultimate answers. This was the great predecessor of secular humanism. Interestingly, Leonardo da Vinci, who perhaps more than anyone else personified the Renaissance, died in 1519, the same year the famous arguments erupted between Martin Luther and his critics. Thus, the Renaissance overlapped the Reformation.

This was more than a mere coincidence of chronology. The Renaissance and the Reformation stand for the two great truth options. In the first view, man was capable of realizing the godlike goals of ultimate understanding and harmony among humanity and with nature. In the second view, man has lost his true understanding and harmony among humanity because of sin; but God, through Jesus Christ, provided a means of obtaining spiritual understanding and reconciled Himself to those who become His children through faith. Those believers have the means of living out a life in harmony with God until He establishes His kingdom—at which time all understanding will be perfect, and man and his new world will be in perfect and eternal harmony.

Five hundred years later we are still living out the struggle between these two polar belief systems. In the 1980s, there was much discussion in the Christian community of the effect of secular humanism on our public education system. Secular humanism was criticized by Christian conservatives as the prevailing mindset of most of our institutions in general, and the public education system in particular. Secular critics scoffed at this idea. In two separate court cases, the Courts of Appeal of two different federal circuits rejected challenges by Christians who claimed that the "religion" of secular humanism was so pervasive in textbooks that it violated the constitutional rights of Christian families whose children were exposed to it. Those who have tried to argue that the worldview of secular humanism is a religion, one officially "established" by the government through public education in violation of the Establishment Clause of the First Amendment, have been soundly defeated in the courts.

These courtroom defeats did not come because the legal arguments were entirely void of any basis. After all, the Supreme Court has, in the past, referred to secular humanism as a form of religion. In *Torcaso v. Watkins*, a 1961 Supreme Court case, the court noted that secular humanism exemplified one of the types of religion that did not posit a belief in a divine being. Whether those comments were capable of providing a basis for a First Amendment challenge to the teaching of secular humanism is doubtful, since those comments were what lawyers sometimes call "obiter dicta"—more like mere asides than direct legal findings that could be cited as precedent.

Yet the Supreme Court has also been clear that religion—any religion—which is officially "established" by any branch or unit of government violates the Establishment Clause. At the bottom of these court decisions were two very real, yet somewhat unspoken, realities. First, most judges simply will not recognize secular humanism as a religion. It is such a pervasive mindset of the 20th century that it is looked at as a guiding philosophy of life or a worldview, but not a religion.

Second, there was a pragmatic reality. If secular humanism was an official religion of the state, illegally imposed on children through public education, a court decision banning it would have radical and catastrophic consequences for the prevailing public education system. Lawyers have quite wisely avoided pursuing these Establishment Clause arguments against secular humanism. But that does not mean it is not a prevailing mindset, or that it does not yield tyrannical consequences that cry out for justice.

Humanism and the Worship of Man

One of the indirect consequences of secular humanism has been the backlash of censorship meted out against those who dare raise questions about this prevailing climate of opinion, particularly in our colleges and universities. In late 1998, Craig filed a Petition for Certiorari with the U.S. Supreme Court in a case of outrageous book banning and censorship. It involved Dr. Dilawar Edwards, a tenured professor in the education department of California University of Pennsylvania, a public university just outside Pittsburgh. In one of the courses, he taught a unit designed to stimulate the thinking of his students (future teachers) on such topics as antireligious bias in textbooks and censorship in the classrooms of America.

Dr. Edwards offered no personal religious opinions of his own. However, he did have his students read a book called *Book Burning* by syndicated columnist Cal Thomas. The book dealt with the anti-Christian bias present in some aspects of our culture, including the media and public education. Another book used was a primer of the role of religion in public education by constitutional attorney John Whitehead, president of The Rutherford Institute.

After one student complained about the course, administrators of the university issued an amazing "cease and desist order" banning the use of *Book Burning!* Also banned was the book by John Whitehead and numerous other materials used in the class. What was the basis for this incredible display of censorship? Such works, the university officials reasoned, were "doctrinaire materials" of a "religious sort." Of course, the officials did not ban *nonreligious* materials that were considered "doctrinaire." And therein lies the rub.

The evidence at trial showed that Dr. Edwards had been targeted as a "fundamentalist," and therefore marginalized. Because he was perceived to be a Christian conservative, he was ridiculed in front of his professional peers. He was subjected to the kind of scathing censorship and professional berating that would never be tolerated if he was a communist, a homosexual, or a liberal of almost any brand or type. In March 1999, the United States Supreme Court issued an order declining to review the case, although a prestigious academic freedom organization had filed its own brief as "amicus curiae" (friend of the court) urging it to take up the issue.

These kinds of incidents are not isolated. A tenured professor at Cornell University was threatened with official censure when he countered a prohomosexual notice on his departmental bulletin board. The Christian professor, in response to the advocacy of homosexuality, posted a notice on that same bulletin board that listed some of the scientific journals and articles that proved homosexuality is a behavior that can be changed. That exercise of free speech almost cost him his job.

There is some historical precedent for this kind of censorship. The temples of the ancient societies, like our modern-day universities and colleges, were impressive and imposing places where gods and idols were worshiped with zeal. But the temple-keepers were jealous for their gods and idols. Competing ideas about the one true God were often given a chilly reception. Paul was derided by the leaders of ancient Greece when he preached the true God in a place populated by the idols of the day.

Yet the ancient Athenians were more open-minded than many of our modern temples of academe. At least they invited Paul to their forum in order to give him the chance to articulate his views. In many of our contemporary temples of idolatry, by contrast, only the gods of man are permitted access. Books and ideas challenging those humanistic ideas are forever barred from entry through the college gate.

This modern form of intellectual idolatry needs to be soundly challenged. The marketplace of ideas in the 21st century needs to be opened up to those ideas that emanate from a Judeo-Christian view of the world. Our universities need to be open to a Christian worldview that challenges the current liberal status quo.

To do this, we need Christians who are intellectually gifted and committed to working within the various academic disciplines. These Christian scholars, however, also need to be tough and battle-hardened. The trenches of their warfare may be intellectual, but they will undoubtedly require hand-to-hand or rather mind-to-mind combat with the forces of anti-Christian bigotry and censorship.

Being able to engage ourselves in the intellectual defense of the gospel in the 21st century is not an option. We are called, within our own spheres of influence, to be Christian apologists to those who hold a variety of ungodly ideas around us. The Apostle Peter said it this way:

> But sanctify Christ as Lord in your hearts, always being ready to make a defense to everyone who asks you to give an account

for the hope that is in you, yet with gentleness and reverence.
(1 Peter 3:15)

Notice that this is a command for *every* Christian. There are several facets to this process of being an apologist to 21st century challengers of our faith.

First is the facet of the heart. Peter calls us to "sanctify Christ as Lord in your hearts." Confronting the false ideas of our age does not merely mean being able to string some clever arguments together or to "win the debate." C.S. Lewis, surely one of the great Christian apologists, once observed that the problem with resting your Christian faith on a clever argument is that it is always at the mercy of a more clever argument. The Lordship of Christ means that our motivation for destroying the false ideas around us is not to win the argument—it is to bring lost people to Christ.

The Lordship of Christ also requires that we engage our deceived culture in a way that is winsome, so we can win them to Christ. Peter says that we are to give a good defense of our faith, but at the same time to do it with gentleness and reverence. If you are a Christian talk show host, it means that when callers vilify you and engage in name-calling, you can challenge their wrong ideas (and their bad manners) but not return the insult.

If you are a Christian trial lawyer, it means that when you do combat against those who oppose the rights of Christians or those who fight for ideas that threaten to destroy families, freedom, and faith, you do not treat them as the enemy. They must be treated as people who have been captured by the false ideas of the enemy. We have to remember that those people who propagate the ideas of Satan are still creatures made in God's image.

The second facet is that of preparedness. Peter's command is not just to be an apologist to *some* people who question our faith. We are to be ready to make our defense to everyone who asks about the source of our hope. This may sound like a staggering task. How can we possibly anticipate and prepare for everyone who will challenge our Christian beliefs? How can we be ready for every conceivable challenge thrown at us?

Janet has an array of trained Bible teachers as guests on her show, *"Janet Parshall's America,"* on a regular basis. They deal with everything from evolutionary theory to the religions of the world, yet even they cannot anticipate every possible call from every skeptic who calls in. While many questions are old standbys, like: "If the Bible is really accurate then where did Cain's wife come from," some of the callers present entirely unique and even weird religious ideas that need to be countered.

The one thing these defenders of the faith have in common is a sure and steady grasp of the Word of God. Bankers tell us we can best spot a counterfeit dollar bill by being totally familiar with the original. In the same way, if we are familiar with God's truth, we can rely on it to pierce the darkness of the lost soul as well as enlighten the mind of someone darkened by false philosophies. We may not be conversant with every false philosophy out there in the marketplace—nor need we be. Understanding God's Word is the necessary requisite to expose any deceptive and devilish idea that comes along.

The third facet involves understanding some of the basics about truth and knowledge. In confidence we should rejoice that truth exists, that God has revealed it, and as Christians we have the means to know truth and distinguish it from falsity.

Francis Schaeffer made this point nearly 30 years ago. Speaking about the unique task of the Church at the end of the 20th century, he challenged the Church to understand the basics about our claims as Christians—and to appreciate what makes our truth claims revolutionary and unique.

> God has given us two kinds of propositional revelation in the Bible. First, didactic statements and commands. Second, a record of how he himself has worked in space-time history. With these two together we really have a very adequate knowledge, both as knowledge and as a basis for action.

God has not given us exhaustive knowledge, but he has given us true knowledge—about himself and about the space-time cosmos. Let me repeat: *It is not exhaustive knowledge, but it is true knowledge.*[1]

In other words, because we can know and have a personal relationship with a God who reveals Himself, several things follow: 1) There is such a thing as truth; 2) this truth is capable of being known (thus truth is not relativistic or situational); and 3) even though this truth, which is derived from Scripture, is not exhaustive truth (we only know as in a mirror dimly now), it is *reliable*. It can be depended on in making decisions about life. Whether our decisions are about how to worship God, or whether to steal from our bosses, or whether to have abortions, or whom we should marry, the Bible contains principles and precepts that are a reliable guide for faith and personal conduct.

The Danger in Ideas

There are two dangers when it comes to the Church and the mind. The first is that the Church will *retreat* from the world of ideas and become profoundly anti-intellectual. This happened with the rise of modern fundamentalism at the turn of the 20th century. Faced with the lies of Darwinism, the advent of Freudian explanations for human conduct that conflicted with the biblical view of sin, and the wholesale assault on biblical truth from modern science, fundamentalists permitted themselves to be cast as reactionaries. Instead, they should have waded into the battle, engaging the false ideas on their own terms and exposing the truth of the Bible to all comers.

The other danger, equally serious, is that we will become so influenced by the world that our beliefs about God and His Word will play second fiddle to the prevailing ideas of the day. We have both heard from time to time the comment from preachers and Christian workers that you cannot rationally argue someone into heaven. And of course that is true. But we have also heard criticisms from fellow Christians that faith is opposed to philosophy. And that is not true. Paul once said, "See to it that no one takes you captive through philosophy and empty deception, according to the tradition of men, according to the elementary principles of the world, rather than according to Christ" (Colossians 2:8).

We are to *beware* of philosophy that is "according to the tradition of men." But we are *called* to a philosophical worldview that is "according to Christ." All else in the world of ideas is idolatry. If Christ has not revolutionized the way we think, then we have denied Him the Lordship of our minds.

This means that we are called to develop, and live-out in our lives, a Christian philosophy of politics and public policy. We are called to a Christian philosophy of music, theater, and art. We are called to formulate, based on biblical principles, and put into action a Christian philosophy of law, of medicine, of economics, and business. It is here the devil has won many of the rounds in America over the last 30 years.

Three decades ago the evangelical Church woke up to the fact that God was being made officially *personæ non grata* in the public schools and the halls of government. We formed organizations and movements that in the 1970s started fighting the battles of religious liberty. When *Roe v. Wade* was handed down in the Supreme Court, Christians were somewhat slower to react. In our family, Craig was in law school at the time. That decision was like a thunderbolt through the legal establishment. As a part-time law clerk for a Catholic lawyer, Craig was given the job of reading and researching the Court decision, then drafting a position paper for presentation to Catholic bishops that the law firm represented.

The Catholic Church, to its credit, had no problem recognizing abortion as murder and denouncing *Roe* as bad law—a disastrous moral and social policy permitting faulty medical practice. This law rested on a mistaken view of Church history on the subject of abortion. Evangelicals waited almost a decade before we, too, recognized the travesty of that decision and added our voices of protest. Eventually, the evangelical pro-life movement was birthed.

The rampant scourge of pornography in America led to a number of pro-decency groups, motivated to return righteousness to our land. Attacks on the traditional family were met by evangelical-led groups formed to fight for the family and for family values. We should praise God for these groups, pray for them, and actively support them. Personally, over the years, both of us have either worked for, or with, almost all of them. Yet the Church has been occupied with a defensive strategy—countering the flood tide of attacks on moral values, innocent human life, and fundamental constitutional liberties. We have neglected a pro-active Christian philosophy that is clear, concise, Bible-based, Christ-inspired—a philosophy that can be a practical guide for America in the new millennium.

It is not enough to merely stop the sewage of bad ideas and destructive behavior that have disgraced our land and destroyed our people. We have to be ready with good ideas that spring from God's eternal Word. We have to be able to articulate in politics, culture, law, and art not just what we must oppose, but also what we support.

Charles Spurgeon once said: "It is mere cant to cry, 'we are evangelical; we are all evangelical,' and yet decline to say what evangelical means." Our task is nothing less than to know what it means to be evangelical Christians in a fallen world, then to apply it to the nitty-gritty problems of the coming, troubled epoch.

CHAPTER THREE

❦

Spirits
New and Old

Shirley was a good student at a major university in the Midwest in the early 1970s. She was a professing believer with strong ties to a Lutheran church. She was also rather lonely and an avid reader. She saturated herself with the poetry of Rod McKuen, but rarely spent time studying the Bible. One day Shirley simply vanished from campus. Her Christian roommate got a call a year later. Shirley had found peace, love, and a sense of belonging, she claimed, from a group that she described as a nondenominational Christian fellowship organization. Then she urged her roommate to come join her group in the State of New York. Shirley was vague about the name of the group, and her conversations about its teachings and identity were always foggy and indistinct. After some digging, it was learned that the group had a name: It was called the Unification Church. Its leader was Sun Myung Moon.

Recently a young college student in the East suddenly and mysteriously dropped out of school. He had been a frequent member of the Christian fellowship group on campus. He claimed to have a personal walk with Jesus, but he didn't care much for Bible study or Christian teaching. He was an emotional and outgoing fellow, always riding the highs and lows of a spiritual roller-coaster experience. Then one day, after dropping out of school, he wrote a letter to some of his Christian friends. He explained how he had found a terrific new "community" of friends to live with. This community was the only way that they could find the Messiah, and only through the community could they prepare the way for the coming of the Lord. He urged his friends to come and visit the group and see how to ready themselves for the Last Days. As it turns out the group was called "The Brethren." They have made national news by separating college students from their parents and convincing young people that Armageddon is only months away.

The Rise of Cults

These stories are true and have been multiplied by thousands around the country. Of course, the threat from some religious cults is easier to recognize than others. When Jim Jones led his followers at the People's Temple to commit mass suicide in 1978 in the jungles of Ghana, the world was horrified. When David Koresh's distortion of Bible doctrine and crazy-quilt amalgamation of Old and New Testament theology led him to justify sexual immorality, it also led the "Branch Davidians" to a siege mentality that created a deadly confrontation with federal authorities at their compound in Waco, Texas. Although there was public sympathy from some quarters for the civil rights of the Davidians to bear arms,

Koresh was vilified in the media. Like Jones, he was portrayed (not unfairly) as a religious zombie whose ideas were dangerous and illogical.

A subtle change occurred, however, in the 1997 news coverage of a mass suicide in Southern California. The group, an advanced computer-literate cult called "Heaven's Gate," dressed as if they were auditioning for Star Trek. Their theology was utterly preposterous: A rocket ship from the other side of the universe was hiding behind the Hale-Bopp comet and would "beam them up" to the ship at the instant they committed suicide. Their bodies, they learned, were merely unnecessary "flesh containers" for the greater spiritual beings inside. They had been training for the day they would be ushered into a greater spiritual dimension.

Despite this ridiculous nonsense, the press gave them a gentle, almost sympathetic hearing. Ted Koppel, host of "Nightline," interviewed a surviving sister of one of the group, carefully handing her the kind of softball questions that never would have been afforded an evangelical Christian leader. Why the difference? Perhaps it was because Heaven's Gate was the kind of cult that had the right appearance for contemporary America on the brink of the 21st century. Its theology, though totally unreasonable and unsupported by any legitimate evidence, had a kind of space-age appeal. An example: its leader, who claimed he received his ideas in a vision, claimed that Mary was not a virgin who bore the Son of God. Rather, aliens had impregnated her. Occasional references to Scripture were only a means to an end—to delude its disciples into thinking that older religions were based on imperfect knowledge of the greater reality in the universe. Heaven's Gate, based on a kind of astronomical fakery, proclaimed itself to be the new enlightenment.

Unlike cults of the past, Heaven's Gate leaders were no prophets of doom. And unlike many other cults before them, the Heaven's Gate crowd made no attempt to distort Christian truth while masquerading as disciples of Christ. Instead, they bypassed

Christianity almost completely, making it a minor footnote in their religious-scientism. They were well-educated, computer-literate, non-violent in their demeanor, and concerned about the mysteries of space and time. In our present age of preoccupation with space travel and interplanetary intelligence, advanced through movies like *ET* and *Contact*, Heaven's Gate was the cult for the new millennium. It was "user friendly," high-tech, and enjoyed a kind of pseudo-science approach. But in the end it was built on a lie and yielded only death and destruction.

Heaven's Gate members denied the "base" aspects of earthly life. They denounced sexuality between husband and wife and the idea of parental rights over children, promoted the practice of castration, and decried earthly possessions. This harks back to Paul's warnings in Scripture written more than 2000 years ago:

> *Let no one keep defrauding you of your prize by delighting in self-abasement and the worship of the angels, taking his stand on visions he has seen, inflated without cause by his fleshly mind.... These are matters which have, to be sure, the appearance of wisdom in self-made religion and self-abasement and severe treatment of the body, but are of no value against fleshly indulgence.* (Colossians 2:18,23)

The Church must wake up to a new appreciation for the increasing number of people caught up in religious cults. The 1992 census indicated the following breakdown for the minority religious sects:

45,000 — Church of Scientology
29,000 — Humanist
28,000 — Bahai
23,000 — Taoist
20,000 — New Age
18,000 — Eckankar
14,000 — Rastafarian
 8,000 — Wiccan
 6,000 — Deity

These numbers may not seem very imposing in themselves. Collectively, however, we get a picture of the changing religious face of America. That census also determined that there were almost a million members of "unclassified" non-Christian religions who did not fit into the traditional religions of Judaism, Islam, Buddhism, or Hinduism. Further, some four million citizens refused to identify the religious group with which they are affiliated. If we combine Jehovah's Witnesses (1,381,000) with these groups, it may safely be said that in 1992 there were potentially more cult members or members of nontraditional religions in America than there were Presbyterians, or Episcopalians, or non-denominational Pentecostals. Further, such people outnumber Jews, Muslims, Buddhists, and Hindus in America.

America, the *cultural* melting pot, has now become the *religious* melting pot. Traditional religions are now blending and mixing with new religions. As one observer has noted, "The new religions are an offshoot of the globalization of practically everything, as formally exotic cultures and religions are suddenly accessible in every way....The idea that one God might be better than another lost its primacy, and people began to think that 'all religions are vital organs in the planet.'"[1]

What makes cults so dangerous, and so effective in recruiting, is their counterfeit appearance. At first blush many look like variations of Christianity. Followers of the Unification Church (the cult that deifies Sun Myung Moon of South Korea) often stop cars at busy intersections or show up on the front porch of homes selling flowers for their cause. When questioned, they describe themselves as part of a "nondenominational Christian youth fellowship." Even after intense questioning about the identity of the actual group they are funding, well-trained followers of Reverend Moon will avoid an accurate and full description.

Others cults disguise themselves behind a veneer of public interest and libertarianism. The Church of Scientology touts such Hollywood disciples as John Travolta, Tom Cruise, Nicole Kidman, and Ann Archer. The group publishes a slick, innocuous-looking magazine called *Freedom* (subtitled "Investigative Reporting in the Public Interest"). A recent issue discusses health care, the treatment of brain injury, court rulings and international developments in the area of human rights, global democracy, a profile on an NAACP leader, and rehabilitation of prisoners. Only on closer inspection does one notice a discreet ad ("What Is Scientology?"), and an article, on the last three pages of the magazine, by the cult's founder, L. Ron Hubbard. On the last page there is a pitch for Hubbard's book *Scientology—The Fundamentals of Thought.* The reader is told that this book deals with "the subject of the mind, spirit and life." There is just enough information to raise the curiosity of the reader, but not enough to tip us off that this philosophical position is radically at odds with the Christian faith.

We cannot assume that Christian believers will be safe from these rising cults, particularly as they use increasingly sophisticated marketing techniques. Cult targets will undoubtedly include spiritually immature believers or those who simply have not made a study of the Word of God. In the coming years, the biggest threat from cults will come from a combination of factors, including ignorance of the Word of God on the part of Christian believers; spiritual immaturity that emphasizes emotional experiences over sound teaching; and lack of accountability to, or fellowship with, other mature believers.

The Threat of the New "Spirituality"

With the abandonment of Scripture as a guiding principle for Christianity, we are at risk of absorbing a strange conglomeration of new-age religion, old-age paganism and earth worship, eastern mysticism, and transcendental meditation. A walk through any of the large secular bookstores bears this out. There may be three or four magazines dealing with traditional Christian ideas. However, it is not unusual to find a dozen or more periodicals on the same aisle dealing with such things as inner healing, spirit guides, and religious mysticism.

PBS, which has a long and consistent pattern of airing programs bitterly critical of Christianity in general and evangelical Christians in particular, exemplifies this new trend. They have aired full-blown lectures of Deepak Chopra, an Eastern mystic. Chopra preaches the classic doctrine of Hinduism he learned as a child in India. What makes his message particularly dangerous to the Church is his ability to do a magician's sleight-of-hand in using references to Christianity and the Bible interchangeably with Hindu teachings from the Upanishads. In comparing his belief in "cosmic consciousness" with "Christ consciousness" Chopra recently said:

> I read the Gospel of John and it was like reading Vedanta [Hindu scriptures] for me....I realized that Christ consciousness is what we are aspiring to and that Christ consciousness is a state of awareness we go into. Christ wasn't about the crucifixion; he was about the resurrection and redemption. God-realized people are those who have achieved that state of Christ consciousness.[2]

Christians must understand what he is really saying. While it was cleverly close to sounding like Christian theology, it is classic doctrinal deception. After all, if Christ's crucifixion—His saving act on the cross as the sacrifice for sin—is not what He "was about," then His resurrection is an empty miracle, a miracle without meaning. The Bible says that the death and resurrection of Jesus conquered sin and death. Chopra is one of many who wish to merge Eastern religion with Christianity, thus emphasizing states of consciousness and turning Christianity into a bland, empty belief system that has no consciousness of sin.

Taking the heart out of Christianity is the only way it can be absorbed into the Hinduism of Chopra. Hindu belief has room only for "Karma" (the sum total of earthly actions which determine one's state of reincarnation in the next). It does not have room for sin. Therefore, the new spirituality has no need for a sacrifice that requires the shedding of blood.

What these opponents of biblical Christianity are looking for is a nonthreatening, nondemanding, spiritually ambiguous Christ who is just one of many "avatars" (holy men who are the incarnation of a god in human form). What Chopra and his ilk want is exactly what the Gospels and the Bible do not have to offer—a christ who is not *the* Christ.

Hinduism clothed as false Christianity delivered in the comfort of your own home thanks to publicly funded television is the wave of the new century. The next time you sit in your easy chair taking in the smooth and comfortable teachings of the sages on the TV screen, remember to listen carefully. Truth is not merely comfort; it is also a sword that cuts away falsehood and deception. The "Age of Spiritual Confusion" is upon us. We will need sharpened swords to cut away the bramble bushes and thorns that threaten to choke the life-transforming message of the gospel.

We can peek through the thorns and notice how Chopra is emphasizing "Christ consciousness." The Bible teaches that true believers have the "mind of Christ," but this does not come as a result of meditation or some higher state of consciousness gained by knowledge or greater awareness. You receive the mind of Christ when (and only when) you become His. And you become His when you "confess with your mouth Jesus as Lord, and believe in your heart that God raised Him from the dead," according to Romans 10:9. When you do that, "you shall be saved."

In John 5:39-40, Jesus says, "You search the Scriptures, because you think that in them you have eternal life; and it is these that bear witness of Me; and you are unwilling to come to Me, that you may have life."

The Lord does not mingle minds with the merely curious. He does not infuse His consciousness into the casual, intellectual seeker. We obtain Christ mindedness only when we obtain all of

Christ through faith in His gracious sacrifice for sin. His holiness is not separable from His mentality; His moral purity and perfection are not divisible from His mind. We receive all of Him—Savior, Lord, and King—or we receive none of Him. Those are His terms.

Chopra's devious emphasis on "Christ consciousness" is the centerpiece of the ever-expanding cult of New Age religion. Helen Shueman's *A Course in Miracles* was a ground-breaking work for New Age philosophy. A proponent of her work, Marilyn Ferguson, spreads this distorted gospel in such books as *The Aquarian Conspiracy*. She has said,

> My definition of Christianity has expanded over the years. After I became involved in meditation, for example, I experienced the vision of Christ more vividly than I ever had through sermons and dogma. You would be surprised, I think, to know how much of the New Age Movement centers on Christ Consciousness. Many Christian churches are seeing that direct spiritual experience offers a revitalization for modern Christianity.[3]

This redefining of Jesus Christ has moved us away from the biblical portrait of the Lord, and toward a watered-down, Hinduistic description of Jesus as nothing more than a spiritual man.

The Rise of Other World Religions

It would be easy to view these strange new formulations of religion as the major challenge to Christian ideas. Yet, in fact, the growth of mainline non-Christian religions in post-Christian America is exploding. Islam, a religion that has never hesitated to brand followers of Christ as infidels, is leading the charge.

Islam originated in 610 when Mohammed, who described himself as the last of God's prophets, claimed to have received divine revelation from an angel in the western regions of Saudi Arabia. Muslims follow the Koran as the word of God, and fiercely maintain a strict obedience to "Allah." Islam maintains a rigid belief in the singular identity of Allah and utterly rejects any possibility of a Trinity. Jesus is acknowledged as a prophet but rejected outright as savior.

Islam has more than one billion followers worldwide. Traditionally, Muslims were found in the Middle East, North Africa, Central Asia, Afghanistan, Pakistan, and Indonesia. There are also more than 100 million Muslims in India. Recently, however, Islam has made sweeping inroads into North America.

In 1990, there were only 500,000 Muslims in the United States. In only seven years that number grew to an amazing 5 million followers. This is roughly equivalent to the increase in the number of Baptists during the same period of time.

In the Newbury Park area of California, one small Islamic mosque has nearly tripled in number of worshipers in just the past few years. In the greater Los Angeles area there are now 50 Muslim mosques. One of them, the enormous King Fahd Mosque in Culver City, is being financed by the Saudi Arabian government at the cost of more than 8 million dollars. In northern Virginia, the Saudi Arabian government is also financing a huge Islamic complex, complete with an elementary and secondary Muslim school, a short distance from Washington, D.C.

Islam is not the only eastern religion that is changing the face of American culture. Buddhism, long the religious favorite of Hollywood with its air of serenity and peace, got a boost in 1998 with two major motion pictures. In *Seven Years in Tibet*, screen superstar Brad Pitt starred as a Nazi sympathizer (Heinrich Harrer, an actual person) who wandered into the mountains of Tibet during the eve of World War II. There he met the young Dalai Lama (the spiritual leader of the Buddhists of Tibet) and was won over to the peaceful, contemplative life. Big-budget director Martin Scorsese was also busy creating *Kundun*, a film about the life of the current reigning Dalai Lama. Scorsese glowed publicly about the movie and described it as a capstone for his film-making career.

The two movies seem to have tapped into the religious vacuum that has been festering in the heart of America. America has become Buddha-infatuated. Buddhism claims followers like actors Steven Seagal and Richard Gere, entertainer Tina Turner, rap-punk singer Adam Yauch, and Phil Jackson, long-time coach of the NBA Chicago Bulls.

Buddhist bookstores are springing up everywhere. Grocery stores now carry Buddhist-inspired drinks like "Tazo Passion Potion," which boasts on its label that it is "the reincarnation of tea." And no benefit rock concert would be complete without an evangelistic reference to the plight of the Buddhists in Tibet who have been oppressed by the Red Chinese government.

The real question is whether America's flirtation with the ethereal promise of Buddistic "enlightenment" is poised to blossom into a full-fledged theological courtship. At present, there are major Buddhist meditation centers in California, Massachusetts, Washington state, New Mexico, New York, North Carolina, and Michigan. Experts now say the time has come for the establishment of formal monasteries in America, for the grooming and raising-up of home-grown, ordained Buddhist monks and Buddhist nuns.

Why do members of mainstream Christian denominations find themselves drawn to Buddhism? Patricia Elam, a 44-year-old mother of three, grew up in an African-American Congregationalist church in Boston. As a child she was bored with Sunday school and church services that she felt were rigid and irrelevant. As an adult she says she longed for "something that, when I found it, would soothe the anxiety and emptiness dwelling in my heart."

Her drifting away from a traditional, but nominal affiliation with Christianity began because she "had trouble connecting to the concepts of 'God' and 'Jesus.' Who were they? Where were they? How did anyone know they existed? Why couldn't I feel their presence? And didn't some mortal men write the Bible, and why should I believe them since I didn't like some of the things it said about women and gay people?"[4]

Patricia's questions are the stuff of basic Christian apologetics. These questions are the kind we must be willing to answer not just to the unchurched, but to the "churched" as well. The pews of churches are filled with people who attend church services through a devotion to tradition. Their lives are as untouched by the fire of the Holy Spirit and the touch of Christ's power as the dead stones of their church buildings. We can no longer presume the continuation of Christianity in America merely because of our Christian heritage or because church spires dot the landscape.

Every time Janet does a program where the phone lines are opened to any and all questions about the basic tenets of Christianity, the lines stay lit the entire hour. The callers, who invariably identify themselves as Christians, will call and ask questions about the Trinity, baptism, communion, eternal security, and the inerrancy of Scripture. This speaks to the need to know what we believe and why we believe it. How can we *share* our faith if we do not *know* our faith?

America grew up hearing hymns wafting from church windows on Sunday mornings. If we do not aggressively evangelize our "churched" unsaved, in the 21st century we may become as accustomed to hearing the chant of mantras from meditation centers and Islamic prayers from minarets.

The Church in America has long focused on the fact that our nation has been a leader in sending Christian missionaries to foreign missions fields. We can praise God for that fact, but the changing face of America in the next century may bring enormous challenges to our concept of "mission field." In coming years, short of a full-fledged revival, the "foreign mission field" will no longer be just the remote tribes in exotic jungles and far-away deserts. The foreign field will be us.

Are we preparing ourselves with the same kind of dedication and training that foreign missionaries undergo? In view of the influx of strange new religions and the rise of other world religions in America, this must be a mandate for all believers. Whether our mission field is to natives in a far-away jungle or our new age neighbors next door, we all have the same great commission. The changing religious face of our own nation means that we must have a missionary strategy for 21st century America.

Just as foreign missionaries learn the culture and language of their mission field, our churches and families must teach the basics of the language of the current religious scene in America so we can better evangelize them. Missionaries to foreign fields are also trained in presenting the gospel and making disciples. Sometimes it takes years of work before the language and cultural barriers in a certain target area can be broken down, interpersonal trust built, and the gospel message clearly communicated to the lost people. In the same way, our churches need to develop a long-range strategy for America. It must be more than just a plan to share the "four spiritual laws," get a decision for Christ, and sign them up for Sunday school. A long-range strategy means really understanding the religious and cultural background of those we evangelize so we can create disciples for a lifetime, rather than just a season.

This long-range plan must involve the strategy to penetrate America with the gospel from the ground up. Our friends on the mission fields tell us that often, after tribal people come to Christ, they are immediately confronted with a conflict between their new Christian walk and their old immoral practices and customs. The missionaries are able to anticipate that, and they can steer them from their old immorality with the guidelines of Scripture and the reinforcement of Christian fellowship. They are also trained to know the difference between the moral mandates of the Bible, which are binding on all of us, and differences in tribal dress, music, or cultural norms, which are to be expected and permitted.

In the same way, we should approach our task as that of missionaries to a pagan America. If we can understand the cultural and religious customs and practices of our future generation, we can anticipate how the moral imperatives of Scripture will challenge the newly converted Christians of the 21st century.

Last, but certainly not least, we should emulate the mindset of the foreign missionary. We have dear friends with New Tribes Mission in South America, Central America, and other parts of the world. If you overheard them talking about their mission field at a restaurant, it would be easy to conclude they were not tourists. They are where they are because they have a *mission* to their *mission field.*

Now is the time for strategic spiritual planning. Every Christian should have in mind a clear mission with an identified mission field. The fields are ripe for harvest, and the workers are few. The new millennium will offer a multitude of strange spirits and half-truths, and the only way to defeat that deception is to communicate the whole truth by being wholly empowered by God's Spirit.

CHAPTER FOUR

Familiar but False Doctrine

Mark Twain once said, "One of the most striking differences between a cat and a lie is that a cat has only nine lives." The corrupting power of a lie is its ability to survive. The best way for a lie to survive is to cloak itself in half-truth.

One of the real dangers of the next century will be the careful manipulation of spiritual half-truths, which are much more dangerous than full-blown lies. They carry the faint glimmer of fact deviously mixed with mythology.

In the Garden of Eden, the serpent ("more crafty than any beast of the field") used the classic half-truth approach. He told Eve that when she ate of the forbidden fruit her eyes would be opened and she would know good and evil. That was true in that Eve would be able to "experience" evil. But he also told her she "would be like God," and that was the false bait that hooked her. Mission accomplished. With a half-truth, Satan convinced Eve to disobey God.

Deepak Chopra and others of the spiritual mysticism movement also rely on half-truths. They talk in terms of the "resurrection" of Christ, which sounds familiar and pleasing to the ear. However, in truth they seek to diminish the significance of Jesus' crucifixion, while retaining His resurrection as an image of spiritual power.

A current heretical movement in the Church is trying just the opposite approach. A group of liberal scholars is willing to accept the crucifixion as historical fact, but they want to deny the reality of the resurrection.

The Threat of Doctrinal Heresy

For 100 years liberal theologians and academics have launched something called "The Quest for the Historical Jesus." These so-called "debunkers" of orthodox Christianity began with the assumption that the divine and supernatural explanations of things like miracles are really just natural occurrences that were reinterpreted or misinterpreted by the religious zealots of the first century. Thus, what we have in the four gospels of Matthew, Mark, Luke, and John, according to these "debunkers," are not historical accounts of what Jesus really said or did. Rather, they are merely the writings of men who lived hundreds of years after the fact, who have embellished the real Jesus of Nazareth with a veneer of religious instruction. The liberal heretics want to strip from the Bible anything that does not fit into their scientific, antisupernatural bias. Whatever is left after their editing job—and not much does remain—is what they believe Jesus was really like.

History is full of examples of those who have tried—all unsuccessfully—to destroy the integrity or the authenticity of the

Gospel descriptions regarding the life, death, and resurrection of Jesus Christ. History is littered with skeptics, from Voltaire in France to Thomas Paine in colonial America and philosopher Bertrand Russell in 20th century England. Thomas Jefferson, while he gave great credence to the moral teachings of Jesus, and although he personally believed in a divine being, once constructed his own version of the Gospels by cutting out the stories with miracles.

Now there is something new in this age-old attack against Christian truth. A new strategy has been mounted, and it is a foreboding of things to come in the next epoch of the Church. For the first time, members of the liberal religious establishment are leaving the ivory towers of their colleges and seminaries, and they are making a full-fledged appeal directly to the churches of America in an effort to win converts to their heresy.

Calling their movement the "Jesus Seminars," these radical deformers of biblical truth are holding community forums around the country. Meetings have already been held in Chicago, Tulsa, Boise, Miami, Sarasota, and Palm Springs. Their leader, Robert Funk, of the Westar Institute in Santa Rosa, California, has published a series of books in his 12-year quest to reeducate Christians on the meaning of Christ. His recent book, *The Acts of Jesus*, claims to be "The Search for the Authentic Deeds of Jesus."

The book is a restatement of the four Gospels with a unique color-coding system. Many of us are familiar with the "red letter" versions of the Bible, which have the words of Jesus in red ink, for easy reference. *The Acts of Jesus*, by contrast, is a kind of red letter Bible for the skeptic.

The book has put in red those parts of the Gospels that are "unequivocally" accurate representations of who Jesus really was. Those parts which may be accurate, but for which the liberal scholars have reservations, are in pink. The parts of the Gospels that may have some relevance to the real Jesus, but which these skeptics believe were not part of the original information that the disciples had about Jesus, are set forth in gray. And those parts the participants consider inaccurate accounts of Christ are left to standard black print. As you might well imagine, the gospel according to the radical religious historians of the Jesus Seminar has become a mass of black print, with very few red or pink passages. The result: Only 16 percent of the Gospel events are deemed to be accurate. And only 18 percent of the Gospel sayings of Jesus can be reliably attributed to Jesus.

As an example, in John 3:1-21 we have one of the most theologically important meetings in all of the Gospel stories. Nicodemus, a Pharisee who has been secretly impressed with Jesus from afar, slips into Christ's camp by night to dialogue with him. Jesus tells him that one can only see the kingdom of God if he is "born again." When Nicodemus expresses bewilderment over that teaching, Jesus tells him:

> For God so loved the world, that He gave His only begotten Son, that whoever believes in Him should not perish, but have eternal life. For God did not send the Son into the world to judge the world, but that the world should be saved through Him.

According to Robert Funk and the fellows of the Jesus Seminar, this entire account is neither accurate nor historical. In fact, Nicodemus, they reason, is a make-believe character in a pretend dialogue that never happened. The entire episode, they argue, was written to symbolize some theological truth, not historical reality.

The Jesus Seminar folks make the fatal assumption that the early believers in Christ treated theological truth as something different from actual events that really happened in time, space, and history. They ask us to believe that those first-century Christians were, in effect, willing to spill their blood, submit themselves to unimaginable persecution, and die as martyrs for something that was in fact not true, but only appeared to be true in some fuzzy and confused theological sense.

Real life, of course, tells us something different. Real life tells us that, in the ordinary course of affairs, most of us will not die for ideas, even beautiful ones. We may love a good sonnet from Shakespeare, but we won't risk the executioner's axe over it. Martyrdom is fueled by sterner stuff than mere ideas. It is motivated by the pursuit of truth—truth so absolute and transcendent that all else pales in comparison. Zealots may be willing to die for what they earnestly-but-mistakenly believe to be such a truth. They may even be willing to die merely for what they *hope* to be the truth. But they will surely not die for what they know to be an untruth.

Early Christian martyrs did not die for a resurrected leader while knowing in truth His body was still in the grave. The Christian zealots of the early Church may have been lacking in terms of scientific sophistication, but they still knew that corpses don't rise up and they stink after three days.

What the Jesus Seminar heretics are really doing is foisting their own 20th century fuzzy thinking onto the common folk of the first century. After all, only a fool would invent a religion that relies on impossible facts like the bodily resurrection of Christ, if what they were really after were just fuzzy religious ideas. If that were the case, why bother with claims that would be difficult to prove? The fact is, claims for the miracles of Christ and His bodily resurrection became the mainstay of Christianity precisely because they had been so clearly capable of being verified and proved.

To find the beginning point in the doctrinal deception of the Jesus Seminar, we must recognize that this group of "scholars" contains no representation of conservative, evangelical Bible experts. As theology professors Michael Wilkins and J.P. Moreland put it, "The Jesus Seminar does not come any where close to reflecting an adequate cross section of contemporary New Testament scholars."[1]

The members of the Jesus Seminar begin with the assumption that the Gospels are not the best evidence of the life of Jesus. This is interesting because, in fact, they are the best *available* evidence, which Funk and company would probably have to concede. The early manuscripts and papyri of the Gospels we have are remarkably numerous, and are much closer to the original events by decades than comparable Roman histories—which our universities would not think twice about accepting as true sources of Roman history.

The problem is that the best available evidence—the Gospels—contains multiple stories about miracles. They also clearly portray this Jesus of Nazareth as a man who both claimed to be God in the flesh and exemplified some rather startling qualities of the nature of God. All four Gospels give us not only the miracles of Christ, but a picture of Jesus as the Messiah.

The Jesus Seminar folks have been confronted with information that will not fit into their assumptions that miracles do not happen and that God did not come down in real flesh, die, and rise from the grave. Therefore, rather than reject Christianity altogether (an alternative that at least would be more logically consistent for them), they attempt to remake it in the image of their own fraudulent philosophy. This takes some doing because the Gospels contain a great mass of factual detail that almost all scholars, both conservative and liberal, have to admit is historically accurate. Instead, Funk and his disciples find nice ways of calling the Gospel writers liars.

As an example, Luke begins his Gospel by claiming to have had access to the original eyewitnesses of the actual events as a basis for his narrative. Luke, a physician, would have been more accustomed than most to the systematic observation of people, events, and conditions. His Gospel, he tells us, was the result of his "having investigated everything carefully from the beginning." He says that he had determined to "write it out" in "consecutive order" so that the reader (a fellow named Theophilus) "might know the exact truth" about the life of Jesus (see Luke 1:1-4).

So, how does the Jesus Seminar handle Luke? By rejecting the obvious: "Luke's claim to have researched everything should not be understood in the modern sense....Luke's aim is fundamentally theological rather than historical."[2] They ignore the fact that a physician, even a first-century physician, knew perfectly well what it took to impregnate a woman and cause her to bear a child. Why would he be willing to abandon all he knew about the natural order of things in order to convey "theological truth" about a virgin birth if he had reason to believe it never happened in the first place?

The obvious answer is that Luke, the physician, was forced to modify some of what he knew about natural phenomena when it came to Jesus, precisely because the evidence for Jesus' miracles and his divine nature was so convincing. In other words, the Jesus Seminar proponents have it backwards. Luke did not give up believing in the importance of historical details so that he could deliver theological truth. Rather, the historical details of the life of Jesus were the very things that convinced Luke (and others) of the theological truth about who Jesus really was! Luke says that very clearly in the opening paragraphs of his Gospel. In order to distort this fact, Funk and his group must turn the normal rules about language and the meaning of words on their heads.

Faced with Gospels they cannot totally disregard but stubbornly refuse to accept, Jesus Seminar proponents make one big, grand leap of faith into the unknown—they speculate that the Gospels are corrupt, embellished versions of an earlier, historical, authentic gospel. But because there is no proof that such a document exists, they cannot give it an accurate name. And because the author of this entirely speculative gospel is also unknown, they simply call him "Q." Like some mysterious, invisible visitor who is always messing up the bedroom of a young boy or breaking his mother's good china, "Q" can be given the responsibility or the blame for whatever the human imagination can devise. "Q" therefore can always be argued, with ease, to be a better, more reliable, more historical account of Jesus precisely because it is safely beyond our ability to verify—or even read—it.

The Jesus Seminar is not the only traveling medicine show peddling false potions. Numerous other religious charlatans are revving up their marketing schemes to bring half-truths to mainstream America. Our propensity to be tricked by these hucksters is determined by our willingness to settle for "gilded truths" that are really cheap lies coated with superficial appeal. The *Titanic* was built at the height of what Mark Twain described as the "Gilded Age." It was a time of opulence and man-made pride. Passengers were willing to believe that it was truly an unsinkable ship because faith in human ingenuity had exceeded common sense and belief in man's vulnerability.

The Church has now been swept into the Gilded Age of the 21st century—a time filled with splendid lies covered with a fresh coat of paint. Half-truths are built, like the *Titanic*, on man's ingenuity and boastful ideas. At first blush, they appear to be unsinkable. Upon examination, they prove heretical.

Gay Theology

The Metropolitan Church movement was founded in 1968 and is now comprised of some 500 congregations, meeting mostly in major cities. This movement has attempted to legitimize homosexuality as an approved family style in the church. Frequently they employ openly homosexual clergy. They make the outrageous claim that Jesus and Paul were homosexuals, and that David and Jonathan were gay lovers. They justify these conclusions by a system of biblical interpretation that forces a preconceived social agenda on Scripture, rather than the traditional method of interpretation that has a high regard for the actual text of the Bible.

Gay theology is just one aspect of the aggressive homosexual rights movement in America. It seeks to force social acceptance, and require legal protection, for its practitioners.

Several mainstream denominations have already either softened their positions or reversed entirely their doctrine on homosexuality as sin. They recognize gay marriages and ordain homosexual clergy. As a result, evangelicals are the newest casualties in the theological battle to advance the homosexual movement.

On November 15, 1998, the Wake Forest Baptist Church, a member of the Southern Baptist Convention, adopted a statement that sought God's blessings on "all loving, committed and exclusive relationships between two people," thus permitting homosexual marriages. The church also authorized its ministers to officiate at same-sex weddings. Abandoning clear biblical doctrine, the church chose instead to embrace heresy.

The homosexual movement has deliberately targeted Christians in their propaganda war. One of the popular pamphlets distributed by gay-rights activists looks like a typical Christian gospel tract. On the outside it says, "What Jesus said about homosexuality." When you open it up the pages are blank. Their point is clear: the right-wing conservative Christians have taken the Bible's statements about homosexuality out of context. If Jesus is not quoted as condemning homosexuality, then how bad can it be?

Homosexual activists have even constructed something called "queer theology," a term activists themselves use. Any portrayal of Christ must be forced to fit into the "queer" worldview. For instance, one homosexual theology leader states: "If the Christ is not queer, then the gospel is no longer good news but oppressive news for queers. If the Christ is not queer, then the incarnation has no meaning for our sexuality."[3]

These radical theologians make no apologies for shredding the basics of biblical belief. And, as a gay theologian has noted, "One of the elements of traditional Christianity that queer Christians must jettison is a belief in a literal resurrection."[4]

Because homosexuality cannot be reconciled with Scripture, Scripture is redefined. Both of us, in debating this issue with leaders of the homosexual movement, have heard the argument that the condemnation of Sodom and Gomorrah in the Old Testament had nothing to do with their perverse practices, but was because of their lack of "hospitality" to the angels. But a reading of Genesis 19:4-5 in any responsible translation gives no doubt about the fact that the men of the town intended to perform forced sodomy on their male visitors. There is no question that "homosexuality and sexual perversion" were practiced, and punished, in this incident.[5] The New Testament verifies this in Jude, a letter which was written by the brother of Jesus. Even further, Christ himself verified the authenticity and historical accuracy of the Old Testament description of Sodom and Gomorrah by referring to it in Matthew 10:15, Luke 10:12, and 17:29.

To pretend that the Bible tolerates or even permits homosexuality ignores the fact that the prototype of marriage was created by God, and consisted of a man and a woman. It further requires that we totally ignore other Scripture such as Romans 1:21-32 and 1 Timothy 1:9-10. Gay theology distorts other Scriptures in an attempt to argue that God even permits homosexuality as a positive good. One of the favorites is 2 Samuel 1:25-27, where we see the loving and brotherly relationship between David and Jonathan. As theologian and expert on the homosexual movement, Enrique T. Rueda states:

> Obviously, none of these passages indicates anything but the existence of a strong affective relationship between these men. The reading of a sexual affair between them is absolutely gratuitous and unwarranted; it assumes that all strong personal relationships are sexual in nature.[6]

This is not a matter of compassion or kindly tolerance. It is a matter of guarding the truth of Scripture against the current tide of political correctness. The Bible is not up for a majority vote, and God is not up for reelection. What His Word says settles the matter. Who He is does not change with the political tides of the times, including the current tolerance of those sins of sexual preference.

The Bible According to Feminism

Along with other counterculture movements that swept across America in the 1960s, the rise of radical feminism has proven particularly destructive in the Church. Birthed partly out of rage against what they perceived as a tyrannical patriarchy and male dominance, feminists engaged in a variety of protest activities that ranged from the merely silly to the outrageous and obscene. Feminists publicly burned their bras before gleeful news cameramen hungry for this kind of visual embattlement of the sexes. At a convention of the National Organization for Women, the attendees were encouraged to participate in a kind of public gynecological examination in order to explore their own sexual identity.

The movement to "de-gender" the "sexist" language of the Bible began in the 1970s. When the Presbyterian Church proposed to create a "gender neutral" Bible lexicon for use in worship, it initially met with a great deal of controversy. But by 1995, Oxford University Press had released a politically correct version of Scripture entitled *The New Testament and Psalms, An Inclusive Version*. In their attempt to be more relevant and more all encompassing, God is changed to "father-mother." Jesus is called the "human one" or "child of God." And when Jesus is dying on the cross, he cries out, in their version, "Father-mother, into your hands I commend my spirit."

Women are told to be committed rather than subject or submissive to their husbands. Children no longer need to obey their parents, now all they must do is "heed." And if you are a left-hander, you needn't feel offended. Now, Christ sits not on the "right hand" of God, but at the "mighty hand" of God.

At least one large religious publisher with an impressive history of evangelical books to its credit stopped just short of publishing a non-gender Bible only after a theological firestorm broke out. The protest from the Bible-believing Church doused the project, for now. But the fire of heresy is still smoldering.

Feminist theologians have dug in and created an intricate system of trench warfare. One battle line is the way in which Christian language will be abandoned in favor of other pro-feminist terms. Another area for reconstruction is the way in which rituals are used in worship. Rita Gross, professor of religion at University of Wisconsin Eau Claire, has proposed a vision for "post-patriarchal" Christianity. In this new millennium religion, we are urged to adopt a radical new acceptance of pagan rituals that have been condemned by Christianity for 2000 years and which are forbidden in the strongest terms throughout the Old Testament. Referring to the pagan cult worship of Wicca and its relationship to feminism, Gross claims, "Magic, exorcism, spell casting, and hexing are all part of contemporary Wicca. Though spiritual feminists disagree over exactly what these terms mean and how these processes work, they are part of the recognized common vocabulary of the feminist spirituality movement."[7]

"Ecological feminists," Gross suggests, may take to describing the universe as "God's body" to fully express their environmental concerns. As to the relationship between the feminist "god" and the earth, she quotes eco-feminist Sallie McFague in claiming that God is in fact "the Mother who encloses reality in her womb...generating all life from her being."

Goddess worship is a full-blown article of faith in the feminist movement. Elisabeth Schussler Fiorenza, Professor of Divinity at Harvard Divinity School, demands that Christianity overcome its fear of the concept of a goddess. These kinds of theological monstrosities are to be expected whenever a system of belief about God is permanently wedded to a radical political/social philosophy. Fiorenza boldly proclaims that theological truth must reside (i.e., "must remain embedded") within the confines of the radical feminist movement: "For that reason I have argued here that G*d language, discourses about Jesus Christ, and Marian symbolism must remain embedded in feminist liberation movements and practices of transformation."[8]

Scripture teaches us that the fear of God is the beginning of wisdom. Feminists like Fiorenza have twisted that and turned it around, preaching that their own faulty feminist wisdom shall be the beginning of their creation of gods and goddesses.

Some feminists, like Mary Daly in her mind-numbing *Pure Lust: Elemental Feminist Philosophy*, simply make no apologies for their rage against traditional Christian belief and their desecration of the holy things of God.

> Indeed, male rape fantasies become high theology and elicit religious rapture when these are vaporized and condensed, elevated and converted, into dogma and art concerning the "Virgin Birth." In the "Annunciation" the male-angel Gabriel brings poor Mary the news that she is to be impregnated by and with god. Like all rape victims in male myth she submits joyously to this unspeakable degradation.[9]

As incredible as it seems, Daly's description of the crucifixion of Christ is even more offensive. And although we would like to ignore her rantings and blasphemies, we do so at our peril. She holds degrees in theology and philosophy, and her ideas are not considered by the American intelligentsia as part of a radical, lunatic fringe, but as worthy of a hearing in the mainstream culture. A leading figure in feminist theology, her twisted ideas have been praised by the *New York Times Book Review*. Even more importantly, like the other religious sorceresses, Daly holds an influential teaching position as an associate professor in theology at Boston College. These radical feminist theologians are part of the academic faculty in colleges where their ideas are influencing generations to come.

The Response of Believers

What should our response be? We could simply condemn them, of course. But there is no support for such a hard-hearted approach in the Gospels. First, let us keep a firm reliance on Scripture that tells us their created gods and goddesses are lifeless, but our God of creation is the giver of life. We must be armed with the understanding of the high price Scripture places on truth.

Thus, their ideas, which are hellish, must be intelligently but firmly condemned.

Second, let us have the courage to admit that the rise of these heretical forms of belief are not someone else's responsibility. They are *our* responsibility. Those who propagate these false messages, and those who believe them, are creating for themselves not just false systems of belief, but dangerous mirages that take thirsty people and lead them into a desert. Damage is being done to people, and lives are being destroyed. We must be the water carriers with the living water of Jesus Christ.

Feminism arose from the ashes of broken marriages, abused women, dysfunctional women, and uncaring and callous husbands who did not practice the recipe for loving relationships set out in God's Word. Gay theology is the product of homosexuals, many of whom are the results of failed same-sex family relationships with their own fathers. It is not enough to condemn their theological perversions, we must see the brokenness that precedes their spiritual confusion and lovingly lead them to Christ, who is the only true source of healing. At the same time we have to be ready to fight for eternal truth within our own Christian community. These two goals—lovingly showing and sharing the gospel to the proponents of feminism and gay theology, yet fighting against falsehood and deception—are not inconsistent. We must learn to do both.

Fighting for truth means recognizing the onslaught of heresy that is increasingly assaulting the Church. Even evangelical churches are starting to show some frayed edges on key issues as a result of 40 years of aggressive feminist attack.

In 1997, *World* magazine, a news publication with an evangelical worldview, published a series of articles dealing with the effects of feminism on the Church. The articles mentioned, in particular, discussions within one Christian publishing house on printing an "inclusive language" New International Version Bible. This issue started with the Committee for Biblical Translation (CBT), the 15-person group that governs the NIV. The CBT had voted on the creation of an NIV *Inclusive Language Edition*. The version would change certain passages of the Bible where the gender reference had previously been male. As an example, instead of God saying, "Let us make man in our image..." the new version reads, "Let us make human beings in our image...."

Bible scholar J.I. Packer called the gender-sensitive version "the feminist edition," and said it reflected an attempt "to pander to a cultural prejudice that I hope will be short-lived." Dr. James Dobson properly wondered if the NIV effort, though well intentioned, "may be hijacked by the spirit of the age, injecting feminist bias and language into the inspired text."[10]

A formal complaint was lodged with the Evangelical Publishing Association against *World* magazine over their series. In the end, however, in the wake of rising objections, the International Bible Society abandoned all plans for gender-related changes in future editions of the New International Version.

While the dust may have settled for the time being on that dispute, it spotlights two urgent jobs for Christians as we enter the new century: maintaining the purity of what we believe along with not sacrificing a spirit of love. As challenges to the integrity of the Word of God increase in the next century, we must do both.

Paul challenges us not to be like immature children, "tossed here and there by waves, and carried about by every wind of doctrine..." but "speaking the truth in love, we are to grow up in all aspects into Him, who is the head, even Christ..." (Ephesians 4:14-15). Growing up in Christ means being bold and uncompromising for the truth in a way that still expresses love. This, in turn, highlights the need for Christian discernment in matters of faith and conduct in a fallen world. Scripture tells us that each of us is to strive to be a mature believer, able to handle the solid food of the Word of God. Mature believers are those "who because of practice have their senses trained to discern good and evil" (Hebrews 5:13-14). To be "discerning," therefore, requires practice in applying the Bible to our lives in order to sharpen our abilities to divide good and evil.

We must be alert to the signs of the times. We must have our eyes wide open if we are to apply biblical standards to the subtle evidence of compromise and shifting standards all around us.

The Threat of Doctrinal Compromise

In the spring of 1994, a profoundly important new movement began. It is called "Catholics and Evangelicals Together." The idea of evangelicals and Catholics working together has borne positive fruit over the last 20 years, particularly in fighting abortion and resisting other destructive social agendas in America. The prospect of finding common ground *theologically*, however, is a different story. Unfortunately, the assumption of "common ground" is that each side will be willing to suspend disagreements on issues that occupy territory on the fringes for the sake of meeting together in the middle on the essentials. Yet when it comes to the truth of what God has said about Himself, about the human condition of sin, and how we can enter into a right relationship with Him both in terms of salvation and our daily Christian walk, separating the "fringe" from the "essentials" can resemble a theological high-wire act.

Catholics and evangelicals met in an historic series of meetings in the spring of 1994. As a result, they produced a joint document entitled "Evangelicals and Catholics Together: The Christian Mission in the Third Millennium" (ECT I). The effort at common ground between Catholics and Protestants has met with criticism. Phil Roberts, director of the Interfaith Witness of the North American Mission Board, part of the Southern Baptist Convention, correctly notes:

> The attempt was ill-advised and seemed to created more confusion than good. The theological reasoning in the document was confusing and at points only served to renew old antagonism between Catholics and Protestants. Several signatories, in fact, had to withdraw their names as a result of pressure from their respective denominations or organizations.[11]

In October 1997, a group of representatives from both sides met again and hammered out a joint statement on salvation, entitled ECT II. That document is troublesome as well. The range of subjects that are admitted to still be in disagreement are so broad as to render the agreed-upon language almost meaningless; the wording on baptism is ambiguous, if not contradictory; reference is made to "Reformation traditions" without any real explanation; salvation and justification are used interchangeably; and the entire subject of spiritual conversion (being "born again") is muddied and vague. Perhaps most important of all, the document leaves unanswered the issue of whether justification by faith involves God's righteousness imputed to us by God, through His grace (that is, by faith alone, as it says in Romans 3:21-31), or whether we are ultimately justified by our transformed lives lived out in faith (in other words, are we saved by works?).

While the Joint Statement appears to present itself in line with the Reformation "tradition," in fact it leaves still unanswered the most important question of the Reformation—whether justification is by faith alone ("sola fide").

The ECT documents have been seized upon by Catholic apologists as clear evidence that the evangelical and Reformation view of salvation is finally falling apart. According to some Catholic authors these "common ground" conferences show that evangelicals are abandoning the Reformation view that we are "justified" in God's eyes, and accepted by Him for salvation by "faith alone" and entirely apart from good works. Robert Sungenis, who is president of an organization whose mission is to defend the teachings of the Catholic faith, has written:

> Further evidence of a breakup in the Evangelical stance on *faith alone* justification is the recent document signed by major Evangelical and Catholic spokesmen. Evangelicals... signed the document knowing that the words *faith alone* were not included in the joint statement on justification....In any

case, the cracks in *faith alone* theology continue to become increasingly evident.[12]

Evangelical Bible teachers R.C. Sproul, John MacArthur, and Dave Hunt have all criticized the Evangelicals and Catholics Together movement as a serious theological mistake.

In the final analysis it is unlikely that the Catholic Church hierarchy will convert to the evangelical view on salvation and spiritual conversion. The ECT movement, after all, does not have the official involvement of Rome. When Pope John II was in Mexico in January 1999, he warned his followers to beware of the evangelicals who have made significant inroads into the Catholic Church. Even further, the Pope recently reaffirmed the validity of the ages-old Catholic doctrine of "indulgences," the ability of the Catholic Church to administer to its followers the avoidance of punishment for sins. It was this practice that was at the core of Martin Luther's objections, later leading to a full-scale Reformation movement in the Christian Church.

The governing leadership of Rome seems light years away from endorsing the ECT effort. What ECT may do, however, is to further confuse those sheep who are simply trying to listen to the Shepherd by adding more conflicting voices to an already noisy sheepfold.

In a sense, this "common ground" movement is history repeating itself. When the Reformation movement was first started, there was an attempt to unify the theology of reformers like Martin Luther with the Catholic Church. In June 1530, a document entitled "The Augsberg Confession" was revealed in Augsberg, Germany. The purpose behind this religious statement was to win the reformers back into the structure of the Roman church. That attempt at reconciliation failed, as well it should.

The Confession, while evangelical in tone, failed to assert the sole authority of Scripture in matters of faith and practice. Such things as the universal "priesthood" of all believers in

Christ (1 Peter 2:9), the nature of the Lord's Supper, and the debate over purgatory were never mentioned in the document. The current attempt to bridge the gap between Catholic and Protestant is no worthier than the efforts in 1530. The evangelical Church must guard against betraying the work of those who paved the way for the Reformation 400 years ago simply for the sake of a religious unification that is as unworkable as it is unwise.

On the other hand, differences of reformationalist v. traditionalist, or fundamentalist v. evangelical should not take our focus away from the common goal of spreading the gospel of Christ to a perishing world. We must not allow differences in worship or practices that may be minor, to become major in the fellowship and work of the body of Christ. Knowing the difference between the two will be a major task before the Church in the 21st century.

CHAPTER FIVE

Knowing Truth, Showing Love, Using Discernment

Although there is a consistent radio audience of cynics, non-believers, agnostics, pagan-worshipers, and atheists listening at any one time to "Janet Parshall's America," there are also many who call the show and identify themselves as born-again believers in Jesus Christ. It is a tremendous privilege to daily connect with the vast network of Christians who are walking the same pilgrimage with the Lord. Yet on this road of faith, there seems to be an ever-increasing number of pilgrims who sound utterly confused over doctrinal issues and deceptive teachings.

This particular problem harkens back to the classic story of the Christian pilgrim. It is a story of a follower of Jesus heading toward God's kingdom through the journey of life, but having to deal with spiritual tricksters and deceptive counterfeits on the way. Next to the Bible itself, the second most widely read Christian book of all time is John Bunyan's *The Pilgrim's Progress*. Why has it been so popular? Perhaps because Bunyan was able to distill the great and profound issues of the Christian faith to the level of our common experience. He took the spiritual walk of the Christian and put skin on it. He took the heavenly pursuit of the believer and translated it into earthly terms we all could understand.

The Christian walk is portrayed in Bunyan's book as a literal walk over the ever-changing terrain of life—some smooth, much of it rugged and up hill. Yet one of the recurring dangers that the main character (appropriately named "Christian") encounters on his journey is the peril of deception. Toward the end of the story, Christian learns to look past the superficial appearance of places and people he meets on the way, and develops a sense of spiritual discernment that is more critical for believers now than ever before.

As a new follower of Christ, just starting out on his faith walk, Christian and his fellow traveler, Hopeful, soon find themselves discouraged by the rough ground underfoot. However, they discover what appears to be a shortcut to the Celestial City, their ultimate destination. Their decision to take the easy and inviting bypass is influenced by another pilgrim, "Vain-confidence," who is heading in the same direction. He is taking this shortcut which, by all appearances, will avoid the dangers and challenges of the proscribed road of faith. They follow his lead, not realizing that the decision-making of Vain-confidence is based on an over-reliance in his own human reasoning. The three friends depart from the mapped-out pilgrim's route that has been given them at the beginning of their journey—a disastrous mistake that Christians should heed in the new millennium.

It is not long before the Christian threesome, after being deceived into departing from God's charted path, meet one cat-

astrophe after another. Vain-confidence falls into a pit. Then
Hopeful and Christian lose their way and make the mistake of
sleeping on the grounds of a forbidding place called "Doubting
Castle."

Bunyan powerfully portrays the consequences of the believer
straying from the narrow, straight path of God's Word. Hopeful
and Christian are caught unguarded by the hulking, hateful lord
of this dismal place—the Giant Despair. He tosses them into a
"dark dungeon, nasty and stinking to the spirit of these two men."

Having thus captured them, the Giant Despair entices them
to end their miserable condition by suggesting they commit suicide. Thus trapped, Christian and Hopeful are the painful but
accurate picture of believers who have been deceived by a world
system that promises quick and appealing answers but, in the end,
makes us slaves to doubt and despair. Their final escape from the
wretched dungeon comes only when Christian remembers to use
the key (which symbolizes the promises of God found in
Scripture) that hangs around his neck. The key is used to unlock
the prison door and represents the victory that belongs to the
believer who turns to God's unchanging guarantees in His Word.

Later in the journey, we see Christian with a more attuned
sense of spiritual discernment. By the end of the story, he has
gained spiritual maturity and has mastered the habit of relying on
and skillfully using God's principles and promises.

Approaching the Celestial City, Christian encounters a fellow named Ignorance. Christian questions this man's basis for
what he believes about the path he is taking and his motivations
for taking it. Ignorance's answers, which are based entirely on
inward feelings of the heart, sound embarrassingly modern. In
fact, from time to time we all may have used this kind of faulty
perspective on our Christian walk:

> Christian: ...But why or by what art thou persuaded that
> thou hast left all for God and Heaven?

Ignorance: My heart tells me so.

Christian: The wise man says, He that trusts his own heart is a fool.

Ignorance: That is spoken of an evil heart, but mine is a good one.

Christian: But how dost thou prove that?

Ignorance: It comforts me in the hopes of Heaven.

Christian: That may be through its deceitfulness, for a man's heart may minister comfort to him in the hopes of that thing for which he yet has no ground to hope.

Ignorance: But my heart and life agree together, and therefore my hope is well grounded.

Christian: Who told thee that thy heart and life agree together?

Ignorance: My heart tells me so.

Christian: Ask my fellow if I be a thief; thy heart tells thee so! Except the Word of God beareth witness in this matter, other testimony is of no value.

Considering the army of spiritual counterfeits that are marching into the 21st century, it would be easy to conclude that this threat to the Church is a particularly modern problem. In fact, just the opposite is true. The early Church in the first century was faced with a considerable number of false teachers, heretical doctrines, and twisted interpretations of the ministry of Jesus of Nazareth.

The Apostle Paul recognized this as a serious problem. After planting the church at Ephesus during the course of his three years there, Paul addressed the critical threat from false teachers in his closing message to the elders of that church. Paul was setting off on a missionary journey that he believed would separate him from his Ephesian brothers and sisters for the rest of his life. His last words to the church leadership reflect an intense and emotional appeal. Baring his heart, Paul shared his greatest burdens for the assembly of young Christians.

He warned of the "savage wolves" that would seek to ravage the flock of believers in his absence. Even worse, he warned that these false teachers who would attempt to draw their own disciples out of the ranks of the church would not appear as outside agitators. Rather, they would come from within the fellowship of the church itself (Acts 20:29-30).

In his letter to Timothy, one of his disciples, the Apostle Paul warned that in "later times some will fall away from the faith, paying attention to deceitful spirits and doctrines of demons..." (1 Timothy 4:1). Even John, one of Jesus' original 12 disciples, admonished believers to "test the spirits" in order to avoid "false prophets" (1 John 4:1). With these clear signposts for us in Scripture, we should know how to avoid getting caught in the clever snares of spiritual deception.

Knowing the Truth: The Central Role of Scripture

Deception-proofing our faith requires us to concentrate on the doctrines of the faith, and unfortunately to many of us this is a dry, confusing, and irrelevant pursuit. Studying the foundations of what we believe, and why we believe it, may seem to some to be lifeless and unrewarding. If we are looking for the emotional highs of the Christian walk, "theology" comes across as a real low. If we think that our greatest need is for a faith that will solve our newest set of problems or remedy the pain in our current life dilemma, then coming to grips with the meaning of sanctification or meditating on the relationship between grace and works may strike us as very much beside the point.

We would be well advised to remember the illustration of the train. The Christian faith is like one of those old-fashioned steam locomotives. The locomotive engine stands for *faith*. Our practice of faith, our personal belief in and commitment to Jesus Christ, is the dynamic force that energizes and directs our walk with God. The coal car represents *facts*—historical and doctrinal truths of Christianity—and they are the fuel, the energy behind what we believe. Last comes the caboose, which represents *feelings*. Our emotional life and physical circumstances are behind everything else because they cannot be relied upon to determine the direction of our faith. Instead, feelings are the byproducts of our spiritual walks. If this were not true, when we experience a sterile "desert" phase emotionally, the truth of Scripture would cease to be true. When we make our inward spiritual feelings the guide for all things, our Christian theology begins to look more like a rollercoaster ride than a pathway of faith. But God continues to be God regardless of how we feel about Him. Our task is to focus on who He is, how He has communicated His truth to us, and what it means to be His children.

The famous evangelist and preacher Dwight L. Moody used to say that the best way to see if your measurement of spiritual doctrine is crooked is to line it up next to the "straight stick of truth." An architect cannot design a great building with a T-square that is crooked. The scientists at NASA could not plan a successful space launch if they could not project a straight trajectory for the rocket. How can we expect to stand firm against the lies of the great deceiver without a command of the truth that is "straight and narrow"? The Bible, the straight stick of God's revealed Word to us, must play the central role in our battle with deception.

This is also important because false teachers can present heresy in a way that looks and sounds convincing to the biblically naive believer. Paul warned that such theological fakes can make very "confident assertions," even though they have no understanding for what they are talking about (1 Timothy 1:7).

Our primary role model in dealing with spiritual deception, as in everything else, must be the Lord Jesus. Notice how He handled deception when Satan pulled out all the stops in an effort to tempt Him. In Matthew 4, Satan presents three temptations. All three were clever because they had a superficial kind of reasonableness to them. They were also particularly devious because his arguments were based on half-truths built on the misuse of Scripture.

Our Lord responded to all three arguments by reciting the Bible in context and rightly applied. But let us not forget the big picture: Jesus had been without food and water, and had been spending days in one of the harshest, hottest deserts in the world. Yet despite this, His response to the deceptive strategies of the enemy were not based on His comfort level, they were based on the Word of God, which is the only infallible guide when faced with lies cloaked in half-truths. God is not interested in our comfort; He is interested in our character.

We should also consider the Christians at Berea. Luke, the author of Acts, observed that they were "noble minded" because they received the gospel message with "great eagerness," and "examined the Scriptures daily" in order to verify that this proclamation of Jesus as Messiah lined up with God's promises in the Old Testament. When Paul was warning the church at Ephesus of the danger of false teachers he had a simple but powerful remedy. After urging them to "be on the alert," he exhorted them to be committed to God's Word: "And now I commend you to God and to the word of His grace, which is able to build you up and to give you the inheritance among all those who are sanctified" (Acts 20:32).

We will need to understand the importance of the inerrancy, infallibility, and inspiration of the Bible in order to meet the challenges to our faith that will come at us in the next century, cleverly cloaked in reasonable-sounding half-truths. We must leave no room for compromise in accepting the fact that "all Scripture is inspired by God and profitable for teaching, for reproof, for correction, for training in righteousness; that the man of God may be adequate, equipped, for every good work" (2 Timothy 3:16-17).

Being armed with a right understanding of, and reliance on, the Word of God is the first step toward preparing for the new deceptions of the new millennium.

Seeking Spiritual Stability and Maturity

Placing too much of an emphasis on getting a "spiritual high" in the Christian walk creates other problems for believers in addition to making us gullible to the lies of the enemy. It also creates a willingness to respond to the invitation of almost all cults and false religions that promise peace, joy, happiness, prosperity, or excitement. Whatever it is that we are craving and feel we are lacking, these false teachers will claim they can provide it.

That does not mean Christianity has to be dour, dull, or joyless. Even though Christ was the "man of sorrows," and lived a life of perfect sacrifice, He lived a life of joy, and promised to share that joy with those who follow Him.

It does mean, however, that while joy is the result of living-out a true faith grounded in His truth, it is not the defining cause for what we believe, nor is it the motivation for us to believe. Rather, our motivation should issue forth from the amazing recognition that God really has spoken, and that Christianity (which is the content of what He has spoken) is true.

As we confront, in the coming millennium, the strategic deception of the three enemies of the Church—the world, the flesh, and the devil—we should prioritize an often ignored and yet fundamental aspect of the Christian walk: spiritual stability. Being grounded and rooted in what we believe, we will not be moved by the winds of change or enchanted by the newest religious fad.

The Christians at Colossae were praised for the "stability" of their faith in Christ. Paul undoubtedly singled out this aspect of their faith for special recognition because of the great onslaught of false philosophies and religions that were bombarding the Church in that area of what today is modern Turkey.

The chief heresy involved variations of Gnosticism. This religious philosophy has been difficult to define precisely, but it basically claimed to possess secret and mystical truths about God, placed Jesus on a continuum along with all of the prophets, and led to acts of self-denial as a means of becoming one with the divine. The Gnostics recognized noncanonical writings as inspired (the so-called "Gnostic gospels"), and their influence would continue to plague the Christian Church for centuries.

In order to resist the deceptive teachings of this philosophy, believers needed to cultivate the commitment to a faith that was stable and rooted in the eternal, unchanging truths of Scripture.

About 100 miles from Colossae was the church at Ephesus. They were likely to have faced the same heresy. And, like the church at Colossae, the Ephesian believers were urged by Paul to cultivate the maturity and stability of their faith: "As a result, we are no longer to be children, tossed here and there by waves, and carried about by every wind of doctrine, by the trickery of men, by craftiness in deceitful scheming" (Ephesians 4:14).

What we need to establish is a Christian walk that will endure through a lifetime of service to the Lord, and not create a spiritual thirst for more gimmicks, bells, and whistles.

The Reality of False Teachers

Most of us never feel comfortable when we find ourselves accused of "judging" others who are talking about the things of God. There is a good reason for that. We are all sinners. We feel there is nothing quite so dishonest as a hypocrite who denounces others while practicing the very same sin. A stream of Hollywood films over the decades has developed the role of the religious hypocrite into a special art form.

Yet there is a risk that the current culture can intimidate us into silence about the differences between those who speak God's Word and those who speak man's word but claim it is from God. To tell the difference is not hypocrisy; it is simply applying God's slide rule to the modern formulas of distortion. If those formulas are found wanting, it is not our judgment that condemns them, it is God's. Scripture is very clear about the fact that we must expect false teachers. It is also clear about some of the major warning signs of religious charlatans.

False teachers very often lack the spiritual stability that Christians are to cultivate. The book of Jude was written by a man who identifies himself as the brother of James, the leader of the Jerusalem church. He was, therefore, also the half-brother of Jesus. Jude's indictment of false religious teachers is one of the most forceful in all of the Bible. We are told that false teachers are "carried along by winds" and are like "wandering stars" (Jude 12,13). They lack grounding in the unchanging truth of God, yet they give the appearance of being as fixed as the stars in the sky! If we navigate our ship of faith by looking to moving and untrustworthy points of light, no matter how bright and fixed they may look, we will end up crashing on their hidden reefs.

We are also warned that false teachers pursue ungodly lusts. This means more than just sexual sins, although it is interesting to note how many notorious false teachers like Jim Jones and David Koresh used their position of influence to gain sexual favors. But it can also be a lust for power, control, or money—manipulating and "flattering people for the sake of gaining an advantage" (v. 16).

The teachings of false prophets are "wordly-minded," according to Jude, rather than based on God's heavenly view of the inadequacy of the world. False teachers can also be detected by their lack of spiritual growth. They are "autumn trees without fruit" in contrast to believers who manifest the fruit of the Spirit (v. 12). In Jude, such teachers are likened to Cain, Balaam, and Korah. All three of those men give us examples of those who advocated false religions and the consequences of their actions.

Cain insisted on his own type of religious sacrifice. When it was rejected by God, Cain gave into self-will instead of conforming his actions to the desires of God. He ignored the clear warning from God that "sin was crouching by the door."

Balaam was a prophet-for-hire whose main concern was collecting his wages rather than dispensing God's truth, and Korah rejected the spiritual leadership established by God through his ordained servants and tried to launch a rebellion among God's people (Numbers 16:1-33). Korah is the classic form of a false spiritual leader who goes among the people and "causes divisions."

Whether we want to admit it or not, as the spiritual confusion of our age increases, false teachers will abound.

Showing Love: A Positive Alternative

Being able to recognize false teachers and deceptive doctrines is critical. But if all we have is the ability to target the spiritual liar with our truth arrows, it will not be enough. We have to go to the next step. Doctrine without love is as dead as the bones in a forgotten and weed-infested cemetery.

The world, which has a woeful ignorance of the message of the Bible, loves to quote 1 Corinthians 13, the famous section on love. We have heard it preached and proclaimed by liberals in a number of situations, perhaps because it can be made to sound nonjudgmental and fuzzy and warm. But there is nothing "fuzzy and warm" about 1 Corinthians 13.

In fact, the subject of love that we are given in that chapter is downright revolutionary. It is an idea that could topple tyrannies, change the hearts of world leaders, and alter the course of history. In fact, it did just that in the ministry of Christ, in the lives of his disciples, and in the history of the Christian Church. This kind of love was no mere cozy emotional feeling. The kind of love staked out through the history of the Church was tough, unyielding, sacrificial, and focused on the truth of Christ. This kind of love "bears all things, believes all things, hopes all things, endures all things" (1 Corinthians 13:7).

Love is also practical when it comes to doctrinal truth. The men and women who serve in our churches, Sunday school programs, and parachurch ministries, and who faithfully share the

89

gospel of Jesus Christ, deserve the real-life expression of our love and our support. If they have stood for the truth of God's Word, they need your encouragement. The pastor who faithfully lays down the straight stick of God's truth needs to hear the expression of our appreciation, not just our complaints that the Sunday service is too long or the air-conditioning is set too high. If the Church has placed a high premium on truth, have we, in love for the Church, placed a high premium on financial giving to it?

Our prayer life should reflect this attitude of love. We must pray for and support Bible schools and seminaries that will continue to train Christian leaders who will teach the Bible without apology or compromise in the coming age. We need to pray for such leaders because we may well be heading into an age that will be quicker than ever to avoid, and apologize for, the often uncomfortable but always life-changing message of Jesus Christ.

This kind of love should lead us to rejoice. We have been called into a time when the land around us is spiritually impoverished. But the Bible tells us that as disciples of the Lord Jesus Christ we are bearers of a great treasure: We have been entrusted with the treasure of the gospel of good news.

What a great privilege to share that immense and eternal wealth whenever and wherever we can. What an honor to bear His love, in our bodies and through our lives, for His kingdom!

CHAPTER SIX

Escape from Darkness

Tal Brooke has been a guest on "Janet Parshall's America" several times. He is always thought-provoking and interesting. He was born into what he describes as a "post-Christian family." His father was a diplomat in England, so Tal experienced the flavor of international culture. He also soon encountered the occult. The family's housekeeper in London was a self-styled medium, and Tal's toys as a boy included a Ouija Board.

During his college years, Tal became a backpacking, LSD-taking seeker. Like many of those who wander into false religions, his trips to the far-flung ends of the earth were a mirror for the wanderings and longings of his soul. In the 1960s, he read the works of Alan Watts, a colleague of Harvard Professor Timothy Leary. Like Leary, Watts was an evangelist for the drug trip, a preacher of the chemically induced religious experience. Brooke was impressed with this new brand of mysticism:

> Here was the testimony of a contemporary mystic. He did not pray in the desert, he did not fast in the wilderness, he did not stick to rigid covenants, nor was he required to spend months in isolation. Rather his meeting with God was as subdued as a New England tea, in part because he took LSD on a farm in the country, and spent the time surveying deeply significant things in this newly altered state of consciousness.[1]

Brooke began immersing himself in books of east-Indian religion. Finally, he left his studies at the University of Virginia and headed for India in search of ultimate enlightenment. At that time, there was a popular "avatar" named Sai Baba living in India. Claiming some 20 million followers, Baba had been called the "Christ" of India by *Newsweek*, and had been credited with performing "miracles" like turning water into gasoline when his car's gas tank was on empty.

Here was perhaps the most famous modern religious figure alive in India. His fame had reached across the ocean to the fertile shores of California. Sai Baba was praised ecstatically in the New Age autobiography of Hollywood's Shirley MacLaine, yet he was inaccessible to almost everyone on an individual basis. His throngs of followers were limited to brief glimpses of him when he would appear at festivals to share his "wisdom" or lead them in Indian hymns as they sat prostrate before him.

Amazingly, Tal gained access to Baba for two full years and followed him as one of his closest disciples. Baba's enticement of Tal began with a simple approach: "Confusion, much confusion," he told Tal. "Not happy, not happy…not happy in America, too much materialism, and no love. Always looking for love, the pure love of

God, but only finding a small sample." Brooke, who had opened himself to the influence of the great deceiver by his meditations on the Hindu scriptures called the Bhagavad Gita, was hooked.

Baba had used the classic approach of the cultist. He knew the soul sickness and emptiness that was in the heart of man. He picked out Tal, who was both receptive and isolated, then offered the perfect "tonic" for the spiritual illness. Tal pledged himself as a servant to this self-proclaimed "Lord of the Universe," offering himself as his property.

But what was promised as the ultimate "enlightenment" soon became a form of spiritual imprisonment. He describes his two "wasted years" by admitting, "Now I could examine my due reward—dogs, beggars, mud, fruit vendors, fleas, photographers and every manner of hawker and hustler and con artist.... My due was a broken heart, a nearly wrecked soul, a penniless pocket, and a grossly undernourished physical body."[2]

Tal Brooke was led out of his captivity by the love of a missionary couple who patiently showed him the truth of God's Word. The seeds were planted, and when Tal returned to England, in the quiet corner of a chapel the pieces fell into place. Looking on the chiseled words of Christ in stone, he wept when he read, "Greater love hath no man than He who would give His life for his friend."

The reality of sin was the great missing element of Baba's phony religious banter. When Tal Brooke was shown the fact of sin through the Bible, he knew why he needed a Savior to be a living sacrifice. "To God and those witnessing my act," Brooke explains, " I faced the wall and utterly denounced Baba. I admitted the depth of my wrongdoing and sin. Then I confessed that Christ alone is the way, the truth, and the life."[3]

Today, Tal Brooke lives and works in California. He is the president and founder of Spiritual Counterfeits Project, an international ministry that helps educate the Church about the constantly changing topography of spiritual warfare and the dangers of new religious movements. God's efficiency and economy is perfect. God did not waste Tal's experience of sojourning in the dark land of spiritual deception. Having wandered in the religious wasteland of eastern mysticism, Tal Brooke is now one of God's "air traffic controllers," guiding others to the one and only way, truth, and light.

Battling for the Bible

Not all battles with doctrinal deception involve religions that are distinctly non-Christian. Some of the most notable examples of tough faith involve struggles against forms of Christianity that have deprived the gospel of its power and its message.

For instance, many of us are familiar with the important work of Wycliffe Bible translators, who place the Word of God into native languages of even the most remote groups and tribes around the globe. We may be less familiar with their namesake. John Wycliffe was a man who boldly broke away from the religious doctrines of his day and contributed to the development of the Reformation idea that the Bible is the true source of God's revealed Word and will, rather than church canons or rules. A noted intellectual in 14th-century England, Wycliffe predated the Reformation by about 100 years, living from c. 1325 to 1384. A teacher at Oxford University and schooled in the medieval scholastic thought of the Catholic Church, he became the advisor to King Edward III and later was the rector of a local parish.

Wycliffe's outspoken writings on spiritual matters put him at the center of a great religious and political controversy, pitting the ambitions of the English Crown against the authority of the pope. Wycliffe had increasingly begun to question the prevailing religious ideas on the power of the medieval Church. Even further, he became convinced that Scripture alone served as the true guide for the Christian life. Wycliffe had also dared to suggest that the Church's property holdings might be subject to civil law, while the true authority of the Church, which extended to preaching spiritual truth, should be forever outside of the reach of the king.

The unscrupulous son of the king, John of Gaunt, and his brand of corrupt nobles seized on Wycliffe's writings as a means of trying to grab the considerable financial holdings of the Church for their own use. Disturbed by this development, the English Bishops summoned Wycliffe to an inquisition, but he was protected by the king from having to appear. Pope Gregory XI issued an order for him to appear at Rome, and similar ecclesiastical proceedings were started against him in London. Wycliffe's popular support among the English people, aided by the fact that he was an asset to the Crown, insured his protection.

John Wycliffe could easily have decided to lie low and hide in the safety of the English Crown. Instead, his writings became bolder, utterly rejecting the traditional structure of the medieval Church and clearly proclaiming that the Bible was the "highest authority for every Christian and the standard of faith and of all human perfection." This was a radical idea. The Bible used by the Church was written in Latin, and the peasant class was thoroughly uneducated. Further, the Bible was treated as the sole property of the Church hierarchy, to use and interpret for the common people. When Wycliffe withdrew entirely from the politics of the English Crown, he became a target of official condemnation from both Rome and the king. When a bloody revolt of the peasants broke out as an aftermath of the Black Plague sweeping Europe, Wycliffe was wrongly blamed for inciting the lower class with his teachings.

The Archbishop of Canterbury condemned Wycliffe's writings and was given authority by the king to arrest and imprison anyone in the realm who spread Wycliffe's condemned evangelical ideas.

Remarkably, Wycliffe himself remained safely in the confines of his small parish and continued to write on matters of faith. He also penned a number of sermons that were used by the "poor priests," itinerant evangelists who had broken away from the medieval Church and were spreading the gospel among the peasants.

But perhaps Wycliffe's greatest contribution to Christians of all ages was his inspiration for translating the Bible from the Latin Vulgate into English so it could be read and believed by the common folk. The power of John Wycliffe's tough and unyielding view of the Christian faith created many enemies. He was so rigorously denounced that 44 years after his death, church leaders ordered his grave be dug up, his remains burned, and his ashes thrown into the River Swift.

It is unlikely that John Wycliffe would have been too concerned. As we enter the 21st century, the Bible to which he was so passionately committed has been translated into more languages, and has been read by more people, than any other book ever written.

The Fortress of Faith

One hundred years after the death of John Wycliffe, the evangelical church was still having birth pangs. The year was 1483. The place was Germany. The man was Martin Luther, born to a father who had raised himself from the peasant class to be the owner of a successful mining company. But he wanted a better life for his son Martin, so he saw to it that the young man was enrolled in law school at the University of Erfurt.

Martin would never graduate. After the sudden death of one of his close classmates, and his own near-death experience with a bolt of lightning that almost struck him, Luther withdrew from law school. Apparently shaken by the fragility of life and convinced of the necessity of pursuing spiritual rather than worldly goals, he entered an Augustinian monastery. Two years later Martin Luther was ordained as a priest and was soon given a position as a lecturer in Wittenberg. He continued his theological studies and was granted a degree of doctor of theology in 1515. Luther's quick mind and immense learning helped him rise to rapid fame in the university community.

But even as he was gaining professional acclaim as a theologian and religious leader, Luther's heart and soul were in great turmoil. He was burdened under the constant weight of guilt and sin. The more he contemplated a pure and holy God, the more lost he felt. When he attempted to solve his sin-guilt problem through the traditional medieval acts of penance and self-denial, his overwhelming sense of condemnation before a righteous God actually seemed to get worse.

Then Luther began to teach a series of lectures on the book of Romans. His study of Romans would end up impacting the course of world history, for Martin Luther's mind and soul exploded with the brilliant light of the gospel. Having narrowly escaped a lightning bolt that could have ended his life, Luther had instead been struck by the lightning bolt of God's revelation.

He concluded that the Bible, and particularly Romans, made it clear that man was not reconciled to God through good works. Just the opposite was true—man lacked the proper motivation to perform good works until he was reconciled to God. That reconciliation, the bringing together of a holy God and sinful humans, could only be accomplished by faith in the saving work of Christ on the cross. God justifies sinners by faith, and faith alone.

By October 1517, Luther was convinced that the true gospel contradicted the existing structure and teachings of the medieval Church, with its emphasis on papal control, good works through rigid religious practices, and the buying of forgiveness through the sale of indulgences. Luther drafted his famous "Ninety Five Theses," soundly condemning those practices and posted them on the castle church door at Wittenberg (the equivalent of the university bulletin board).

He was immediately denounced as a heretic. Doubly painful was the fact that his chief accuser was Johann Maier, a theology professor and his former friend. The established church leaders sought to summon Martin to Rome to be vilified and condemned, but like John Wycliffe in England, Martin Luther had a friend in high government. Prince Frederick intervened and placed him under his protection.

Rome issued an edict (a "papal bull") formally condemning Luther and all of his works throughout Christendom. Luther's books were publicly burned in several cities. But Martin Luther responded by taking a copy of the edict against him and publicly burning it in front of his university students and the amazed onlookers from the City of Wittenberg.

In April 1521, with an official guarantee of safe travel, Martin appeared before Church authorities at Worms to answer for his teachings. It was there, before Charles V, Emperor of the Holy Roman Empire, and before representatives of Pope Leo, that Luther was confronted with a row of his own books spread out before him. He was asked whether he would denounce and recant them. Luther refused. The officials gave him a day to reconsider.

Tradition has it that on his return the next day, Luther proclaimed to the watching group that he could not recant what he had not been convinced of "by the testimony of the Scriptures or by clear reason." The Emperor was astounded at Luther's audacity and cut him off, but Luther cried out, "Here I stand. I can do no other. God help me, Amen."

Prince Frederick was in attendance and was undoubtedly instrumental in at least ensuring that Luther was not physically harmed. Had there been a strong central governmental figure in Germany at the time sympathetic to the Emperor, Luther would probably have been executed for his faith. Instead, his books were banned throughout Europe. Although Luther survived, a formal arrest warrant was issued for his imprisonment. He was never apprehended. For the remainder of his life Martin Luther wrote boldly on the doctrines of justification by faith and on the abuses of the medieval Church, even though he did so under the constant shadow of an active arrest warrant.

Not all of Luther's theological ideas were correct, but history records that the course of the Christian Church was changed in

October 1517 when he nailed his faith to a church door. His convictions would powerfully influence John Calvin, the great reformer of Geneva, and John Knox, irrepressible advocate of biblical Christianity in Scotland.

It is hard for us to imagine a world where doctrinal disputes over biblical truth would lead to the threat of imprisonment in a cold, airless dungeon or even to death. But even more unimaginable is a world where the gospel is secretly hidden from those who need its message of hope and redemption by the very religious institutions that ought to be proclaiming that message from the rooftops. Can we imagine a world where the gospel message is universally distorted and twisted by a ruling church hierarchy that imprisons the souls of its followers with man-made rules and corrupt and vain religious practices?

If the 21st century cries out for more John Wycliffes and Martin Luthers, will we respond? The course of precise events in the immediate future is uncertain, but one thing is sure: The future will need a strong, clear, and bold proclamation of the gospel.

The shifting sands of a soul-sick world demand that we take our stand on the rock-solid truth of God's Word and, standing there, declare, "I cannot do otherwise." Here we stand. God help us. Amen."

CHAPTER SEVEN

Souls Aflame

The history of the Christian Church reveals many examples of believers who backed what they believed through their actions and death. These examples of tough faith should encourage us to be strong in our faith and step out for Christ, trusting in God's mercy and grace to see us through difficult times.

About 30 miles north of Jerusalem, near Mount Gerizim and surrounded by other mountains, there was an ancient city known as Shechem. It had an illustrious history throughout Bible times. According to Genesis, Abram traveled through that area before he was renamed Abraham. It was there that God renewed His covenant. Jacob dwelled in Shechem, and Scripture records that he was buried there.

In A.D. 70 the Jewish Wars erupted in Jerusalem and outlying areas, pitting the occupied Jews against the Roman government that had been ruling over them with an iron fist. The Jewish revolt was ruthlessly crushed, and Shechem was renamed with a Roman title—*Flavio Neopolis*.

As a result of the destruction of Jerusalem by the Romans, and the growing persecution of the early Christian Church there, Christianity spread outward into the surrounding areas. Paul extended the reach of the gospel as far as Asia Minor and Europe. By A.D. 113 all of the apostles—the men who had personally walked and talked with Jesus—had died, and yet the spread of the Christian message was continuing to pick up miraculous momentum even in the midst of a hostile, pagan world. Pliny the Younger, a Roman governor, wrote to the emperor at that time, complaining that "the contagion of that superstition [Christianity] has penetrated not only the cities but also the villages and country places." By A.D. 150, Flavio Neopolis was overtaken by the prominent influence of Roman and Greek culture, but the growing influence of Christianity was being felt. Justin, a young man who resided in Flavio Neopolis, was a student of philosophy at that time when one of the most prominent intellectual doctrines was that of the famous Greek philosopher Plato. Justin would later write that the teachings of Plato offered him the answers to the great questions of life. He said that he "expected forthwith to look upon God, for this is the aim of Plato's philosophy."

The ideas of Plato had taken a powerful hold on the ancient world. Though Plato died in 347 B.C., his philosophy persisted from the refined and airy Greek world into the more militant and imperialistic Roman culture. His doctrines and writings had become the predominant way of viewing the big questions of life.

Plato taught that the world of our senses, the world of sight and sound and physical experience, was but a mere shadow of the greater forms of eternal reality that lurked behind the three-dimensional "theater set" of everyday life. The promise of Plato was that philosophical contemplation could provide a portal through which the mind could pass into an understanding of the eternal.

In a complicated parable called "the cave," Plato gave a word picture for man's inability to gain true insight into reality by merely relying on our senses. Imagine, Plato explained, that each of us, from birth, are captives in a cavelike world. Chained to the wall of the cave, and with our backs facing the faraway opening to the outside world, we must rely on reflected light onto the cave wall to tell us what the world outside is really like. Our senses are but interpretations of shadows, according to Plato. The great and eternal reality lies beyond the land of flickering shadows and dim light.

As a student of the teachings of Plato, Justin had taken up this view that pursuit of the eternal must be through the rigorous exercise of the intellect rather than through the physical senses. But soon he began to develop doubts about this system of belief. One day Justin became involved in a conversation with someone he described only as "a certain old man," who convinced him that Plato's ideas were faulty. More importantly, he became convinced that if the pursuit of philosophy (literally, the "love of wisdom") involved knowing truth, which ultimately resides only with God, then the only reliable source of knowledge was what God Himself chose to reveal to the human race.

Thus, Justin was led into the study of the Old Testament prophets and the recently written Gospel narratives. What he found there convinced him not only to acknowledge Jesus as the revealed Son of God with his mind, but to accept Him as Savior of his soul. Ignited by the fire of the Holy Spirit, Justin discovered a new direction for his profession. He chose to continue wearing his philosopher's robes, however, because he believed that the honest pursuit of truth through the asking of tough questions can bring one to the truth of Christ. Justin himself was living proof of that.

In A.D. 153, Justin moved to Rome and launched into the writing of his work, *Apology* (which means "defense"). In his position as the philosopher-Christian, Justin would become the defender of biblical faith in the midst of a culture violently and viciously hostile to the message of Jesus. During his lifetime, Christians were under increasing persecution by the Roman government and often found themselves treated as the scapegoats by suspicious pagans who misunderstood their faith. Justin's *Apology* first addressed the unfairness of treating the followers of Jesus like criminals when they had not committed any illegal conduct. Often, Justin argued, they were punished simply because they were Christians. Justin argued in his book that these Christians were no threat to the welfare of the Roman government. They did not seek to overthrow the civil government, but instead, they sought a heavenly kingdom where God reigned.

Justin went on to describe the excellency of the gospel story as truth in opposition to the prevailing pagan beliefs and showed how Jesus' divinity was proven by His amazing fulfillment of the prophecies of the Old Testament. For the remainder of his life, Justin was an outspoken defender of the Christian message, and his writings formed an indispensable link between the age of the apostles and the young, but exploding, Christian church of the second century A.D.

But the Roman Empire of the second century was jealous to retain the absolute allegiance of its citizens to its emperor; therefore, ideas often had costly consequences. Justin never compromised his message. He died by the executioner's sword, earning the name by which he has been known ever since—Justin Martyr. Yet to the end, Justin Martyr refused to return to the intellectual idolatry from which Christ had rescued him. He penetrated the unbelieving world with a mind committed to God's kingdom. To that end, he refused to flinch in his absolute certainty that in the life, death, and resurrection of Christ is the ultimate truth. He popularized a creed that concisely summarized the truth of the gospel that his philosopher's mind had accepted and his heart had received: "Jesus Christ, who came in our times, was crucified, and died, and rose again, has ascended into heaven, and has reigned."[1]

In the end, it was not only Justin Martyr's tough mind that was a witness to God's truth, but his tough *faith*, even to death, left its mark on the early church.

Tough Faith in Action

Fifteen hundred years after Justin Martyr there was another example of great intellect acknowledging the Lordship of Christ. On November 23, 1654, in Paris, France, we find Blaise Pascal, the renowned scientist, inventor, and mathematician struggling with a seemingly unsolvable problem in his late evening hours. Pascal is in deep despair, having spent the better part of that year reading Epictetus, with his view on the greatness and nobility of man's nature. Yet he had also read and believed the truth of Montaigne, who explained that human nature is base, ruthless, and corrupt.

Clearly this was more than a matter of the scientist's dispassionate curiosity. The conflict in Pascal's mind was not mere frustration over a game that could not be solved; undoubtedly Pascal, who had been nominally raised in the predominant church of his day—Catholic—and who was familiar with the general doctrines of the faith, was personalizing in his own mind and soul this philosophical question. If he was a noble creation of God, then what was the source of his sense of moral guilt? And if he was morally corrupt, then how could he hope to achieve meaning in his life and acceptance in the eyes of God?

But Pascal had an encounter with the truth. One evening, shortly after midnight, the light of the gospel broke through his gloom and darkness. Pascal was filled with joy. He was overcome with a peaceful sense of certainty about who he was—a creature with the potential for greatness because he was created by God. Although he was unable to live the life he should because of his fallen and sinful state, the answer to Pascal's dilemma lay in God's grace.

Through Christ, who is provided to us because of the unmerited grace of God, we are taken out of the misery that the control of sin brings and brought into the family of the Lord. While it makes us uncomfortable to fully understand what miserable sinners we truly are, it is necessary if we are to recognize our need for a Savior. That evening was a watershed for Pascal. From that point on he devoted himself to writings that sought to explain our need for a Savior and extolled the sufficiency of Jesus Christ to fully and joyously save us.

Interestingly, it has been suggested that the death of his father a few years before had tilled the soil of Pascal's heart, to ready it for the roots of the gospel to fully take root. Yet this is not unique to Pascal. It seems that God often uses a bruised heart to confound and redirect the highly tuned intellect and to open the soul to His plan of salvation.

The Oxford Skeptic

When C.S. Lewis experienced the death of his father, it began a quiet but profound shift in his spiritual journey. As a young man, he had abandoned any allegiance to the church. Later, as a brilliant scholar and professor of medieval literature at Oxford, Lewis dabbled in theosophy and had an interest in Freudian psychology. But in the end, he found such theories empty. They failed to furnish the answers for the questions that nagged and haunted him. Lewis would later write that, at the bottom line, the general worldview of Sigmund Freud was "in direct contradiction to Christianity." His philosophy that sought to explain human behavior and the nature of the human heart could not be correct. A choice had to be made. Lewis was a brilliant thinker, and he could tell a checkmate on the chess board when he saw one.

It was not as if Lewis rejected the idea of God from the outset. Rather, he grudgingly had concluded that God might be the landlord of this universe and we His tenants, but God was surely an absentee landlord. Before his spiritual conversion he once wrote to a friend: "The trouble about God is that he is like a person who never acknowledges your letters and so, in time, you come to the conclusion either that he does not exist or that you have got his address wrong."

Ultimately, to the great blessing of many who would later read his post-conversion Christian writings, there was a third option. What if God has already answered our letters and telegrams in His own love-letter written 2000 years ago, but we have not bothered to check our mailbox and discover it?

C.S. Lewis circulated in a small group of some the greatest minds in England, including Lord Adrian, the winner of the Nobel prize for the medical study of nerve cells; Gilbert Ryle, the linguistic theorist and philosopher; and J.R.R. Tolkien, the scholar in ancient Anglo-Saxon languages and literature who authored the Lord of the Rings trilogy.

Tolkien was unapologetic about the underlying Christian themes that ran through his fantasy stories of gnomes, kings, dragons, and wizards, and he was instrumental in Lewis' conversion. A frequent debater, conversationalist, and professional friend of Lewis, Tolkien had been with him the night of September 19, 1931, at a dinner party. After dinner they strolled around the grounds of the college. Conversation drifted onto the subject of myths.

Lewis remarked that he enjoyed reading ancient mythic stories, but took no stock in their truth. Tolkien challenged him. What if the ancient mythic stories about gods who die and then come back to life, while fanciful in themselves, are harkening back to the one mythic story which was really true? What if God, at one point in history, really came down in human form and permitted Himself to be killed, and then triumphantly was resurrected, all so that He could transform those who believed in Him? The point, Tolkien explained, is to commit, to plunge in, to personally encounter the author of that grand drama.

Two days later Lewis was riding in the sidecar of a motorcycle being driven by his brother Warren on the way to the zoo. "When we set out I did not believe that Jesus Christ is the Son of God," he would later write, "and when we reached the zoo I did." His conversion was undramatic. He was like a "man, after a long sleep...[who] becomes aware that he is now awake."[2]

From such small and humble beginnings, God creates great effects. The conversion of C.S. Lewis led to his authoring a host of Christian writings that arguably introduced more people to the basics of the Christian faith than any other writer in the 20th century. He explained the fundamentals of the faith for the worldly skeptic and the searching mind in *Mere Christianity*, helped us face the dilemma of evil and suffering in a world created by a perfect God in *The Problem of Pain*, and soundly refuted the errors of humanistic educators and moralists in *The Abolition of Man*. In *Miracles*, Lewis showed us the irrationality of those who deny the very notion of a Supreme Being who can perform supernatural acts, while reminding Christians of the dangers of the more mundane (but highly effective) strategies of the devil in *The Screwtape Letters*.

C.S. Lewis, the "most reluctant convert in all of England," became another example of what God can do with a mind yielded to His Kingship.

Blinded by the Light

As we plunge into the new millennium of startling ideas, breathtaking discoveries, and vain speculations, there is no better intellectual standard for us to follow than the man who humbly described himself as marked by "weakness, fear, and trembling." A man who declared that "My message and my preaching were not in persuasive words of wisdom, but in demonstration of the Spirit and of power" (1 Corinthians 2:4).

Without doubt, Saul of Tarsus was a brilliant man. In fact, history has shown that this "Saul," who became Apostle Paul, may have been one of the most powerful intellectual forces in recorded history. He described himself as "educated under Gamaliel, strictly according to the law of our fathers" (Acts 22:3). Gamaliel was a highly regarded Jewish teacher who taught according to the tradition of Hillel, the famous Rabbi. Gamaliel is described in the earlier verses of Acts as a man who was "respected by all the people." When he spoke, the religious authorities of the Jewish temple not only listened, they deferred to his learned advice (Acts 5:34-40). For Paul to have studied at the feet of such a teacher is testimony to the apostle's great background of learning.

Festus, the Roman governor to whom the apostle preached while under arrest, acknowledged Paul's "great learning." He was schooled in classical Greek literature. Twice in Scripture, Paul cited parts of an ancient poem attributed to Epimenides:

> They fashioned a tomb for thee, O holy and high one—
> The Cretans, always liars, evil beasts, idle bellies!
> But thou art not dead; thou livest and abidest for ever;
> For in thee we live and move and have our being.

His familiarity with the Greek poets was also illustrated when he addressed the philosophers in Athens: "In Him we live and move and exist, as even some of your own poets have said..." (Acts 17:28).

Yet despite his brilliant mind, great learning, and training in the classics of his day, prior to his face-to-face meeting with Jesus Paul was blind to the truth. As a result, he had become an obsessed enemy of the early Church. Paul was present at the execution of Stephen, even giving his consent to the murder of the first recorded Christian martyr. We are told that he "began ravaging the church, entering house after house; and dragging off men and women, he would put them in prison" (Acts 8:3).

The word "ravaging" gives a ferocious picture of violence, like a wild animal ripping and tearing at its prey. Prior to his setting out on a trip from Jerusalem to the city of Damascus, he obtained arrest warrants from the high priest in order to apprehend believers in Jesus and to "bring them bound to Jerusalem." In the darkness of a soul that did not know Jesus as Lord, Paul was "breathing threats and murder against the disciples of the Lord" (Acts 9:1). Though his eyes could see and his mind could reason, Paul was spiritually blind. Though he was intellectually brilliant, he was mired in a mindset that was brutal and conceived in darkness.

It was only when Paul had a life-altering encounter with Jesus Christ on the road to Damascus that he understood the truth. It was in the brilliance of Christ's light that Paul was temporarily blinded and rendered helpless. Then, and only then, did he embrace the truth and gain spiritual insight. From that point on, we see Paul not as the persecutor but as the apostle. His mind and heart illuminated by the mind of Christ, and his life empowered by the Holy Spirit, Paul used his great learning and mental powers to one end: to preach Christ crucified, resurrected, ascended, ruling in heaven, and coming again. What a triumphant picture of a mind set free! On his missionary travels, Paul incorporated his intellectual gifts into his ministry. His goal was never to outwit his opponents or impress the crowds, but it was always to press home the main point: the preeminence of Christ and the excellence of His sacrifice on the cross.

When Paul moved in the Greek world with his message, he was able to understand the mind-set of these non-Jews who had no Hebrew Scripture, no history of prophets, and no one to tell them of the transcendent and holy God who nevertheless deals directly with the human race. Instead, the Greeks had been captive to worldly speculations and complex philosophies that sought to explain the world only in the limited terms of what human reason could conjure up. Paul was eager to share that the truth can be known, and known with certainty, for God, in Jesus, has revealed it to us.

When he engaged the great minds of his day on the high hill of the Areopagus in Athens in Acts 17, Paul challenged the idolatrous speculations and beliefs of the city. The learned Athenians had known only the human reasonings of the likes of Socrates, Plato, and Aristotle. He used the literature of the Athenians' own poets, and capitalized on their own religious symbols to lay out an apologetic of the Christian faith.

Paul began his message by commenting on notions with which the Athenian philosophers could relate: their desire to know God and their cultural awareness of Him. He also appealed to the evidence that we can know something about who God is from the world of nature and the rise of nations (see Acts 17:22-28). Paul directed his message specifically to the mind-set of his audience.

Two of the prevailing philosophies of Athens at the time were those of the Epicureans and the Stoics. In Acts 17:25, he creates a bridge to the Epicurean belief that God needs nothing from man by pointing out that God does not need what man can create with human hands in order to make Himself known. In that same verse, Paul also appeals to the Stoic doctrine that the divine is the source of all life by sharing with them that "He himself gives to all life and breath and all things." But Paul does not miss the opportunity to take his audience to the ultimate point: God has a standard of righteousness, and our fall from that standard requires us to repent, and to look to that "Man whom [God] has appointed, having furnished proof to all men by raising Him from the dead" (Acts 17:31).

Paul was a soul aflame doing battle with the intellectual idolatry of his day. We have to follow his example into the 21st century. In our lifetimes, there will be countless new challenges to the truth of Scripture. Man-centered science and human reason will perfect its arrogant attack on the truth of God. Our task is to understand the failings of the world's ideas and to expose their insufficiency in solving the eternal dilemma. What will bridge the gap that sin created between God and man? Then we must be able to communicate the truth of the gospel, that Christ—and Christ alone—is the bridge to the 21st (or any other) century.

In order to bring this timeless message to the world in an effective way, in order to win lost souls to Christ, we cannot afford to be intellectually lazy. We cannot leave our brains in neutral when it comes to the most important subject in the universe—the truth that Jesus is both Savior and Lord. The modern "Athenians" of today are perishing for want of the Word of Life. Will we bring it to them?

Part Two

꩜━✦━꩜

The Persecution of the Pious

꩜━✦━꩜

"Christ, hearing the confession of Simon Peter, who first openly acknowledged Him to be the Son of God (Matt. xvi), and perceiving the secret hand of His Father therein, answered again; and alluding to his name, called him a rock, upon which rock He would build His church so strong, that the gates of hell should not prevail against it. In these words three things are to be noted. First, that Christ will have a church in this world. Secondly, that the same church should be mightily impugned, not only by the world, but also by the utmost strength and powers of all hell. And, thirdly, that the same church, notwithstanding the efforts of the devil and all his malice, should continue."

—Foxe's Book of Martyrs

"My God, Sir, they've gone down with her. They couldn't live in this cold water. We had room for a dozen more people in my boat, but it was dark after the ship took the plunge. We didn't pick up any swimmers. I fired the flares....I think the people were drawn down deep by the suction. The other boats are somewhere near."

—Titanic's Fourth Officer Boxhall,
upon being rescued by the ship *Carpathia*

"And indeed, all who desire to live godly in Christ Jesus will be persecuted."
—2 Timothy 3:12

CHAPTER EIGHT

The Coming Persecution of Christians

A Christian preacher in early America by the name of Jonathan Maxcy once made the observation that we can judge our freedoms in the civil realm by determining how much freedom we have in the religious realm. Indeed, if our religious liberties evaporate, the other civil rights become meaningless.

It is true, of course, that judged by global standards Americans have an enviable amount of religious freedom. Unfortunately, the freedom of the Church in America has lulled many Christians into a false sense of security that there is no clear and present danger of religious persecution. Even if we assume that Christians have no need to anticipate future persecution on American shores (an assumption that may be wrong), we must respond to the rising evidence of worldwide mistreatment and even torture of believers. We are commanded that "if one member [of the body of Christ] suffers, all the members suffer with it" (1 Corinthians 12:26).

Jesus exemplified this. When Christ appeared to Paul on the road to Damascus, He made it clear that He associated intimately with those believers who were being persecuted in His name (see Acts 9:4-5). As followers of Christ, we must do the same.

The worst maltreatment of Christians has taken place in the strongly Islamic nations. It has been estimated that eight out of the ten worst nations for anti-Christian persecution are governed by strict Muslim regimes. Those "top ten" are:

1. Saudi Arabia
2. Sudan (South)
3. Somalia
4. Sudan (North)
5. Yemen
6. North Korea
7. Iran
8. Morocco
9. China
10. Libya

If we look a little closer at the persecution in just a handful of countries, it becomes clear how serious a problem persecution is.

Saudi Arabia

In Saudi Arabia, freedom of religion does not exist at all. It is an officially Islamic nation and all citizens are required to be Muslims. As the guardian of two of the most holy shrines of Islam (The Dome of the Rock and Al-Aqsa), the government of Saudi Arabia believes it must oppose all other religions, including Christianity. The *Mutawwa'in* (the Islamic religious police) roam the streets looking for violators. Foreigners who conduct clandestine

Christian worship services are often subjected to harassment, including lashings and arrest. The International Operations Subcommittee of the House of Representatives has received reports (apparently still not verified by firsthand witnesses) of the crucifixion of Christians in the Saudi Arabian desert.

This has implications for American foreign policy as well. In Rihad, Saudi Arabia, anti-Christian censorship has already taken place in the American Embassy. Traditionally, American embassies are considered an extension of American soil, even though they are located in a foreign nation. In Saudi Arabia, on the demand of the Islamic religious police, American officials have banned Christian worship services that had been taking place within the walls of the embassy. During the Persian Gulf War, American soldiers could not openly read their Bibles, and our military chaplains were prohibited from displaying their crosses.

It is not inconceivable that our reliance on the oil-exports of the Islamic nations, and our political need for peace in the Middle East, may lead to future accommodations toward Islam at the expense of Christian freedom.

Sudan

In the Sudan the atrocities against Christians are shocking. An Islamic nation, the Sudan permits Christian nationals to be rounded up and placed into forced slavery. The problem began in 1989 when a radical Muslim regime took over. They view forced conversions of Christians to Islam as a duty. One way they force conversions is by physical threats or violence. Their "jihad" (holy war) is being waged against anyone who is not a Muslim.

Young Christian girls are captured and turned into sexual concubines. Those Christian slaves who try to escape are beaten to death, thrown down wells, or have their feet and hands cut off.[1]

Cal Bombay, who has investigated this cruel phenomena for Crossroads Christian Communications, reported his findings to a Canadian newsreporter. The reporter wrote a three-part series in the *Le Journal De Montreal*. Shortly after the series appeared, the reporter, Pierre Richard, received death threats that were later traced to a radical Muslim who had ties to Sudan.

Iraq

In the village of Dokuk, in Northern Iraq, evangelicals have been openly attacked. A local evangelical church and the home of the pastor was invaded by Muslim mobs. The pastor (and his family) barely escaped, but armed Muslims have issued an order to kill him. Prior to that, Mansour Hussein Sifer, a Christian bookstore worker, was murdered. Violent persecution of Christians has become the norm in Iraq.[2]

India

In January 1999, a mob of Hindu radicals surrounded a jeep occupied by Christian missionary Graham Staines and his sons Philips (10) and Timothy (8). The group of about 40 Hindus doused the vehicle in gasoline and set it ablaze, watching the father and his sons burn to death. They also assaulted bystanders who attempted to rescue the Christians. The atrocities were part of a recent sweep of violence through India against what the World Hindu Council calls the Christian attempt at "fraudulently converting" Hindus. Twelve churches have been attacked in the pattern of violence.[3]

Egypt

In Egypt there are some six million "Coptic" Christians, a group of people who have populated Egypt since the first century. Recently reports have verified serious religious persecution. Paul Marshall, in his book *Their Blood Cries Out*, documents that every year between 7000 and 10,000 Christians are kidnapped as part of an attempt to forcibly convert them to Islam. Ever since the Egyptian government declared Islam the official state religion in 1980, Christians have been the subject of consistent violence and murder.

China

The rampant official persecution of Christians in China is a perplexing and disturbing reality. Yet President Clinton, with full knowledge of the atrocities that occur there, has pushed for full trading with China, granted them Most Favored Nation status, and authorized a flood of new American technology into the world's largest and most dangerous communist country. Secretary of State Madeleine Albright believes linking human rights and trade is the wrong approach for China. Sadly, the Clinton administration has a track record of putting profit over principle.

The politics of Washington has attempted to whitewash the problem with superficial junkets and good-will visits. After an agreement was worked out by President Clinton and Chinese President Jiang Zemin in 1998, a delegation of religious representatives from Judaism, Evangelicalism, and the Catholic Church was permitted to visit China to investigate human rights violations in the area of religious faith. Rather than assisting the persecuted Church, the superficial visit has been criticized as actually adding to the level of violations. The family of at least one evangelical prisoner was forcibly removed from their home and quickly relocated to a far-away province so they would not be interviewed.[4]

In its annual human rights report, the State Department said the situation in China "deteriorated sharply" in the last half of 1998. The report told of killings, torture of prisoners, and forced confessions. China has imposed new rules on social organizations, the publishing industry, and the Internet.

The plight of evangelical Zhao Mu Na is typical. She graduated from the government theological school and was required to join the Patriotic Three-Self Movement, the government unit used to monitor and control all church activities. Her problems started when she quit the Movement and began to spread the gospel on her own. Her husband disappeared and is believed kidnapped by government authorities. Zhao was later arrested because of her evangelistic activities and placed in a labor camp. Rather than being unique, Zhao's situation has become the norm for Christians in China.[5]

The Rough Road Ahead

While "human rights" problems around the globe catch media attention from the liberal press and organizations like Amnesty International, the persecution of Christians has been a quiet scandal. Nina Shea, Director of the Center on Religious Freedom, points to the fact that many journalists simply view Christianity as a "white man's religion." They conclude that attempts to spotlight anti-Christian persecution in other countries is just one more type of "Western imperialism." The irony is that three-fourths of the Christians in the world today live in third-world nations. These Christians need our prayers and our support. They also deserve to have their stories shared with the world.

Meanwhile in the United States, some progress has been made toward coming up with a way to combat international persecution of the Christian Church, but not nearly enough. A strong bit of legislation by Congressman Frank Wolf from Virginia, "The Freedom from Religious Persecution Act," was introduced in Congress in 1998. It originally provided for direct and powerful penalties for nations that persisted in this kind of official religious persecution. Unfortunately, Congress lost its nerve and ended up passing a watered-down and lifeless version of the bill.

Finally (and grudgingly) President Clinton looked into the problem. But instead of creating a permanent office within the State Department to deal with religious persecution abroad (a solution that held out some hope of real and immediate action), the president instead created an Advisory Committee on Religious Freedom Abroad. This committee was formed to "call attention to problems of religious persecution around the world." The committee is likely to end up being a mere showpiece of politics.

Interestingly, the committee's task is to make recommendations on how the U.S. Government can "bring about reconciliation in regions where religious enmity is a threat to peace...."

Think about that last phrase for a minute. The State Department wants to negotiate religious "reconciliation" between Christians and Muslims under the guise of creating peace. The implications are mind-boggling and disturbing. The probability is that little substantive help will be given to Christians who are mistreated and tortured abroad by the same governments that we trade with, and with whom we attend polite embassy dinners. In addition, there is a possibility that this kind of initiative might actually increase the loss of rights of Christians as a means of achieving "peace."

With this sort of thinking becoming official U.S. policy, what impact can we expect on Christians in America in the decades to come?

CHAPTER NINE

Tried by Fire, Refined as Gold

I n "How Firm a Foundation," a hymn dating back to 1787, we sing of God's faithfulness even as we are tested and tried:

> When through fiery trials thy pathway shall lie,
> My grace all sufficient shall be thy supply.
> The flame shall not hurt thee, I only design,
> Thy dross to consume, and thy gold to refine.

The trying and testing of our faith is a fact of life. Second Timothy 3:12 promises that "all who desire to live godly in Christ Jesus will be persecuted." That is not a verse most of us enjoy reading. It tells us, in essence, that if we do what we are most called to do (live godly lives in Christ) we can expect to receive that which we most want to avoid (punishment from the world).

The problem is not with the theology of that verse, but with our understanding of faith. We are to live lives that mirror the life of Christ. We fail at that, of course, but that is the ideal—to live like Christ, in His power. Why, then, should it surprise us that when we do that, we should also be mistreated? Was Christ not misunderstood, ridiculed, misrepresented, and mistreated? Was He not unjustly accused of crimes He did not commit? Was He not subjected to an illegal procedure that violated both Jewish and Roman law? And in the end, although He was without sin and spoke absolute truth and acted in perfect conformity with God's law, did He not suffer torture and execution? Even one of the criminals on the cross next to Him, suffering his own execution, had to acknowledge that Jesus was totally undeserving of the punishment He was receiving.

The history of those who have taken a stand for God in godless surroundings has been one of persecution. When Daniel "made up his mind that he would not defile himself with the king's choice food or with the wine which he drank" (Daniel 1:8), he was tested. When he refused to stop praying to the God of Abraham, Isaac, and Jacob, he was thrown to the lions. When his three fellow believers persisted in their godliness, they were tried in the kiln of persecution. Shadrach, Meshach, and Abed-nego were tossed in a furnace so hot the palace guards who threw them in were burned alive by the flames (see Daniel 3:22).

The history of God's prophets is filled with persecution of the worst kind. Just moments before becoming the first Christian martyr, Stephen reminded his executioners, "Which one of the prophets did your fathers not persecute?" (Acts 7:52). Stephen was soon followed by James, who was executed by the sword (Acts 12:1-2). It looked as if Peter would be next, as he was arrested when the early church started to grow, but he was miraculously saved through the direct intervention of God's messenger. Paul's missionary journeys in the book of Acts are replete with stonings, beatings, illegal arrests, and imprisonment. Many of his letters were written from the inside of jail cells. Yet much was accomplished while he was in chains.

The example of the early Church bears out Paul's warning: If we intend to live godly lives, we will suffer persecution at the hands of God's enemies.

In the latter days we are promised that iniquity shall abound and love will grow cold (Matthew 24:12). That is a powerful and disturbing thought. Love will literally escape from the world in the last days, like air from a leaking tire. At the same time, the love of Christ, which will be evident in His people, will be ever more apparent, and even more miraculous!

In the final days, the Church must be prepared to be delivered up to the authorities, to be afflicted, or even killed. Christians can expect to be "hated by all nations" for the sake of Jesus Christ, according to Matthew 24:9. At the same time, the message of the gospel will be seen most clearly and most powerfully in our beaten and persecuted bodies.

Remember, as Christ hung on the cross, one of the criminals hanging with Him was saved by the power of His witness amid suffering. As He lived out the message of His ministry in the manner of His death, Christ shook the battle-hardened heart of a Roman centurion. The guard was standing right in front of Him, and he had a front-row seat to every detail of the agonizing and unjust persecution of the Lord of lords. When it was through, he could only declare, "Truly this man was the Son of God!" (Mark 15:39).

The Future of Persecution

John, through the inspiration of the Holy Spirit, gives us the future of the Christian Church. It was no accident that God picked him, the apostle of both love and suffering, to be the receptacle of God's picture of the future Church: abounding in love while experiencing unimaginable suffering.

Through the vision imparted to him by God, John gives us a description of seven churches that handle the challenges of persecution and trial in a variety of ways.

The church in Ephesus, described in Revelation 2:1-7, is a picture of believers who are pure in their doctrine, but who miss an essential of the faith. That church was bold and fearless in exposing false teachers, and its members persevered in the face of strong persecution. However, they were lacking in one important regard: They had grown cold in their love of God. When persecution comes, it will not simply be the rightness of our doctrine that will change hearts; it will be our devotion to the Savior and our declaration of love to those who persecute us that reveals the true nature of God to the world.

The church at Smyrna, in Revelation 2:8-11, is the fiercely persecuted church. It suffers tribulation, poverty, prison, and even worse. To them God says, "Be faithful until death, and I will give you the crown of life." In those few words there is a universe of meaning. Persecution can lead to separation from husbands, wives, children, and friends. It can mean a cold, forgotten jail cell and hearing the boots of the executioners as they come for us with mechanical, uncaring faces. It might mean pain and death in a lonely and forgotten place, surrounded by filth, indignity, and hate. There are Christians who are suffering like that today around the world. Yet the Lord tells us, "Do not fear what you are about to suffer....He who overcomes shall not be hurt by the second death." Only when we get God's view of eternity and of our future with Him can we understand how we can be true overcomers. Against those who know the Father of heaven, death can never claim victory.

In the church at Pergamum, the followers of Jesus are praised for being faithful to the cause of Christ, even while being surrounded by the worst of the pagan and anti-Christian world. Yet John, in Revelation 2:12-17, warns them that they have been too tolerant of false teaching. Pergamum was the Washington, D.C. of the ancient world. It had the second largest library of that day and was home to some of the greatest temples dedicated to Caesar. It was an obvious seat of political and cultural power. We can reasonably speculate that the church there had bowed to the influence of its surroundings. When persecution comes, it is easy to tolerate compromise, and we can easily rationalize how our bending in matters of truth will not hurt anything, compared to the pain of persecution. But in God's view, compromise when it comes to truth is not an option.

The church at Thyatira had a similar problem. In addition to tolerating false teachings, it willfully engaged in immoral and sinful conduct. In Revelation 2:18-29, God's judgment on that church is clear and awesome: sickness, death, and pestilence. To those who keep themselves pure and faithful, however, they are promised to be part of God's ruling and eternal kingdom. We are being prepared for an invisible city that is not made by human hands. Even in the midst of pressure from a pagan world, we must always conduct ourselves as ambassadors for God's city.

When the heat and pressure of tribulation come, one unfortunate response can be to merely go through the motions of a Christian walk while being spiritually dead. The church at Sardis is described as "alive, [but] you are dead." Believers there are told in Revelation 3:1-6 to "wake up, and strengthen the things that remain." The time for sleep is not when you're walking through the challenges of the future.

The church at Philadelphia was relatively powerless in the measurements of the world. It was small, and had "little power." Philadelphia was not a major center, but a small area with a limited population located in a spot plagued by earthquakes. Yet in Revelation 3:7-13, God reminded this modest group of believers that He had not forgotten them. "I know your deeds," He assures them. Because they had been faithful to His name amid persecution, and had kept God's Word, the believers were given great spiritual power. They were blessed with an open door of gospel opportunity "which no one can shut." Persecution ultimately reduces the persecuted to a position of being powerless. That is when we must rely on the power of God, who does not forget us, and who will never abandon us. Praise God that He rescues His remnant of faithful followers!

Last, and perhaps most sadly, is the church at Laodicea. That city was a major banking center, and was located in what was considered a prosperous area. It received its water source from hot springs some six miles away, but by the time the water got to Laodicea it was neither hot nor cold. It was simply tepid—lukewarm. The wealth and prosperity that surrounded the city had infected the faith of this church. In Revelation 3:14-22, we read Christ's shocking reaction: "I will spit you out of My mouth." The corrupting effect of prosperity and self-indulgence can be devastating. Better to be poor and persecuted than rich but disenfranchised from God Himself.

Regardless of the circumstances of our persecution, we are commanded to "hold fast." That is one of those commands that seems easy to understand, and yet sometimes impossible to apply. How do we "hold fast" when we know that the job promotion was denied because we have shared our faith at work? How do we "hold fast" when our neighbors scandalize us or ridicule us for being conservative Christians?

Some time ago the two of us were working together on a very public and controversial issue to which we both felt called to respond as a matter of biblical principle. We were both featured in newspaper and television programs for taking a stand that was not politically correct. Within days, we started receiving death threats against ourselves and, even worse against our children. Our property was vandalized in a way that was the trademark of one anti-Christian group. Envelopes started arriving, each containing a picture of a family (obviously meant to represent ours) with the eyes burned out. The message was dark and twisted—but very clear.

These were small matters, certainly, compared to the real persecution that has been suffered by Christians through the ages, but it gave us a little bit of a glimpse at the inside view of what persecution does, how it feels, and how we are to react. The first question we were forced to confront was this: Was it our message that was offensive, or were we, in our manner and delivery, the offense? This kind of introspection is always necessary. We must not let our mode of communication mar the eternal message we have to deliver. Mistreatment by others can create some beneficial times of meditation and reevaluation for us individually.

Second, we had to make sure that we did not respond in kind. The Bible is clear that a "soft answer turns away wrath" and that we are not to "overcome evil with evil." Instead, we are to overcome evil with good.

Third, we realized that there are occasions when the truest message, delivered in the most Christlike way, will still reap anger and punishment from those who do not know His love. When persecution comes, as it will always come in a variety of times, places, and methods, it is very easy to adopt the "duck and cover" mentality. Yet survival is not the primary goal the Bible charts for us. We are not called to be merely "survivors," we are called to be "overcomers."

The ultimate message in Revelation is that God is triumphant and His love unfailing, and that we are to be overcomers in the midst of the worst situations. Remember, we are given the command to be overcomers in the context of the book of Revelation, which depicts the most egregious persecution the world has ever known. We are able to overcome because, as we are told in John's Gospel, Christ has overcome the world, the flesh, and the devil. We can overcome these formidable opponents not because of our strength, but because He lives in us.

Who are "overcomers," and how do they "overcome" the fiery trials of persecution? The answer is clear, simple, and infinitely powerful: "Whatever is born of God overcomes the world; and this is the victory that has overcome the world—our faith. And who is the one who overcomes the world, but he who believes that Jesus is the Son of God?" (1 John 5:4-5).

We do not need some magical formula to become conquerors in the midst of earthly defeat. We need only call upon the power of Christ in us, the hope of future glory. Peter, who experienced a myriad of persecutions in his life and ministry, reminds us that persecution should not come as a surprise. In fact, for the mature believer, persecution is the norm:

> Beloved, do not be surprised at the fiery ordeal among you, which comes upon you for your testing as though some strange thing were happening to you; but to the degree that you share the sufferings of Christ, keep on rejoicing; so that also at the revelation of His glory, you may rejoice with exultation. If you are reviled for the name of Christ, you are blessed, because the Spirit of glory and of God rests upon you. (1 Peter 4:12-14)

CHAPTER TEN

Sifted, Weighed, and Found Faithful

It is a sober and undeniable fact of history that the growth and spread of the Christian faith has been watered, from time to time, by the blood of Christian martyrs. We do not always know when the strength and authenticity of our faith will be sifted, weighed, and tested in a significant way, but we do know that the sifting has come to others in the past, and it will come to followers of Jesus in the future.

How different are the results when the mockers of God are sifted and tested. Belshazzar was a corrupt king of Babylon, a pagan who "praised the gods of gold and silver, of bronze, iron, wood and stone" (Daniel 5:4). In the middle of a drunken orgy, while he and his nobles were defiling the Jewish vessels captured from the temple, he received a message on the palace wall. Written with the hand of God, the indictment against Belshazzar informed him that he had been sifted and weighed by the Lord and was "found deficient." Ancient historians Herodotus and Xenophon tell us that the armies of the Persians were already camped outside the palace, waiting to attack. When they invaded the royal rooms and killed Belshazzar and his noblemen, they found them unprepared, totally absorbed with their drunken festival.

Peter was warned by the Lord Jesus in the dark hours at the Garden of Gethsemane that "Satan has demanded permission to sift you like wheat" (Luke 22:31). Peter faltered in that first test, watching Christ's interrogation by the authorities from afar and denying his association with Jesus. But after the empowering of the Holy Spirit, Peter did not fail in his bold proclamation of the gospel, even when he was arrested and his own execution looked likely (see Acts 4:1-14; 12:1-4).

History verifies that, in the end, almost all of the disciples died for their faith. In the centuries that followed, Christianity did not grow in the midst of peace, but it spread in the midst of suffering, sacrifice, and death. While the severity of persecution varied from emperor to emperor depending on the political needs of Roman domination, it was a continuing reality in the Church for hundreds of years.

It took centuries of Christian martyrdom before the pagan societies began giving some grudging respect to these executed Christians. For at least 100 years, the Roman empire, relatively unmoved, watched the spectacle of those who were willing to give themselves to horrible pain and death rather than deny the Lordship of Jesus Christ.

Persevering Perpetua

Just after the end of the second century, in A.D. 203, Carthage was a typical Roman-controlled city. Located in Northern Africa, it was a heavily populated, key commercial area. The message of Christ was new to the people there, but it was starting to win converts. Perpetua, a 23-year-old mother of an infant son, was one of them. She had a reputation as a woman of beauty and grace, sharing her considerable social position and wealth with others. Her husband is not mentioned in any of the accounts of her life, and it is likely that he abandoned her when she became a Christian.

Roman Emperor Severus had just issued an edict prohibiting conversions to Christianity, and Perpetua was arrested along with five other fellow believers with whom she regularly worshiped and prayed. She was brought before the Roman procurator and asked one simple question: "Are you a Christian?" To answer in the affirmative meant certain death. We can imagine how easy it might have been for Perpetua to flinch in the face of Roman execution. She was a new Christian, hardly mature in the faith, and the mother of an infant child. If she died, who would look after her son? Her aged father had pleaded with her to deny Christ for the sake of her family. Yet when the question came, for Perpetua there was only one answer: "I am," she stated confidently. "I cannot forsake my faith for freedom." Her father, who was in the audience, tried to run to her aid, but was beaten back with a club.

The martyrdom of Perpetua, like the executions of many other second century Christians, is preserved by reliable first-hand accounts.[1] On March 7, A.D. 203, Perpetua was led out into the arena where she would be confronted with wild animals. If she survived that, she and her fellow disciples were to be put to death by Roman gladiators as the cheering crowds looked on. Perpetua's grace and faith under horrible persecution was described this way, as she was thrown out onto the open ground of the arena:

> Perpetua was tossed first and fell on her back. She sat up, and being more concerned with her sense of modesty than with her pain, covered her thighs with her gown, which had been torn down one side. Then finding her hair-clip that

133

had fallen out, she pinned back her loose hair, thinking it
not proper for a martyr to suffer with disheveled hair.[2]

Moments later, after being torn by the animals, Perpetua was
run-through by the sword of a gladiator. To the end her affect was
serene, and her countenance was confident. Those of us who
know the Lord Jesus Christ personally will surely rejoice when we
meet this gracious saint in the heavenly city!

One Hundred Years of Testing

Between A.D. 210 and 250, Christians were given a measure
of rest from the worst kinds of persecution. There were signs that
public opinion was slowly starting to change its opinions about
the torture of Christians, and the Church was starting to become
vocal in opposing it.

In A.D. 250, the Christian Pionius was executed when he
refused to participate in pagan sacrifices. His stand of faith struck
the public as curious because even the local Christian bishop had
compromised and indulged in the required pagan ceremonies.
"Faced with the alternative of obeying the emperor or suffering for
their faith, the great majority of Christians went with the
emperor," according to church historian William H.C. Frend.
Nevertheless, even Pionius's executioner pleaded with him to
compromise his faith in order to avoid death. Pionius refused and
was killed. There seemed to be little enjoyment by the pagan
onlookers at his death.

When Bishop Cyprian was to be executed for his faith in
A.D. 258, the Christian minority in the city held a public vigil the
night before in support for him and opposition to his death. This
public act was a sign that the Christian Church was growing and
ready to make itself visible in times of persecution.

The Great Persecution of 303–312 was ordered by Emperors
Diocletian and Maximian in an attempt to utterly destroy the
spread of Christianity. But, by that time, there were too many

Christians in the empire, and their persistent refusal to abandon their faith had impressed the rest of the population. Many believers were killed, but this was the final showdown between Spirit-filled Christians and the Roman Empire. The Christian historian and leader Eusebius described the resolve of the Christians this way: "As soon as sentence was passed on one, another from one quarter and others from another would leap up to the tribunal and confess themselves Christians."

In 313, inspired by a vision that he would be led to victory by the God of the Christians, Constantine defeated the Roman army at the battle of the Mulvian Bridge. The bloody war against Christians waged by Rome was over. In an amazing turn of events, the following decades would see an end to official persecution of Christians, and Christianity would be institutionalized as the official religion of the realm.

Faith in the Fire

History certainly teaches us that Christian martyrdom did not end with the close of the Roman Empire. Twelve hundred years later in Scotland, some of the most vicious persecutions of the Reformation took place. The killing of evangelical Christians in Scotland was not in massive numbers, but the cruelty endured by the saints was impressive. The first known martyr was a young scholar named Patrick Hamilton. His faith and sacrifice for the gospel is marked by an interesting inscription just outside the academic buildings of St. Andrews University.

St. Andrews is an ancient city, monopolized by the darkened brick buildings of the University and by the famous St. Andrews Golf Course, which lies a few blocks away along the coast. In the cold and dreary month of February 1528, Patrick Hamilton was a 24-year-old student with a nobleman's lineage. Even more remarkable, he had previously traveled from his homeland in Scotland to Wittenberg, Germany, and had personally studied under Martin Luther. After studying the principles of justification by faith, and after embracing the Lordship of Christ, Hamilton expressed a desire to return to Scotland and share the gospel there. He was warned repeatedly against such a plan. The Scottish Parliament had banned the works of Luther, calling them "filth and vice," and banned any ships from bringing them to Scottish shores. But Hamilton would not be dissuaded. The truth needed to be shared with his countrymen.

He returned to Scotland and immediately began preaching the gospel. Archbishop David Beaton was then ruling the religious life in St. Andrews with a cruel hand. He lured Hamilton to St. Andrews under the guise of having a debate over spiritual matters. Instead, he had the young evangelical arrested and condemned to death for heresy. John Knox himself describes Hamilton's slow sacrifice of faith this way as he was burned at the stake:

> The innocent servant of God being bound to the stake in the midst of some coals, some timber, and other matter appointed for the fire, a train of powder was made and set on fire, which neither kindled the wood nor yet the coals. And so remained the appointed death in torment, till men ran to the Castle again for more powder, and for wood more able to take fire; which at last being kindled, with loud voice he cried: "Lord Jesus receive my spirit! How long shall darkness overwhelm this realm? How long wilt Thou suffer the tyranny of men?"[3]

Today, students walking to the campus buildings of St. Andrews University step on the letters PH arranged in the bricks of the sidewalk. The initials of Patrick Hamilton mark the spot where he gave his life for the truth of God.

Twenty-eight years later, almost to the very day and but a few blocks from that site, a St. Andrews teacher named George Wishart suffered the same fate for the same reason. Wishart had previously been warned by church authorities to stop having his students read the Greek New Testament in his classes. He refused. Wishart obtained a license to preach, and boldly proclaimed salvation by faith in Christ wherever and whenever he could. He was the first preacher in Scotland to gain wide numbers of conversions during his open-air evangelistic meetings. Church authorities fought back by issuing six articles of heresy against him, and Wishart fled the country.

In 1543 he returned, accompanied by a young devotee who was converted to the Reformation gospel and served as Wishart's bodyguard, carrying a two-handed sword. The young man's name was John Knox. Wishart knew his days were numbered, so he told his good friend and companion to depart from him so that only Wishart would be captured. Knox was unwilling to do so, but Wishart prevailed on him. "One is sufficient for sacrifice," Wishart told him. Shortly afterward, he was captured and taken to the Castle of St. Andrews where he would await trial for heresy.

There are only ruins of that castle remaining today. A few walls of that foreboding building stand upright with gaping holes, like empty eyes that look out to the ocean beyond. But there is a peculiar place beneath the floor of the castle, called the "bottle dungeon." It is likely the place where Wishart was kept for several months before his execution. From an earthly perspective it is a hopeless looking place, a small hole in the brick floor protected with an iron grate, perhaps two feet in diameter, opening into a large, windowless well some 20 or 30 feet below. From above you can feel and smell the dampness of the place. Those who found themselves in the bottle dungeon knew their days of life were numbered.

But George Wishart knew a hope that began and ended far beyond that dreary and dreaded place. He knew that the truth of Christ, which he had preached and for which he would die, would preserve his soul and grant him peace in the middle of torment. The day of his execution, he was lashed to a post in the street and an iron chain was fastened around his middle. Presumably the chain was for additional effect, as it would radiate red-hot heat into his body with the fire of the flame. As Wishart was burned alive, the noose around his neck was tightened. But he was able, in the last moments before entering eternity with Christ, to forgive his tormentors, to commend the onlookers to read the Word of God, and to state, "I know surely that my soul shall sup with my Savior this night."[4]

John Knox was spiritually ignited as a result of the sacrificial death of his mentor. He became a preacher of the gospel and proclaimed the message of salvation without fear or hesitation across Scotland. He was captured by the bloody Archbishop of St. Andrews and banished for life. He was chained to the bottom of a French galley ship as a rowing slave. During the almost two years of that wretched confinement, lashed to the ship and rowing from dawn till dusk, Knox became convinced by God of one irrepressible fact. He knew he would one day return to St. Andrews, to his beloved Scotland, and there freely preach the saving blood of Jesus Christ.

Knox's prayers and his vision were answered. The king of England would later order his release and his return to Scotland. Not only would Knox preach at St. Andrews, he would deliver the sermon at the inauguration of King James.

Unfortunately, John Knox is often portrayed only as the wild-eyed, black-robed adversary of Mary Queen of Scots. In fact, inspired by the evangelical martyrs who preceded him, John Knox, more than any other man, unleashed the power of the gospel throughout Scotland and into England.

The Harvest of Faithfulness

The seeds of persecution can plant an awesome spiritual harvest. The persecution of the early church in Jerusalem scattered Christians and led to a missionary movement in other regions. The astounding sermon of Stephen, the first Christian martyr, was approved by a Pharisee named Saul of Tarsus, who looked on (see

Acts 7:54-58). That murder proved instrumental to the ministry of Paul, and therefore helped catapult the gospel around the known world.

Does all this mean we should not oppose persecution by lawful means? As we debate and discuss issues of religious liberty in and around the nation's capital, we have heard well-meaning Christians suggest that we should welcome persecution and not oppose it. They suggest that this response is the duty we have as believers.

Nothing could be further from the truth. On the one hand, Scripture is clear beyond debate about what our attitudes should be during persecution when it is inevitable. According to Peter, we are to count it all joy when we are chosen to suffer for the name of Jesus Christ. At the same time we have examples of godly opposition to persecution. When Paul was wrongly arrested, flogged, and thrown into a Philippi jail in violation of his rights as a Roman citizen, he protested. When it appeared he would be captured and possibly killed, Paul slipped out of Jerusalem, carried in a basket by fellow Christians. The early Christian Father, Justin Martyr, in his "apologia," specifically argued his case to convince the Roman government that Christians were being wrongly persecuted. John Knox's writings, as most of the writings of the Reformers, are filled with a practical denunciation of governmental abuses of Christians.

There are some practical ways we can follow in these noble footsteps of our spiritual ancestors. Congress has drafted legislation that would revoke aid and support to those nations that persecute Christians. This needs our support. China continues to arrest, imprison, and kill Bible-believing Christians, yet President Clinton has continued to send economic and technological aid to China. It is imperative that Christians speak out on these issues. When Washington actually proposes legislation that would stop anti-Christian persecution, how dare we fail to give it our attention—and our voice!

There are a number of nonprofit organizations that monitor anti-Christian persecution around the globe. They need our dollars and our prayers. There are pagan countries that need Bibles to help break the back of religious bigotry, superstition, and darkness. We should be sending our personal resources to support such missions. Our local churches need to participate in the International Day of Prayer for the Persecuted Church, which has been commemorated every year since 1995. And we need to pray for our brothers and sisters who are languishing in jails and prison camps for the sake of the gospel.

Perhaps most importantly, we need to live our lives seriously for Christ. We may never be called upon to give the last, full measure of sacrifice, but we need a walk with the Lord Jesus Christ that will be ready to do so, if that should be necessary.

We have a number of precious friends who have been, and are, serving Christ in dangerous lands, under dangerous circumstances. They have been an inspiration to the two of us. They do not serve God to be heroes; they do it do be faithful. If the Lord should come back to this sin-weary world in the next millennium, will He find us faithful?

CHAPTER ELEVEN

Suffering in the Next Century

In the old section of Jerusalem, on the palm tree-lined boulevard along Nablus Road, there is an aged but elegant hotel called the American Colony. Inside, you get the feel of the Middle East of 100 years past. With its high-backed wicker chairs, potted palm plants, and stone floors that sweep through the arched doorways and courtyards giving a cool respite from the desert heat, the hotel has many stories to tell.

On the walls are memorabilia and pictures of T.E. Lawrence, with his English face framed in Arab headdress and robe. There is a photo of English General Edward Allenby, who led British soldiers to the gates of the city, driving out the Turks, then dismounted in respect so as to enter the holy city on foot. But also on a wall, off to the side and behind the

French doors, there is a small and unassuming display. Many visitors probably pass by without notice. It is a framed piece of paper, the letterhead of an ocean liner. The prior occupant of the hotel wrote the words on the letterhead. He was to become the head of a Christian mission that operated in the building in 1880, a man named Horatio Spafford.

On that piece of paper, in Spafford's handwriting, are the words of a hymn he wrote. Many of us know that wonderful hymn but perhaps do not know the man and the life experience behind it. We know those reassuring refrains that remind us how God can keep us in spiritual peace, though the world is crumbling around us:

When peace like a river attendeth my way,
When sorrows like sea billows roll,
Whatever my lot, Thou hast taught me to say,
It is well, it is well with my soul.

Behind those words, penned while Horatio Spafford was on board an ocean liner, is a lesson of spiritual endurance and joy that triumphed over unimaginable loss. Spafford started out as a successful lawyer in Chicago. He and his wife raised four daughters, were active in their local church, and were strong supporters of D.L. Moody. But in 1871 the great Chicago fire swept through the city, and in the process wiped out all of the Spafford's considerable real estate properties.

Moody was planning an evangelistic campaign in Great Britain, and Horatio Spafford decided to take his family over to Europe to participate in the meetings. On November 27, 1873, at the last minute, urgent business detained Horatio, so he sent his wife and four daughters ahead on the steamship S.S. *Ville du Harve*, while he stayed behind. He planned to join them as soon as possible.

Halfway across the Atlantic Ocean, the ship was struck by another vessel and sunk in a matter of minutes. While Mrs. Spafford was miraculously saved, their four precious daughters were not. Tanetta, Maggie, Annie, and Bessie Spafford drowned with 226 other passengers. Horatio received the devastating news in a telegram from his wife, who stated simply, "All lost save one."

Mr. Spafford immediately boarded a ship that would take him to join his grieving wife who was waiting for him in Wales. Horatio walked the deck of the ship as it took him across the ocean. One can only imagine what a profound sense of grief must have washed over him as he walked the decks of that ship alone, thinking of his lost daughters. As he finally neared the area where the ship bearing his beloved girls had gone down, Spafford was filled with a supernatural power of God's comforting touch. There, facing the ocean deep that had claimed the lives of two-thirds of his family, Horatio Spafford jotted down the words that would become one of the great Christian hymns, and which call us to remember God's ultimate and future plan:

> Though Satan should buffet, tho' trials should come,
> let this blest assurance control—
> That Christ hath regarded my helpless estate
> and shed His own blood for my soul.
> And, Lord, haste the day when the faith shall be sight,
> the clouds be rolled back as a scroll,
> The trump shall resound and the Lord shall descend,
> even so, it is well with my soul.

As Horatio Spafford sailed on the ocean waves, he discovered the hope that comes from a soul fully steered by God. He found rest in the heavenly Father who sheds His unconditional love on us, and who comforts us with a compassion that passes all understanding. Tough faith means seeing Him and His eternal love in the midst of temporal pain. It means knowing He has the perfect answer to every bit of human suffering, even though He does not answer all of our questions about our suffering in this life.

Today, we must also be prepared to exercise tough faith. If we extrapolate the amazing scientific advances of the last 40 or 50 years, and the ever-increasing speed with which such breakthroughs are occurring, we can easily conclude that in the next decades we will see some impressive discoveries. Along with this, we can predict an increase in the human confidence index. If we can design fiber optics and send probes into deep space, surely we can minimize the problems on our own planet. Unfortunately, one of the major myths of modern life is that we are gaining more and more control over our world.

As Christians we should see just the opposite: The world system, which is controlled by the prince of the air and which is opposed to God's eternal truth, is gaining more and more control over the hearts of people. We are in a fallen universe, and Paul tells us in Romans 8:22 that the "whole creation groans" under the weight of sin and fallenness. The reality is that there are painful experiences in our lives that are universally guaranteed and are beyond our control. We use catch phrases like "time and tide stop for no man" and "nothing is constant except death and taxes" as familiar reminders of the inevitability of those unpleasant forces in life.

The lie of the new millennium may be the illusion that pain, war, and perhaps even death itself can be mastered through scientific achievements. We need only remember the spread of AIDS as one example of how new disease processes constantly evade our ability to anticipate them. Tornadoes, hurricanes, even the vagaries of "El Niño" mock our idea of predictability, safety, and control in our lives. These kinds of occurrences are reminders of our own frailty.

When El Niño hit in December of 1997, it brought scorching heat that caused 30 deaths in Texas alone, and was responsible for decreased harvests in Brazil and huge fires in Borneo.

When its climatic sister "La Niña" hit in July 1998, we saw torrential rainstorms in Asia and an increase in hurricane activity along the eastern seaboard.

Some of us have grandparents who remember the great Midwest dustbowl drought in the 1930s. It turned farms into deserts, plunged people into poverty, and hit America right in the breadbasket. Two researchers have published a report that indicates the dustbowl was mere child's play compared to the megadrought that may be heading our way in the next century.

In the *Bulletin of the American Meteorological Society*, Connie A. Woodhouse and Jonathan T. Overpeck have reviewed the cycles of drought over the last 2000 years. According to their data, it is more than a remote possibility that in years ahead we may be hit with the kind of 20- to 30-year drought that struck the planet in the 13th and 16th centuries. These kinds of forecasts were made solely on the history of climatic conditions and quite apart from the controversial theories about "global warming" and the "greenhouse effect."[1]

These trends could be aggravated by the over-cultivation of the lands in the midwestern United States and the excessive demands being placed on the Ogallala Aquifer, the underground source of about one-third of America's irrigation water. Any drought to hit us would be exacerbated by these factors. Have you ever stopped and wondered how we would fare in the face of a worldwide drought of the kind that takes food off your table and makes you wonder about your own survival?

Suffering and the Freedom of Choice

The positive lesson from these disasters is not necessarily what we can do to avoid them. (Though if you live in a hurricane belt, sturdy construction, knowing your evacuation route, and having insurance is a good start!) Instead, we ought to consider how we will choose to respond when the Lord allows disaster to come our way.

Dietrich Bonhoffer, a Lutheran pastor and radio preacher in Nazi Germany, was arrested by the Third Reich as he was preaching over the airwaves against the atrocities of that regime. (Janet spends a lot of time doing talk radio, and she never ceases to thank God for the freedom of radio communication in America. As she sits in front of a microphone for four hours every day, she is filled with gratefulness at not having to listen for the sound of stormtroopers' boots outside the studio door.) He was jailed for his radio addresses, and eventually he walked down a stone path from his cell to a spot where he was summarily executed. Before his death, Bonhoffer observed that no matter how bad our personal circumstances get, no matter how we may suffer a loss of freedom of comfort, of family, of shelter, or of food, one freedom remains—the freedom to *choose our attitude*.

The Apostle Paul said something that should rivet all of us heading into the new millennia:

> *Not that I speak from want; for I have learned to be content in whatever circumstances I am. I know how to get along with humble means, and I also know how to live in prosperity; in any and every circumstance I have learned the secret of being filled and going hungry, both of having abundance and suffering need. I can do all things through Him who strengthens me. (Philippians 4:11-13)*

Paul did not write these words from a luxurious penthouse or a palace. He wrote them from jail. He wrote them under the inspiration of the Holy Spirit after years of deprivation and hardship. "We are afflicted in every way," he notes in 2 Corinthians 4:8-9, "but not crushed; perplexed, but not despairing; persecuted but not forsaken; struck down, but not destroyed."

Where did Paul's source of strength come from? The apostle stated clearly that it was "the Lord who strengthens me." And how was he able to be content in all circumstances, not losing heart in the face of disaster? Paul boldly proclaimed that "though our outer man is decaying, yet *our inner man is being renewed day by day*. For momentary, light affliction is producing for us an eternal weight of glory far beyond all comparison, while we look not at the things which are seen, but at the things which are not seen; for the things which are seen are temporal, but the things which are not seen are eternal" (2 Corinthians 4:16-18, emphasis added).

Anyone who has battled a serious disease or had a loved one struggle with cancer can relate to the picture of the "outer man decaying." It isn't pretty, this process of decay and death. Several years ago, Janet's brother was diagnosed with cancer. Two weeks later her other brother was also diagnosed with cancer. Ten months later her mother was diagnosed with cancer. In less than a year their world was turned upside down.

We wept, waited, and prayed. We spent countless hours in hospital hallways as this invisible but deadly enemy ravaged her family. "Why God?" we asked. "Why us? Why so many in one family? Are we being punished? Where is the guidebook for appropriate behavior in circumstances like these?"

It's amazing how "real life" can make you do a very thorough inventory of what matters and what does not. For five years, Janet's family was poked, probed, radiated, filled with drugs, diagnosed, and tested. But the *real* work was being done on our hearts, away from the peering eyes of microscopes but completely transparent to the God of the universe.

Janet had to come to the realization that suffering was a guarantee in this life; the rain does indeed fall on the just and the unjust. As hospital personnel asked us how we were coping with such a tragedy, we began to realize we had been given a heavenly opportunity. How do we cope? Because we know that death has been conquered; the grave no longer can claim victory because the tomb is empty. That's how we cope. We knew beyond any doubt that each one in the family knew Christ as his or her personal Savior, and that knowledge secured the reality of seeing each other again on the other side of the grave. To the Christian, death in a family of believers is only a separation; it is not an end.

Instead of seeing this as some cosmic blunder, we began to realize that God, in His tender love for us, was giving us the opportunity to lift Him up. To make the proclamation, through pain, that we can indeed "do all things through Christ who strengthens us." The greatest fear that any of us can have is the fear of death. We became keenly aware that wearing a white hospital coat doesn't mean that the wearer has peace with the concept of death. To doctors and nurses, to lab technicians and orderlies, we found a mission field. We would pray for opportunities to share our faith in the midst of this trial. And God was faithful.

After five years, Janet's younger brother and mother went into complete remission with experimental chemotherapy and, praise God, remain that way today. But Janet's other brother, Charlie, was a different story. This good-looking, superior athlete was a world-class bond trader on the Chicago Board of Trade. He drew people to himself with his quick wit and spontaneous laugh. He had courage both on and off the trading floor, he was sharp with numbers, and became a financial success. He was compassionate with people, and his benevolent giving was well-known and much-appreciated.

Charlie's battle was with non-Hodgkin's lymphoma. He fought like a medieval warrior for five long years—even trading while wearing a flack jacket because his body was so battered from surgery and radiation. But Charlie knew he was losing this fight.

Janet's mother was a hospice nurse and we were all strong believers in patient advocacy, so we created a system of having at least one family member at Charlie's bedside each day he was hospitalized. The night of our 20th wedding anniversary it was our turn to be with Charlie. In the quiet of his room, Janet asked what she could do for him. Through an oxygen mask and with labored breathing, he asked her to just hold his hand. As she watched him bravely draw each new breath, she was flooded with memories that only a brother and sister can make—wrestling on the living room floor, trying to make each other laugh in church, and debating the politics of the day. But mostly she just sat there and loved him. He was her brother forever. Nothing and no one could change that. But for the first time, she was about to witness that which was promised to all of us...death.

Charlie suddenly sat upright in his bed and gazed out the window into the inky night. A look she will never forget came over his face. His eyes widened, he managed a faint smile, and he looked at something or Someone she could not see but knew was there. Here it was—the moment when Charlie was suspended between heaven and earth. As he placed his head back down on the pillow, Janet gently put her hands on his cheeks and said, "Charlie, you tell Jesus that I'm coming too!" It was a line from an old Sunday school song her mom loved to sing: "If you get there before I do, tell all my friends I'm coming too!" As he slipped deeper from this life into the next, she stroked his hand and sang, "Softly and tenderly Jesus is calling." Charlie did get there before her, but she *is* coming too.

This young man, in the prime of his life, had beaten one of the world's toughest financial markets before reaching 40. Then he met one of the immovable and unbeatable realities of life. But, more important than anything else, He met his Savior face to face. Tough faith is the only answer when no easy answers are at hand. Faith that is tried, tested, and true. Faith that lets you stare death right in the face.

We cannot always choose the difficulties we will face in this life, but we can certainly choose how we will respond to them.

Suffering and the Glory of God

Why God permits suffering has been one of the great debates throughout the ages. There are no easy answers. But there are some *clear* answers. The Bible tells us that sometimes pain and loss, even the most excruciating kind, is linked to the very essence of who God is, and it has a connection to something called the "glory" of God.

In the eighth chapter of the Gospel of John, we find Jesus in Jerusalem, the capital city of Israel. There in the great temple, we see Him debating with the hostile religious establishment of His day. The Pharisees condemn Him with every attack they can muster. They accuse Him of being demon-possessed, they call Him a "Samaritan" (a nationality considered undesirable by the Jews in those days), and even make reference to the current gossip that Jesus was born illegitimately. Then, in a burst of self-congratulation the Pharisees boast that they are the kin of Abraham.

Surely, they argue, Jesus cannot claim to be greater than Abraham and the prophets. But Jesus answers them by pointing out, "If I glorify Myself, My glory is nothing; it is My Father who glorifies Me, of whom you say, 'He is our God'" (John 8:54). It is God who glorifies Jesus, and it is the glory of God that is displayed in Jesus.

Then Jesus makes the most astounding statement of all: "Truly, truly, I say to you, before Abraham was born, I am." Here is a clear proclamation to the ruling religious class that Jesus was no mere man—indeed, not even a prophet. Jesus is clearly claiming His own divinity.

The outrage of the Pharisees was immediate. They scurried for rocks in order to stone him, which was the penalty for blasphemy. But the appointed time for Christ's death had not yet come, so Jesus hid Himself as He left the temple. And then, as He was leaving, the Lord caught sight of a blind beggar. The sight of a blind man begging for enough coins to buy bread must have been a common sight in the temple, particularly around the time of holy days and feasts. Certainly with the influx of worshipers the meager prospects from begging might be a little bit better.

The plight of this blind man struck a chord with the disciples. They wanted to know the explanation for this kind of suffering, and asked the Lord if he was being punished for his sins. Jesus gave them an answer they had not considered: "It was neither that this man sinned, nor his parents; but it was in order that the works of God might be displayed in him" (John 9:3).

The truth of Christ shattered the popular thinking of the day. Suffering may not be a matter of sin. It may, in fact, be the way God displays Himself through the brokenness of our lives. Jesus miraculously gave sight to this man, who for most of his life had been one of the wretched and neglected of the community. Suddenly, by the touch of Christ, his eyes were flooded for the first time with the brilliant colors and images and faces of the crowded streets of Jerusalem.

The Pharisees demanded he "give glory to God" for his healing, and not Jesus, who they considered a mere sinner. How ironic it was that they would have made that kind of demand as the Son of God stood nearby. God had been glorified because the works of God were displayed in that beggar through his healing. But *the healing could only have been possible because he had suffered* in blindness for years.

A little later Jesus was confronted with the death of Lazarus, the brother of Mary and Martha of Bethany. Amid the wailing and grief of the family, Jesus did the miraculous. He told them to roll the stone away from the tomb where Lazarus had been buried for four days. While the family protested loudly because they focused on the decaying body, Jesus focused on the glory of God: "Did I not say to you, if you believe, you will see the glory of God?" (John 11:40). Then, in the presence of witnesses, Jesus called forth from the grave a man who had lain dead for several days. We are told that "Many therefore of the Jews, who had come to Mary and beheld what He had done, believed in Him" (John 11:45).

We Shall See His Glory

Suffering can glorify God even when there is no miraculous healing, no supernaturally bestowed sight, no resurrected life out of death. Our personal hopes for physical comfort or the lessening of pain, no matter how legitimate those hopes may be, does not limit God's glory. He can be glorified even when we get the answer we fear most. When the diagnosis from the doctor is the one we dread, when the knock on the door brings news that God wills *not* to reverse, He is still glorified. Indeed, God *has* been glorified when the faith of His faithful servants has resulted in miraculous rescues. The writer to the Hebrews tells us:

> ...Who by faith conquered kingdoms, performed acts of righteousness, obtained promises, shut the mouths of lions, quenched the power of fire, escaped the edge of the sword, from weakness were made

strong, became mighty in war, put foreign armies to flight. Women received back their dead by resurrection. (Hebrews 11:33-35)

God has been glorified when the sufferings of His children were permitted, and when the endings were not pleasant. Hebrews 11 continues by reminding us:

Others were tortured...experienced mockings and scourgings, yes also chains and imprisonment. They were stoned, they were sawn in two, they were tempted, they were put to death with the sword; they went about in sheepskins, in goatskins, being destitute, afflicted, ill treated (men of whom the world was not worthy), wandering in deserts and mountains and caves and holes in the ground. (verses 35-38)

So what is this "glory" of God that can be manifested in our sufferings? Our puny minds can hardly comprehend it. The greatest poets of history can barely give us but slim shadows of what it means. The human imagination pales in an attempt to describe it.

The Bible tells us that when we finally see Jesus as He really is, as Lord of lords and King of kings, we shall see His glory. The Apostle John, given an opportunity to observe Jesus in all His glory, described it this way:

And I saw heaven opened; and behold, a white horse, and He who sat upon it is called Faithful and True; and in righteousness He judges and wages war. And His eyes are a flame of fire, and upon His head are many diadems; and He has a name written upon Him which no one knows except Himself. And He is clothed with a robe dipped in blood; and His name is called The Word of God. (Revelation 19:11-13)

It is a glimpse of this glorious presence of God that can be reflected through the prism of our sufferings. We seek the status quo, the comfort of our present state. When we feel the grinding wheel and the sanding belt at work on our glass edges, we moan and complain. What we must see are the fine crystal lenses He is making out of us, so others may look through them and see Him. In the middle of our trials, we are not to lose heart—even though our bodies may be decaying. Our inner spiritual persons are being renewed every day as we fix our eyes on the future weight of glory that God is preparing for us. Whether in health or disease, in adversity or triumph, we are to fix our eyes on Jesus who is the example we are to follow for endurance and victory amid suffering.

Tough times will come to each of us in the future. We are told to expect trials and tribulations, for they are the rule, not the exception. In fact, if truth be told, most of us from time to time feel as if the trials of life outweigh the pleasures. The "preacher" in Ecclesiastes got to the point when he exclaimed that it seemed as if it would be easier if we were never born at all!

Trials come to everyone, and we should anticipate an acceleration of trouble as our world gets closer to the end of the Church Age. The Bible warns that false teachers, wars, famines, earthquakes, tribulation, and persecution of believers will be the signposts of the end. Even the capacity of humans to love one another will wane when the really tough times hit.

So how do we find victory when our circumstances are screaming "defeat"? God's Word tells us that we are to be "overcomers." Not just survivors, but *overcomers*. We are victors! Not simply gritting our teeth, putting our head down, and charging forward in order to survive, but living through our difficulties in a way that brings glory to God. As 1 John 5:4 tells us, "This is the victory that has overcome the world—our faith."

An overcoming life in the next millennium will be a life lived in faith. As Paul puts it,

> *We also exult in our tribulations, knowing that tribulation brings about perseverance; and perseverance, proven character; and proven character, hope; and hope does not disappoint, because the love of God has been poured out within our hearts through the Holy Spirit who was given to us (Romans 5:3-5).*

As we encounter the great trials to come, we are not alone. The God whose Son walked before us has given us the path to follow through the life of Christ and the enabling power of His Spirit to walk it. Not only that, He has encouraged us by revealing the footprints of those who have gone before us. They have faced difficulties and, by faith, overcome them. Through faith in Christ, we can do the same.

The Credential of Credibility

As a young teenager, Ron Hagy discovered that a wave has two sides, and even when you find yourself on the wrong side of a million gallons of water God can bless you in unexpected ways.

Ron had everything a young high school boy could want. At 17 he was handsome and athletic. He had a crowd of friends at his Oregon high school, and he felt he had the world by the tail. It was spring break, and Ron had decided he would head down to the beaches of southern California. Ron's 13-year-old brother begged to come along, but Ron would not consider it. However, as younger brothers often do, he kept pestering Ron until they struck a deal: If his brother did all of Ron's chores, Ron would take him to the beach.

When they finally arrived, Hagy could not wait to try surfboarding for the first time. Looking back, Ron remembers his excitement: "We got up early, and the sun came through the window. I remember stretching, and thinking this is going to be the greatest day. I didn't know it would be the last day I would put my own shoes on."

Ron hopped on his surfboard and gleefully prepared to meet the huge wave approaching him. But instead of lifting him up onto the top of the curl, the massive wave pulled him straight down to the bottom. Ron rolled downward under a world of water. There was a sandbar, and his head was thrust into it, snapping his head back violently. Then there was a terrible cracking sound.

Lifeless under the water, Ron could not move his arms or legs. Suddenly, two skinny arms reached down and pulled him to the surface. It was his young, 13-year-old brother, saving his life. Ron Hagy, a young man with a future as bright as any teenager could wish, had just hit one of the biggest potholes the road of life has to offer.

When he woke up in the hospital, the nurse had to tell him what day it was—March 18, his eighteenth birthday. The break in his vertebrae was terrible, completely paralyzing him. He had to be hooked up to a ventilator to breathe, and he faced the substantial odds that he would not survive at all.

God does not play the odds. Ron survived, but was left with the ability to only move his head. When he realized the reality of life in a wheelchair, not being able to walk or tie his shoes, the sky fell in. Laying there helplessly, Ron lashed out at God, life, and the world. Sobbing and yelling out from his bed, Ron felt the unfairness of it all.

But then, from behind the curtain that separated him from the bed of Jimmy, his 8-year-old roommate in the hospital, he heard a voice. Jimmy was himself recovering from a massive head injury. Ron had been ignoring him during his recovery, except to yell at him when Jimmy would moan because of his head pain. This time the voice from the other side had something to teach him. "I love you, Ron," Jimmy said.

Somewhere, the darkness was starting to fade. "God reminded me of His love through this little boy," Ron told Janet on her radio program one day. "At this point the lights came on."

Ron had been to the bottom of life's oceans. Now God was slowly pulling him to the surface, where he could feel the warmth of daylight, see the blue sky, and find victory in the midst of disappointment.

Ron Hagy has a message to tell the world. He is quick to tell you about the tremendous support he received from his family during those dark days. He also has a message about the love of God and the tough faith that was forged out of helplessness and built on God's promises. One of the Bible verses that became a living reality to Ron was Matthew 6:33-34. His father had taped it to the ceiling of his hospital room when all he could do was lay on his back and stare straight up:

> *But seek first His kingdom and His righteousness; and all these things shall be added to you. Therefore do not be anxious for tomorrow; for tomorrow will care for itself. Each day has enough trouble of its own.*

Ron has since gone on to college and graduate school, earning his master's degree. He has written a book about his encounter with life's tidal wave, called *Life Is an Attitude.* We may not know a fraction of the reasons why a young fellow like Ron Hagy had to face life without the use of his arms and legs, but one thing is very certain: When he talks to us about "attitude" in the midst of difficulty, we listen. Ron has earned the credentials of credibility when it comes to matters of endurance and personal victory.

If the waning years of the 20th century are any indicator, the next century will continue to place a high premium on personal comfort and the increase of self-indulgence and instant gratification. We lose patience when we have to sit in snarled traffic during rush hour. Regular mail delivery time has become an intolerable wait. Not being able to afford the luxuries that Madison Avenue panders to us in slick ads in magazines or those tantalizing offers of the "good life" on television, becomes our measure of "sacrifice." One wonders what kind of loudspeaker God needs to call us back to the eternal things, the things that really matter, to lives of service to Him rather than self-service.

This kind of talk will probably not be popular in the coming decades. The issue of human suffering is at the top of the "don't get into that" list for any social gathering. Yet, it is the tough parts of real life that we need to get right the first time. After all, the lives we live in the midst of suffering do not count for nothing. In God's economy, they count for everything. So what should we focus on? Being overcomers.

CHAPTER TWELVE

A Black Cloud
in the Silver Lining

In order to understand where the 21st century may be taking us economically, there are two financial realities we must remember. As a couple, the two of us share a running joke about our mutual lack of economic sophistication, therefore these two realities will probably strike you as monumentally basic. But like so many other things, the basics are the most important. Living and working in and around the beltway of the nation's capital, we have heard the ever-present mantra that "the economy is everything." To those in that chorus, we would say it is time to remember the two truths.

First, we are an extraordinarily prosperous nation. Every four years, when we go into an election, we are hit with the political banter from one party that the "other party" has caused a current economic downturn. The truth is that, compared to both past American standards and current standards in other nations, we are incredibly prosperous.

Economic indicators indicate we have been financially blessed. Compensation and benefits have increased steadily since 1947, income for families has made modest but steady increases since 1967, and measured by "purchasing power parity" (the ability of Americans to buy), we are clearly the richest country in the world.

Per capita income has nearly doubled in the United States during the last three decades, and only six other countries of the world have higher per capita GNP than we do. The average hourly compensation in America for production workers was recently charted at $17.74 per hour, much higher than Canada's $16.66 per hour, and far greater than the rock-bottom $1.50 of Mexico. Americans also have fewer worries about affording the necessities of life than citizens of other countries. In India 52.4 percent of the average person's total expenditures is devoted entirely to buying food to survive. In the United States we spend less than 10 percent on the same concern, leaving a substantial amount of our income free for the purchase of items that would be considered luxuries in almost all other nations of the world. About 97 percent of all Americans own color televisions and, as of 1993, 63 percent of us had cable TV.

If you travel to even the wealthiest of the European nations, you soon notice that the average person has less than we have. Gone are the designer jeans, personal pagers, expensive cars, and mega-sound CD players and stereo systems that have become fixtures for American teenagers. Absent, too, are the several new cars, multiple cable-TV televisions, vacations to Disney World, and large homes that have become a way of life in America.

Let's admit the truth: On average we are a prosperous, economically blessed nation. And most of us, if we were candid, would admit that we've become quite attached to the luxuries of life in America. But if this is true, why are the headlines and the evening news always telling us that we are experiencing economic labor-pains?

Syndicated columnist Ben Wattenberg makes an interesting observation in his book *Values Matter Most*. After reviewing the economic trends over the last few decades, he describes why we are always complaining about money pains: "Having become the richest people in all history, Americans are growing somewhat more prosperous very, very slowly, and this causes relative pain."[1]

Second, our prosperity is subject to radical change. America's economic picture is getting more and more complex. Financial markets are no longer local, regional, or even national. Markets are now worldwide. We are becoming more and more dependent on an intricate web of economic ties with other nations of the world. What if this ever-increasing web of economic ties results in massive financial failures? Is our faith tough enough to survive even in economic hard times?

The perils of this interconnectedness of world markets were well illustrated recently. When the Asian money markets collapsed in May 1998, and foreign banks started closing, tremors were immediately felt on Wall Street, and the Dow Jones average plunged. A second shock wave was felt in diminished American exports. The Asian financial crisis caused a substantial increase in America's trade deficit, hitting a record high of 13 billion dollars for one month.

Speculation abounds about why this recent crisis occurred. One theory has the ring of common sense: These newly emerging economies in Asia were unable to control the huge influx (and retraction) of international money. As financial analyst Robert Kuttner noted: "It is impossible to run an efficient economy when your currency swings by 100% in just a few months."

No sooner had the Asian financial crisis hit than a second tidal wave of financial woe swept out of the chilly regions of

Russia. The Dow Jones average plunged hundreds of points when American investors started a panic sale of stocks in the wake of financial collapse in Russia. It was the third worst point drop in the history of Wall Street. Further uncertainty was felt in world stock markets as Venezuela gave signs of its inability to repay its debts.

Of course, when the American stock market crashed in 1929 and the great depression hit, we responded with national economic regulations in banking and on Wall Street to prevent similar catastrophes. As international financial interdependence between the nations of the world increases, how will the world's experts try to prevent a worldwide financial crash?

The obvious solution is worldwide regulation in the areas of trade, monetary policies, investments, and banking. If you think this sounds overly sinister and conspiratorial, consider the following comment from Linda Y.C. Lim, professor of international business at Michigan Business School:

> Today, even the World Bank has lent its support to some forms of capital controls for small open economies that can be severely disrupted by massive inflows and outflows of foreign capital. There is a growing consensus that, at a minimum, some international monitoring and perhaps risk-insuring agency is necessary to oversee these currently largely unregulated flows."[2]

We must not miss what professor Lim is saying because it is what most international economists will soon be saying. We must construct, "at a minimum," some type of international monitoring system to oversee the flow of money around the globe. This worldwide "risk-insuring agency" will be demanded vigorously as the amount of American investment in economies of foreign countries increases.

Potential for Disaster

The Christian Church cannot merely receive this information in a vacuum. We must know how a global, centralized monitoring of world economics fits in with the clear prophetic message of Scripture. This is not "out there" in the misty future somewhere—it is facing us right now. This news ought to thrill us with the anticipation of the imminent return of Jesus Christ, but it should also energize us with the passion to make the most of our short pilgrimage.

For example, dependence on increasingly complex and highly interconnected commercial technology such as satellite links may portend disaster. When the commercial satellite Galaxy IV failed, service to millions of pager customers ceased, all of National Public Radio's 600 stations lost programming, and credit card purchases at 5400 Chevron gas stations were blocked. This was just one out of some 600 satellites that regularly provide service to businesses from outer space. Multiply this shutdown of services by a factor of 100,000, and you begin to see the potential impact of a major computer crisis. As our dependence on complex technology increases, the chances of unforeseen failures in those man-made systems increase, and with them the risk of catastrophic economic failure.

Our reliance on certain necessary goods is another potential for disaster. One ominous indicator is the prospect of an oil crisis worldwide. A recent article in *Scientific American* notes that "within the next decade the supply of conventional oil will be unable to keep up with the demand." The study concludes that "the world could thus see radical increases in oil prices" as we enter the new millennium.

Recall, for a moment, the "oil crisis" during the 1970s. When gasoline supply at neighborhood gas stations temporarily slowed down, tempers flared, panic started to spread, and some angry drivers even brandished guns and shot at each other. There seems to be a consensus of opinion now that this "crisis" was no real crisis at all, yet when Americans felt their ability to drive their automobiles was threatened, an ugly "every person for himself" sense of survivalism sprang up quickly.

We all remember how riots broke out in Los Angeles following the court verdict involving the police officers who attacked Rodney King. The images on television of violence and brutality were shocking, but we also recall how stores and shops were immediately plundered as if they were part of some bizarre giveaway TV game show. In the same way, when catastrophe hits a major city, whether by flood, tornado, or hurricane, and the economic and material status quo is disturbed, wholesale looting and thievery become the instant reaction. How then, would America handle a major economic crisis involving the scarcity of necessary goods or the disruption of our material lives?

Another economic indicator of potential disaster is the future impact of our soaring national debt load, both federally and individually. This fact has been noted repeatedly over the last 20 years from every corner of the financial world, and the reality led Christian financial counselor Larry Burkett to predict, back in 1990, the coming of an "economic earthquake." Burkett also noted the solid historical data for the phenomena of economic cycles—simply put, the world has seen major financial depressions about every 60 years. The year 2000 is ripe for another.

Recently a member of one of America's premier think tanks, an international computer executive, and a Washington, D.C., editor teamed up to depict the global future of the next millennium. What they see, by the year 2040 is this:

- Social Security alone will take up 55 percent of each paycheck (compared to 17 percent today);

- Public entitlements (like Medicare and Social Security) will exceed all federal revenues;

- Japan and Germany will become nuclear powers;

- A "holy war" will break out between Muslims and Christians;

- China will become the world's largest economy.[3]

Of these predictions, the last one—the rise of China as a world economic leader—is probably shared by the most experts who deal in the business of prognosticating future trends.

The Coming World Power

Hamish McRae, an editor of the London newspaper *The Independent*, and whose book is reputed to be on Bill Clinton's reading list, has made the following prediction regarding the first two decades of the new millennium:

> Yet if the US does not deal with the high cost of running its diverse and complex society, by 2020 its days as the only superpower will be drawing to a close. Its chief rival for dominance will probably be China. Unless the Americans of the next generation are better educated and show greater self-discipline than their Chinese contemporaries, economic might, and hence world leadership, will gradually but inevitably shift to China.[4]

Remember how China, at the end of the 100-year lease on Hong Kong, recently accepted the hand over of complete and total ownership of this Asian economic "jewel" from Great Britain? Our televisions brought us the images from the other side of the world as gala celebrations and fireworks burst forth over Hong Kong while international dignitaries smiled politely. The television commentators smiled politely too, for no one was mentioning the obvious. Like the superficial conversation at the funeral where no one seems to know the deceased, the media, capturing all of the fanfare, ignored the casket at the end of the room.

Here was the potential death of freedom for Hong Kong occurring before our very eyes as an entire region was being handed over to one of the most ruthless and powerful nations on earth. But all would be well, we were told, because mainline China had promised not to disturb life as it had grown to exist on this affluent little empire of international free trade.

The delivery of Hong Kong to China was a symbolic picture of things to come. President Clinton has consistently conferred on China "Most Favored Nation" (MFN) status. As a result, China has enjoyed all of the benefits of full trade relations with America. When the United States began downsizing its military and closing bases around the nation, one of them was at Long Beach in the San Diego area. The base was to be sold to China though public outcry has forestalled the sale.

No sooner had we seen the disintegration of the Soviet Union as the chief communist rival to America's world leadership than China, the sleeping giant, raised its tyrannical head as the new challenger. Ironically, the United States may be sowing the seeds of its own destruction by its warmhearted welcome to China's expanding economy. In June 1998, President Clinton paid an historic visit to China. As he strolled down the broad plaza of Tiananmen Square in Beijing, smiling, an ocean of camera shutters clicked as he walked with Chinese President Jiang Zemin before the People's Liberation Army, standing smartly at attention with rifles raised.

This was the same Tiananmen Square where, in 1989, this same army rolled in with tanks and brutally crushed a political protest by Chinese students. Some 225 of the students arrested for those protests are still in jail, victims of a legal system in China that sentences citizens to "labor reform" in prison camps without the benefit of a trial. Torture of citizens who are arrested is an ongoing fact of life in China. Yet President Clinton rejected the pleas of his critics to avoid meeting China's leader at a place so symbolic of that country's iron-fisted tyranny. He was so eager to be a good guest that he refused to meet with political dissidents. An Associated Press photographer took a picture that revealed more than a thousand words—as Clinton met with China's leaders, the photo caught the sight of an American flag waving in the breeze, hanging over a huge picture of China's communist founder, Mao Tse-Tung in Beijing's famous square. It was obvious that President

Clinton was bent on one primary objective: to continue strengthening the economic ties between the United States and China.

Gone was Bill Clinton's tough election year rhetoric from 1992, when he had ripped into his opponent George Bush as someone who "would do business as usual with those who murdered freedom in Tiananmen Square." This was the new Bill Clinton, and this was the new plan for China It means tons of high technology and computers and millions of American dollars sent to communist China.

As China's economy leaps forward, racing into the next millennium with the help of the United States, our present administration is banking on the fact that finances will grease the wheels of freedom. At a speech at Beijing University, President Clinton proclaimed that "in the Global Information Age, freedom is a powerful engine of progress." Yet what kind of freedom was Bill Clinton talking about? What kind of freedom is being enjoyed by the Protestant and Catholic leaders languishing in prison for the practice of their faith? In anticipation of President Clinton's trip, these kinds of questions had been asked by a delegation of visiting U.S. clergy. Ye Xiaowen, director of the State Administration for Religious Affairs for China had the typical communist response: "We do not allow anyone to use religion to disrupt normal public order."[5]

It remains to be seen whether ignoring China's repressive charter against political and religious freedom and its history of atrocities will haunt the world scene in the coming years as it expands its financial world dominance with American know-how and dollars. However, one thing is relatively clear. If China has no real "conversion" to freedom, as it brings itself up to par with the United States in its wealth and trade power, the next few decades may reveal a new kind of sinister terrorism being used against the free, democratic countries of the world. A kind of economic terrorism may become a new weapon for China, along with its developing nuclear ability. China may soon be in a position to impose trade restrictions, embargoes, or economic sanctions against nations that do not agree to assist its international agenda. If the economy of the United States should falter, we could see the specter of America looking to China for essential trade. What freedoms would we be willing to give up to communist China in the next 20 years in return for increased jobs for Americans or to prevent an economic depression?

The New Order

As the borders of the distant future become sharper, some visions for the economics of the end of the 21st century become more shocking. It has been suggested that our 5000-year-old notion of nation-states, with borders, political structures, and laws, may become of secondary importance to global financial forces. Futurist Alvin Toffler notes:

> As finance is globalized, nations risk losing control over one of the keys to their power. The proposed all-European currency, for example, would reduce the flexibility of individual nations to cope with their own unique economic problems. Another proposal would arm the EC commissioners with far greater control over the budgets of supposedly sovereign nations than the federal government of the United States exerts over its fifty states—a centralizing power shift of massive proportions."[6]

The power of global money and world economics may become so instrumental that some financial analysts predict a 21st century world where international borders will not be so much defined by what country you live in, as by what economic unit you are working for.

In the new millennium, it is predicted that "governments [will] fade into immateriality and corporations [will] emerge as the lords of a new, borderless world order."[7] No longer will predictable, traditional management systems based on organization and logic prevail. Instead, we are urged to prepare for the "chaos world," where the ability to adapt to change will be one of the highest virtues. The new rules of the new millennium corporations that will govern the world are clear, blunt and unforgiving:

> The only test should be whether employees share the organization's core business values. If they don't, they are wrebels—rebellious workers who seek to wreck an organization's value system. And if they are wrebels, they must be gone, whatever their race, sex, or cultural heritage.[8]

The reality check for all Christians is that economic hard times may be coming. Perhaps it will happen because of disruption of necessary goods (whether it is oil or food), or we may face an economic crash because of the reality of financial cycles. Perhaps the sheer complexity of our computerized, international web of interdependent economic ties will be unable to adjust to sudden social, political, or environment upheavals, and our monetary systems will collapse like a house of cards. Or perhaps China, having grown to such world financial power with the help of the free world, will turn on us, like a Frankenstein monster turning on its inventor.

If that happens, sound financial strategies both national and personal will be critically important. But financial planning will not be enough. The real question is whether our faith will be tougher than our economic circumstances. When prosperity wanes and our comfort level disappears, it is our spiritual perspective and our perseverance that will determine how successfully we function as believers in Christ.

This is not a new message. We have been warned before that our culture has become bloated with wealth, indulgence, and sensual decadence. Such indictments against the lavish excesses of the palace are often most effectively delivered from the hermit who has just stumbled in from the desert. Alexander Solzhenitsyn delivered such a message to America on June 8, 1978. The Russian novelist created a firestorm of controversy when he delivered his commencement address at Harvard University, condemning our materialism, immorality, and greed. The Harvard intellectuals should not have been surprised.

Solzhenitsyn's views on our national obsession with the pursuit of prosperity and pleasure were forged from within the ice-shrouded walls of a "gulag" in Soviet Kazahstan. He had been sentenced to banishment there because his writings had grown increasingly critical of the communist government in the Soviet Union. Through the suffering and deprivation of that experience he gained a unique perspective on the materialism of our culture. Years later he was released by the communists from his isolation and stumbled into America, bringing with him a warning about the perils of prosperity and personal comfort. Solzhenitsyn scolded our nation that:

> Two hundred or even fifty years ago, it would have seemed quite impossible, in America, that an individual be granted boundless freedom with no purpose, simply for the satisfaction of his whims. Subsequently, however, all such limitations were eroded everywhere in the West; a total emancipation from the moral heritage of Christian centuries with their great reserves of mercy and sacrifice. State systems were becoming ever more materialistic. The West has finally achieved the rights of man, and even to excess, but man's sense of responsibility to God and society has grown dimmer and dimmer.[9]

Solzhenitsyn never really changed his theme. The threat to the soul of our nation he visualized from his Vermont retreat after gaining his freedom he had also seen from his imprisonment in Russia. When he accepted his 1970 Nobel Prize for Literature, his words were even sharper. Solzhenitsyn's speech had to be delivered in his absence, in written form, because the communist officials refused to permit him to travel to Stockholm, Sweden, to give the address. On this day he cried out,

I even venture to say that the spirit of Munich is dominant in the twentieth century. The intimidated civilized world has found nothing to oppose the onslaught of a suddenly resurgent fang-baring barbarism, except concessions and smiles. The spirit of Munich is a disease of the will of prosperous people; it is the daily state of those who have given themselves over to a craving for prosperity in every way, to material well-being as the chief goal of life on earth. Such people—and there are many of them in the world today—choose passivity and retreat, anything if only the life to which they are accustomed might go on, anything so as not to have to cross over to rough terrain today, because tomorrow, see, everything will be all right. (But it never will! The reckoning for cowardice will only be more cruel. Courage and the power to overcome will be ours only when we dare to make sacrifices.)[10]

In the 21st century, will our faith be strong enough to engage in sacrificial living? Will the Christian Church be able to separate itself from the mad dash of the world to gain and maintain financial prosperity no matter what the cost? If not, we fear the power of the Church will have dissipated, having been traded for comfort and luxury.

CHAPTER THIRTEEN

A Faith for
the Future

L ife is unstable. Everything changes. We change jobs, we
change homes, we change churches, we change the style of our
clothes, we change hairstyles, we change hair colors, we change
diapers, we change channels on the television, and we change our
majors in college. Some changes are simply more difficult to handle than others. As we get older and slower, we lose our pace, we
lose our hair, we lose our memory, and even lose the ones we love.
Things continue to change, no matter how much we try to keep
them the same.

In this unstable world, people are seeking something unchanging, something secure. Many have chosen to put their faith in

wealth, or possessions, or the stock market. It is inviting to believe that wealth and financial security are the best hedge against change and insecurity, but to place that idea in perspective we need to look at the financial ups and downs of recent years. During April 1997, the emerging "Asian Tiger" markets of the Far East that had experienced phenomenal economic growth in the early 1990s started collapsing. In July of that year, the values of the currencies of Thailand, Philippines, Malaysia, and Singapore plunged. In August, Indonesia's currency dropped, then in October the Hong Kong stock market did a dead fall downward, dropping 40 percent.

Despite the Asian crisis, the U.S. stock market remained strong. By June of 1998, the Dow Jones Average (stock prices from a group of 30 major companies that trade on the New York Stock Exchange) hit a record high of 9337.97. However, due to the instability of foreign markets, American investors started selling off. In August of that year, Russia's currency lost 50 percent of its value, and in desperation Russia froze payments on its debts. Investors, concerned that other nations might freeze their debt payments as well, triggered a massive sell off, putting the stock market into a fast downward plunge. By August 31, 1998, the stock market had dropped by a whopping 500 points—a 19 percent tailspin in just six weeks.

President Clinton described the global financial scene as the worst economic crisis since the end of World War II. America was facing the threat of a major recession. But the recession never happened. Instead, economic growth increased when the Federal Reserve cut interest rates. As confidence in the market rebounded, the Dow Jones leaped up to a new high. In the course of one year, all of the major markets of the globe, linked by new international economic ties like roller coaster cars hooked together at an amusement park, had taken a wild and unprecedented ride. The market was up; the market was down. By early 1999, the Dow Jones hit 10,000 for the first time in history. Then the analysts began predicting a crash.

How do we plan for financial stability in an economic scene that seems to be growing increasingly unstable and more unpredictable? Our choice is basically simple: We choose to have faith that will get us through the ups and downs of the market, or we choose to have faith in the markets themselves.

Prioritizing Your Finances

If we want to survive the financial future, we're going to have to know, and apply, God's priorities for our finances. We are commanded to be practical in our earthly work, applying ourselves to the task of providing for our families. The Apostle Paul instructed the believers at Thessalonica to "attend to your own business and work with your hands, just as we commanded you; so that you may behave properly toward outsiders and not be in any need" (1 Thessalonians 4:11-12). In 1 Timothy 5:8, he was even more blunt: "But if anyone does not provide for his own, and especially for those of his household, he has denied the faith, and is worse than an unbeliever."

God's first priority for finances is that we work hard and use our money wisely. The Lord knows we have needs, but He asks, in Matthew 6:33, that we look to His kingdom as our destination, and to His righteousness as our primary activity: "But seek first His kingdom and His righteousness; and all these things shall be added to you."

It is clear that God has placed an emphasis on the concept of "value." He wants us to understand those things that have eternal value, and to distinguish those from the lesser things that have only fleeting value. In Matthew 13:44 Jesus tells His disciples: "The kingdom of heaven is like a treasure hidden in the field, which a man found and hid; and from joy over it he goes and sells all that he has, and buys that field."

Things of eternal value must take precedence over temporal things. Jesus told a parable of a man seeking a pearl of great price. That man so valued the pearl he was willing to sell all he had in order to possess that treasure. In other words, his actions revealed the priority in his life. In the same way, our actions should reflect God's eternal priorities.

There is a heavenly profit and loss formula that departs from the wisdom of the world. Jesus asked, "What will a man be profited, if he gains the whole world, and forfeits his soul?" In God's economy, our concept of "profit" should start with what enriches the spirit, even though it may end with the material things that care for the body.

Jim Bakker, former host of the *PTL Club* television program and the founder of Heritage U.S.A., learned that lesson the hard way. Having amassed and spent a fortune on the running of his huge Christian "empire," Jim was charged and convicted of federal crimes relating to financial fraud. He spent a number of years in a federal prison, and is now sharing his hard-earned lesson about heavenly and earthly values.

He preached a "prosperity" gospel that measured God's faithfulness by a financial yardstick. But during the months and years in prison, as Jim read his Bible, he came to the startling conclusion that he had missed the point of prosperity:

> How could I have taught and even written books on the subject of how to get rich, when Jesus spoke so clearly about the dangers of earthly riches? One of the statements of Jesus that kept echoing in my head and heart was in The Parable of the Sower, where Jesus said that "the cares of this world, the deceitfulness of riches, and the desires for other things entering in choke the word, and it becomes unfruitful" (Mark 4:19 NKJV). *The deceitfulness of riches!* The more I thought about it, the more I had to admit that I had fallen into that snare.[1]

God knows how dependent the world is on material things. He knows our longings, our fears, and our needs. What He wants us to do is to look to Him as the ultimate source of blessing, and as the sovereign provider. When we look to Him, and follow His principles, He can take the modest things we have and multiply them.

When Jesus fed the 5000, He started by challenging the disciples to evaluate what they had. It might have seemed ridiculously small for the task: five loaves of bread and two fish. But it was more than enough—not only were the thousands of followers fed, they were "satisfied" and had 12 full baskets left over!

Jesus was handed the modest food the disciples had found. We have to hand Him our possessions, our material things, and make them His. They belong to Him anyway. If we put those things in His hands, then he can bless them and use them. But if we dedicate our possessions to Him, we must have the faith that knows He will bless them in a way that will glorify His kingdom. In the feeding of the 5000, that blessing was shared by many. Even more important, it meant that thousands were eyewitnesses to the miraculous power of Jesus Christ to provide for our material as well as our spiritual needs.

We can only wonder whether Cleopas and his friend were among the 5000 that day. When Christ was resurrected and appeared to those two on the road to Emmaus, they did not recognize Him at first. Luke 24:30-31 tells us it was only when He sat down with them to eat and "*took* the bread and *blessed* it" that "their eyes were opened and they recognized Him." When we allow Jesus to have possession of our material things, He can make them a blessing to others. In so doing, He will leave an indelible mark on their hearts and souls.

The Gift of Giving

Scripture gives us clear guidelines on giving. We are to be regular, committed, and cheerful givers to God, and to those ministries involved in His work. In 2 Corinthians 9:6-7, Paul writes,

> *Now this I say, he who sows sparingly shall also reap sparingly; and he who sows bountifully shall also reap bountifully. Let each*

one do just as he has purposed in his heart; not grudgingly or under compulsion; for God loves a cheerful giver.

There are three principles here that are essential for guiding our giving in the coming decades. First, there is the *principle of the harvest.* Pastor James Summers, a friend who heads a large church in Miami, recently drove this point home during a dinner conversation. He pointed out that we tend to emphasize only the negative aspect of this principle. When we talk of "reaping what we sow," we usually think in terms of doing evil and getting evil in return. Yet we are missing a tremendous opportunity for a positive blessing. Good will results in further good. If we handle our giving wisely and biblically, we will reap bountifully. Christians need to start taking God's promise of blessing seriously.

This does not mean that the Bible teaches a "prosperity gospel," where we ensure wealth by the measure of our giving to the church. What it does mean is that God will be faithful to meet our needs, and He will bless in untold ways our generous and cheerful giving. In fact, the next verse makes clear that "God is able to make all grace abound to you, that always having all sufficiency in everything, you may have an abundance for every good deed." In other words, our aim should be to maximize the abundance from the Lord so we can use it for good deeds. The more God gives to us, the more excited we should be to use it as a blessing for His work.

The second principle is one of *planning:* "Let each one do just as he *has purposed in his heart*" (2 Corinthians 9:7, emphasis added). As life gets more complex and time-intensive, we feel we have less time to plan. Yet, as Paul told the church at Corinth, their giving should be according to a *purpose.* Giving should be planned, not willy-nilly. Christian financial expert Ron Blue drives this point home. He points out that there are three questions which need to be asked and answered in establishing a plan for giving: *When should I give? Where should I give? And how much should I give?*[2] Giving in the First Century Church was not haphazard; it was systematic, planned, and generous.

Taking into consideration the trajectory of recent years as we peer into the future, it is reasonable to conclude that our lives will only become busier and more complex. This makes a plan of giving even more important. If we do not plan, our giving to the Lord's work will fall between the cracks—and with it, the great blessing God has for us.

The third principle is *attitude*. We should not give to the work of God because it is an obligation; we should give out of joy. Our giving should be cheerful! This should be the natural response of every believer in Jesus Christ. We are the recipients of the greatest gift of all—salvation through Christ, who willingly gave Himself to us on the cross.

The Church is to do the work of Christ until He comes again. At present we are doing that work in the midst of relative prosperity. What will happen if there is a sudden or drastic change in our national or international economic picture? A cheerful attitude toward giving is not limited to times of prosperity. In fact, it becomes even more important as the financial times become more desperate. A panel of 17 financial futurists have agreed that the possibility of a global economic collapse in the imminent future is a feasible scenario.[3] This is not doomsday fanaticism or fear-mongering. It is a matter of looking at the approaching skies and wondering, if a tornado should hit, how we would manage in our storm cellar, and whether we could cheerfully provide room for others there.

Around A.D. 46, much of the Roman Empire in and around Judea was hit by a famine. It was due to a series of poor harvests during the reign of Emperor Claudius. A Christian prophet named Agabus warned the church at Antioch that the famine was coming. In Acts 11:28 we read: "And one of them named Agabus stood up and began to indicate by the Spirit that there would certainly be a great famine all over the world. And this took place in the reign of Claudius." The response of the church during this time of impending financial crisis is instructive: "And in the proportion that any of the disciples had means, each of them determined to send a contribution for the relief of the brethren living in Judea. And this they did, sending it in charge of Barnabas and Saul to the elders." (vv. 29-30)

It was determined that the church in Jerusalem would be hardest hit by the coming famine, so believers in Antioch sent a relief-fund there by way of Paul and Barnabas. Paul later advised the believers in Corinth to also contribute to the needs of the poverty-stricken believers in Jerusalem. During the early days of the Church there was a great disparity regarding collective giving, just as there is now. Unfortunately, only one local congregation, the church at Philippi, contributed to Paul's ministry, and they did it repeatedly and generously. Their attitude was cheerful, apparent, and consistent.

Like the church at Philippi, our churches need to stand ready to give to ministries and churches in need. We ought to be willing to respond cheerfully and generously to those parts of Christ's Church that may be hit hardest in the economic uncertainties of the future.

Capitalizing Your Assets

In the world of business, "capital" is the so-called fixed asset needed to carry on the enterprise. Capital includes things like land, buildings, equipment, and furniture. When a business is "undercapitalized," it does not have sufficient assets to carry out its primary task. If a business is "overcapitalized," too much money has gone into fixed assets. A small sales office of three employees does not need a fleet of ten vehicles or several branch office buildings.

Being overcapitalized is usually not the problem in running a small business. In order to maximize profits, the temptation is to undercapitalize the business, to "get by" with the least amount of investment in capital assets while increasing the income as much as the capital structure of the business will permit.

In our personal lives, by contrast, most of us run the "business" of our homes and families in just the opposite way. The temptation is to overcapitalize—to have cars that are more expensive than we need, houses that are too big, or lifestyles that exceed the needs of the business of our lives. Given the uncertainties of the economic future, we need to define what the purpose of our families and our lives really is. We can do this by prioritizing, based on God's principles. With the right priorities, we will engage in biblical giving because that reflects God's economic design and desire.

We need to capitalize our families and personal lives in a way that maximizes their effectiveness in reaching spiritual goals and fulfilling biblical mandates. We have to make tough decisions: What spiritual return on our investment will we realize by sending our children to a Christian school? Is a college education for our son or daughter a wiser and more biblical "capital asset" than a new boat and motor? Should we invest in those things that will aid in the ministry to which God has called us, rather than increasing our leisure and recreation activities?

On the other hand, God intends for us to have leisure time and recreation. It is necessary for a balanced and happy life. Any good business recognizes that workers need break times to maximize productivity, and our families are no different. It is paramount for married couples to be able to invest in activities that give them time together and enrich their relationship. One of the smartest things we have done as a married couple is to insist on those times when we can go off somewhere together. It does not require a bundle of money, it only requires planning, thought, and a dedication to the importance of your relationship.

The balance we achieve in these areas will be a result of prayer, being immersed in God's Word, and having a good "business philosophy" for our lives. Like any other business, our lives should be attuned to the market forces around us. We have to be mindful of the changing financial environment in America; we have to understand what it means for us now that markets are global. We cannot afford to be naïve when it comes to the electioneering of politicians who promise easy economic solutions.

Remember Jesus' warning that we should be like the farmer who knows the seasons, or the sailor who carefully watches the skies. Jesus reminded the Pharisees and Sadducees of the popular wisdom that says, "In the morning, 'there will be a storm today, for the sky is red and threatening.'" There is an old saying that goes, "Red sky at morning, sailors take warning; red sky at night, sailor's delight." We cannot gauge the weather signs if our noses are always to the grindstone and our eyes are fixed on the ground beneath our feet. We need to watch the economic signs of the times with God's Word in our hand, relying on it as the ultimate weather map.

Looking to the Future

We take seriously Christ's directive that no one will know the day or the hour of His coming. Nothing could be more foolish than for Christians to try to predict the dates of end-times events. By the same token, we are not only instructed by Jesus to *watch* for the signs of the times, He has given us a map of some of the events that will occur. It seems reasonable to conclude that we are to use the knowledge of the future to prepare for the future.

In the last days, the ultimate control of Satan is not just political or spiritual, but economic. In Revelation 13:17, we are told that the end-times "beast" will have the authority over global economies and will be able to control every sale and purchase transaction. As we get closer to the latter days before Jesus' return, the economy of the world will suffer catastrophically. Jesus warned us of devastating famines and economic upheaval. Therefore, as we prepare for the future, we are to glory in the hope that we have in Christ. We should rejoice that God is in control, even as world events may seem to spin out of control. In the area of finances, as with every other aspect of life, we will be faced with two lifestyle choices that face every generation, every community, every family, and every human being: Will we be takers or will we be givers?

Part Three

⊂═══⧓═══⊃

Living Righteously
in a Ruined Culture

⊂═══⧓═══⊃

"Then conquer we must, when our cause it is just,
And this be our motto: In God is our trust!"

—Francis Scott Key,
The Star Spangled Banner

"The committee is forced to the inevitable conclusion that the
California, controlled by the same company, was nearer the Titanic
than the 19 miles reported by her captain, and that her officers and crew
saw the distress signals of the Titanic and failed to respond to them in
accordance with the dictates of humanity, international usage, and the
requirements of law."

—Final Report of the U.S. Senate subcommittee,
May 28, 1912

CHAPTER FOURTEEN

The Deadly
Hedonism of Our Culture

There is strong evidence that the ship *California*, the nearest vessel to the sinking *Titanic*, received distress signals but chose to ignore them. In fact, during an official inquiry conducted in Great Britain, the bone-chilling conclusion of the inquiry was that "many if not all of the lives that were lost" would have been saved if the crew of the *California* had simply responded to the distress flares being fired into the night sky by the floundering *Titanic*.

Why did the crew of the S.S. *California*, only 19 miles away from the desperate *Titanic*, ignore the clear signs of disaster? It appears that the captain of the *California* was fast asleep. He had a reputation as a quick-tempered tyrant, and the crew quite simply preferred to permit a catastrophe to occur rather than risk waking him and incurring his wrath.

It is easy for us, in hindsight, to condemn the cowardice of those crew members. But will the Christian Church of the 21st century stand by, like the S.S. *California*, ignoring the distress signals from a nation that is sinking in an ocean of immorality?

One of the major problems in America is ungodly personal conduct that inevitably has had a devastating public impact. At the root of this is a bondage to hedonism, that pattern of life that seeks, above all, immediate satisfaction for personal cravings, the pursuit of pleasure, and the attainment of well-being at almost any cost. America's captivity to this can be clearly seen by its citizens' preoccupations with sexual immorality and drug use.

In the 1960s and 1970s the debate over the legalization of drugs started getting widespread attention in America. One of the main arguments for legalization was that drug use was a "victimless" crime. If anyone was going to be hurt, the argument went, it was only the user. Why should that user's private behavior concern our government, our laws, our courts, and our police?

In the decades that followed, that argument should have been buried forever. An enormous percentage of crimes are committed by persons under the influence of drugs, alcohol, or both. We are forced to spend huge amounts of money to set up substance abuse programs to help recovering addicts and alcoholics. American industry loses millions of dollars in lost productivity due to this problem. Worst of all, marriages and families are torn apart and lives are shattered. What could be more public than the damage done by the use of addictive substances which give us a false, but immediate, sense of well-being?

Sexual immorality has been promoted since the "free love" years of the 1960s with the same argument. Even prostitution has been defended as a "victimless" crime. Yet today, can anyone deny that sexual immorality has not victimized the whole of American society? The AIDS plague stands as a deadly example of uncontrolled sexual desire. The highest percentage of carriers of HIV, according to the studies at the Centers for Disease Control, has consistently been those engaging in promiscuous sex. As a result, public blood supplies were tainted when these carriers donated blood, resulting in countless victims who have died of AIDS because they received contaminated blood transfusions. Insurance companies have paid out millions of dollars in benefits, and millions more in public money are being focused on treatment or cure for this sexually transmitted disease. Families have been ravaged by this terrible illness, yet despite these ugly realities, Americans seem unconcerned about the consequences of sexual immorality.

The Culture of Sexual Immorality

The dilemma of hedonism and immorality facing our nation has no better example than our commander in chief, President Bill Clinton. Many of us remember tuning in to watch President Clinton's televised statement to the American people denying "sexual relations" with an intern. But later, when the facts came out, we shook our heads in disbelief. The president of the United States on live prime-time television, looked America in the eye on August 17, 1998, and admitted having had a "wrong" relationship with a 21-year-old White House intern named Monica Lewinski. By the time his short television statement was concluded, there was no doubt about two basic facts. First, that Bill Clinton had engaged in sex acts with an intern in the Oval Office, and second, that his previous denials of the sexual affair just a few months earlier had been blatant lies.

In fact, as the evidence would later seem to show, the president probably committed perjury while presenting sworn testimony about it. He had denied having sexual relations with Ms. Lewinski in sworn testimony presented before a federal judge in a deposition in the Paula Jones sexual harassment lawsuit and, again, in testimony before a grand jury.

It must be admitted that, as a *legal* matter, sexual immorality of a president does not mandate his impeachment. The Constitution of the United States is specific in requiring proof of "treason, bribery, and other high crimes and misdemeanors." The language of the Constitution itself, and the historical context of that phrase, make it almost impossible to argue for impeachment on sexual misconduct alone. The actual vote on two articles of impeachment against President Clinton, however, did not relate to sex. They were based on his having committed perjury in sworn testimony, and having obstructed justice in attempting to hide the truth about his sexual misconduct.

But there is a separate question about moral duty, apart from the legal and constitutional questions. The president had a *moral* duty to resign from public office when his personal character was shown to be so flawed that he became morally disqualified from serving in America's highest office—an office served in the past by the likes of George Washington and Abraham Lincoln.

President Clinton and his "attack-pack" of advisors not surprisingly went on the offensive. They arrogantly refused to consider resignation, perhaps banking on the moral indulgence of a lax and lazy American people to look the other way. Like the citizens of the declining Roman Empire, the American populous was counted on to be satisfied with the status quo of Washington, as long as they had been bribed with the "bread and circus" of our prosperous culture. The president's team was banking on that picture of America, and, sadly, they got it right.

Very quickly, the fact of Bill Clinton's sexual immorality and his attempts to cover-up his lies about it took a backseat to a media debate clearly designed to help refocus public attention. The twisted semantics and strategies in the reframing of that debate were all too characteristic of America at a moral crossroads as it nears this new century. The culture was flooded with questions about the immorality of casual and repeated sex acts by the President of the United States with a young, low-level federal employee. Questions about the breach of marriage vows; questions about the judgment of a president who sexually manipulated and used a young intern; questions about a president who engaged in "phone sex" in the late evening hours. These questions were pushed aside. They became buried under the jargon that followed four devilishly clever, yet related tracks.

The four ploys used by the Clinton team are clear evidence of how far we have fallen as a nation. The first tactic was to trivialize the immoral aspect of the president's conduct. Second, the conduct itself was "privatized," so that the public was led to believe sexual morality is something that concerns only the participants. Third, those who dared to call the president's conduct into question (chiefly Special Prosecutor Kenneth Starr) were themselves vilified and cast in the role as prudish, hypocritical, right-wing, religious busybodies. Fourth, the conduct was excused because it was portrayed as "popular" behavior.

Before the president's news conference and "confession" of August 17, 1998, former White House Counsel Jack Quinn presented the trivializing defense in a manner that would be typical of the president's defenders: "This is a matter of sex between consenting adults, and the question of whether or not one of the other was truthful about it.... This doesn't go to the question of his conduct in office. And in that sense, *it's trivial.*"[1]

This defense was a popular one, particularly with Clinton loyalists like James Carville, Clinton campaign strategist, who was fond of repeating over and over again on the TV talk shows, "It's just about sex." The modern translation of this statement is: "Listen, folks, this is just about whether a man and a woman were having sex; this is no big crisis. It is not something that undermines the integrity of the president, and frankly, it's no concern of yours."

Bill Clinton used the second tactic, the "privatization" approach, in his testimony before the grand jury. In explaining his refusal to answer certain questions in the legal proceeding he complained that the investigation had "frankly, go[ne] too far in trying to criminalize my private life." President Clinton used the same theme in his televised statement to the American people later that night: " I intend to reclaim my family life for my family. It's nobody's business but ours. Even presidents have private lives. It is time to stop the personal destruction and the prying into private lives and get on with our national life."

But the third strategy—attacking those people who dare criticize those who violate standards of decency—was the most outrageous. Kenneth Starr, a highly respected former Federal Court of Appeals Judge and a former United States Solicitor General, was nightly subjected to excruciating criticism. On television talk shows like "Rivera Live," Judge Starr was painted as the stiff-necked son of a zealot-fundamentalist preacher who was blinded into obeying a deep-seated inner hatred for Bill Clinton and all things liberal.

Congressman Henry Hyde, as chairman of the Judiciary Committee of the House of Representatives, was vested with authority to lead the House inquiry into possible impeachment. When it was clear that Hyde was not going to "roll over" for the White House, an internet news magazine called *Salon* trumpeted the news that more than a decade before Hyde had had an affair. Of course that news was entirely irrelevant to the Clinton issue. Hyde's affair, as wrong as it was, did not involve misconduct in office, and it certainly did not involve false testimony in a federal lawsuit or false testimony before a grand jury, as was the case with Bill Clinton. Yet the polls consistently showed that at least half of the American people did not care that the leader of the United States committed the most outrageous kind of sexual immorality while on duty in the Oval Office. Almost as many did not care that he lied under oath to cover it up.

Clinton backers explained the polls by pointing out that sexual infidelity is a common occurrence, and that the most natural thing in the world is to lie to hide that kind of behavior. That was the fourth, and perhaps, the most effective lie that softened the Clinton scandal. It is similar to the teenager's plea that "everybody's doing it." As parents we rarely let our children get away with this kind of argument. Whether bad conduct has been popularized or not is really beside the point. But Americans willingly accepted this argument and the other flimsy excuses offered by the office of the president.

Why have Americans been so eager to divorce sexual fidelity from the business of public responsibility? To understand this, we need to take a quick history lesson.

America's Sexual Revolution

The first 100 years of the American experiment had been one of relative family stability, with a reasonable view of the husband's primary responsibility toward his family. In the early 1800s, French historian Alexis de Tocqueville traveled to America to survey how the United States was faring under its new constitutional form of government. His monumental work, *Democracy in America*, is as much a cultural review of life in America as it is a comment on the success of our system of government. In his work, de Tocqueville makes some important observations about the family in early America:

> There is certainly no country in the world where the ties of marriage are more respected than in America or where conjugal happiness is more highly or worthily appreciated....While the European endeavors to forget his domestic troubles by agitating society, the American derives from his own home that love of order which he afterwards carries with him into public affairs."[2]

But in the later half of the 19th century, America faced a complex constellation of factors including the industrial revolution, urban poverty, and America's own civil strife. Much of denominational Christianity had been embroiled in interdenominational splits, nonbiblical church movements (like the Christian Science church) arose, and a new emphasis on "social gospel" theology concentrated on social welfare rather than personal conversion.

The authority of Scripture itself became a battleground at seminaries such as the liberal Union Theological Seminary, which broke away from the Presbyterian General Assembly. Even in the churches themselves the role of women was changing. Some denominations, including Baptists, Congregationalists, Disciples, Unitarians, Universalists, and Holiness and Pentecostal bodies began ordaining women for the ministry. Theological liberals were gaining footholds in many denominations. With the authority of the Bible under attack, the spiritual and moral underpinnings of our views toward marriage, men-women relationships, family, and sex were ripe to be challenged.

This was the social and religious landscape inherited by Margaret Sanger, one of the most powerful sexual revolutionaries of the 20th century. She was a 17-year old in Corning, New York, when the 20th century began. A few years later she became a nurse, and while working with low-income mothers she became impressed with what she perceived as the subjugation of women, particularly in matters of birth control. Sanger made the availability of birth control products her *cause célèbre*. But her influence on American culture went far beyond issues of birth control. She became a pivotal figure in sexual politics, feminism, and the sexual revolution. Ultimately Sanger would sow the seeds of social dissent that would force the Supreme Court to decide *Roe v. Wade* a few years after her death. Sanger joined the Socialist Party, left her husband, and led a life of open and well-publicized promiscuity. She started a publication called *The Women Rebel*, which promoted the slogan, "No Gods! No Masters!" In the first edition, marriage was called a "degenerate institution." The idea of sexual modesty was ridiculed as a form of "obscene prudery." Sanger's fight for birth control led to the founding of Planned Parenthood. The battle lines for free love, sex without responsibility, and the slippery slope of personal privacy as a constitutional right had been drawn.

The misguided idea of constitutionally protected privacy in matters of sexuality was extended to a woman's right to have an abortion throughout all nine months of pregnancy in *Roe v. Wade* and its companion decision *Doe v. Bolton*.

Although Sanger did not live to see the *Roe* decision, she would have been pleased. She was a proponent of abortion globally and had written in *The Pivot of Civilization* that our government should mandate the sterilization of the "feeble-minded" in our population. In Sanger we have the pernicious mix of feminism, eugenics, and sexual immorality. She paved the way for the sexual revolution of the 1960s, and the modern scourge of sex education.

In 1948, 50 years before the Clinton scandal broke, the "Kinsey Report" on sexuality was first published. The report (officially called *Sexual Behavior in the Human Male*) caused a national sensation. Kinsey became an American icon, with his portrait on the cover of *Time* magazine illustrative of the way in which his sexual revolution was embraced by the press. Kinsey's portrait was a warm, inviting watercolor, with his face framed by blossoming flowers and buzzing bees. He was proclaimed "the Columbus of Sex." He had interviewed 5000 men to arrive at his conclusion that more than one-third of all men engaged in some form of sexual encounter with at least one other man. In a 1953 study, "Sexual Behavior in the Human Female," Americans were told that half of the women in the nation were not virgins when they married, and one-fourth engaged in extramarital sex after marriage.

The social and cultural effect of Kinsey's report was staggering. It legitimized promiscuity under the guise of the "scientific method." His findings indicated that premarital sex was actually beneficial for women, and that children (even infants) were sexual beings who could, and in fact should, have pleasurable sex with adults.

Unfortunately, what was passed-off as science was based on outlandishly rigged test samples and stilted data. For example, 1400 of the males interviewed were convicted sex offenders in prisons scattered over a dozen states, as one of Kinsey's own researchers later admitted. The test group interviewed by Kinsey was rounded up by a sad and frightening category of sociopaths, deviates, and social misfits. These "contact" persons who were responsible for collecting volunteers were described as "male prostitutes, female prostitutes, bootleggers, gamblers, pimps, prison inmates, thieves and hold-up men."[3]

Further, Kinsey relied on volunteers to participate in his sex experiments and interviews. Children aged 2 months to 15 years were sexually stimulated by a group of sex offenders. One researcher, Lewis Terman of Stanford University, published a critique of Kinsey's research in 1948 that concluded Kinsey's use of sexual volunteers stacked the deck in favor of false and misleading conclusions about the frequency and nature of American promiscuity. Terman found that the volunteers used in Kinsey's interviews were, in all likelihood, more prone to have been involved in promiscuity by the very nature of their desire to participate in sharing such personal and intimate information.

But these kind of intellectual and statistical niceties do not make good print on newsstands. It would be several decades before the fault-lines of the Kinsey method would be known. In essence, what Americans were unwittingly sold as the scientific explanation about modern sexuality was in actuality shoddy science passed off as social gospel by the popular media.

The timing of Kinsey's report was perfect for the budding sexual revolution. Hugh Hefner gave credit to Kinsey in his first issue of *Playboy*. The Kinsey report, as flawed and fantastic as it was, became self-fulfilling prophecy.

According to one recent study, almost one-third of all Americans have had or are now having a sexual affair.[4] In May 1997, the National Center for Health Statistics reported that 75 percent of all women interviewed admitted to having had premarital sex; and more than half of all women had multiple sexual partners. Everyday in this country, 4219 teens get a sexually transmitted disease, 1106 get abortions and 1000 unwed teenage girls become moms. Even worse, in the face of these troubling figures, we appear to be entirely incompetent in carrying on any kind of intelligent national debate on the social, spiritual, and health implications of America's obsession with unrestrained sex.

The spectacle of the president of the United States seeking to avoid the consequences of rank sexual depravity and corruption was shameful. It degraded the presidency and made the greatness of that office a mockery. Regardless of his acquittal in the trial before the United States Senate, the president was clearly guilty of sexual immorality and lied repeatedly to cover it up. Yet in the end, Bill Clinton was merely the bitter harvest sowed by America's sexual revolution. In his shame and humiliation we see America in the mirror.

The Curse of Pornography

America has become so saturated with sexually explicit information, advertising, entertainment, and art that it has become one of the most consistent backdrops in our culture. Sexually enticing females pose in front of cars, shaving cream, soft drinks, motorcycles, and shampoo. One of the worst ads on television is a woman feigning a sexual experience while showering. The product? A new-and-improved shampoo. Name it, and sex has been used to sell it. In the last decade, male sexuality has been added to Madison Avenue's arsenal of sales techniques. A shirtless male model portraying a muscular construction worker on break is ogled by a bevy of secretaries looking out from an office building. The point of this television commercial? A can of soda.

This is merely the "soft" side of commercialized sex in America, but it signals a dramatic change in the popular mores of this nation. Within present memory, television used to ban the appearance of women or men in anything less than full dress. Now it is standard fare to see male and female models semi-naked and in provocative poses, accompanied by blatant appeals to the sexual impulse. When we see the old black-and-white commercials of the 1950s, with their traditional role models and conservative values, we shouldn't feel nostalgic. We ought to weep for the decline of decency that has occurred in the last half of the century.

At the same time, cinema continues to push the outside of the frontiers of obscenity and child pornography. *Lolita*, based on the 1955 novel that shocked the world when the world was, alas, more easily shocked, has now been filmed and purchased for airing on cable television. The film shows an explicit sexual relationship between a 12-year-old girl and a 45-year-old man. It should be noted that the role of the sexual temptress is played by a 15-year-old actress. There is no state in the union that would not criminally prosecute a middle-aged man for having sex with a 15-year-old girl, and in fact the general rule of law is that teens are presumed not to be mature enough to give a voluntary, meaningful consent. The law treats it like rape. The social service agencies that campaign regularly against child abuse in every hamlet, village, and town ought to be making *Lolita* a *cause célèbre*. Instead, there is only silence. They have left it to the conservative Christians to make the outcry, again allowing the Church to be painted as America's moral busy-bodies.

Yet, all of this is but the glossy and superficial exterior of a business that at its core is one of the most devilish and destructive forces at work in our nation. As the American Civil Liberties Union (ACLU) and its ilk cry "free speech," the pornographers continue to feed the worst of human depravities.

The civil libertarians were naturally up in arms when the Reagan administration formed the Attorney General's Commission on Pornography in 1985. Among the commission's members was Dr. James Dobson, founder and president of Focus on the Family. When the commission finished its work and issued its report, Dr. Dobson predicted that "America could rid itself of hard-core pornography in 18 months" if the recommendations of the report were implemented. Some of the recommendations have been implemented. Most have not. America, it seems, lacks the moral and political will to get serious about hard-core pornography.

After the commission had finished its work, serial killer Ted Bundy, who was sitting on death row awaiting execution, called

Dr. Dobson, inviting him in for the historic filming of Bundy's "confession." This was not his confession for having committed the murders because he already had been convicted and sentenced to death for them. Rather, it was his account of how an addiction to pornography had contributed to his sadistic thirst for the deadly combination of sex and violence.

But the mainstream media discounted the filmed interview. It was portrayed as a political ploy by a right-wing "pro-family conservative" to attack pornography by using Bundy as a willing pawn. And then came Jeffery Dahmer.

This boyish-looking, blond-haired Milwaukee man dominated the headlines, magazine covers, and television news in February 1992, as he went to trial for the murders of 15 men and boys, most of whom were homosexual. He had sex with all of them before and after taking their lives. The killings were so grotesque and bizarre they almost defied belief. Victims were cut apart, and their organs stored in the refrigerator. Skulls were saved as ornaments in his apartment. Unspeakable acts of cannibalism had been committed. Even though Dahmer was clearly emotionally tortured and troubled, the jury found he had been legally sane when he committed these horrible acts. In fact, Dahmer's long, detailed, and vivid confession to the police seems to corroborate this. He expressed regret at the murders, and more than once described shock that he was capable of committing such heinous crimes. All of this was part of the news coverage at the time. Though he had few possessions, and no permanent address, a trunk filled with hard-core pornography was his constant companion. In his confession, Dahmer told police that his involvement in homosexual pornography, and the seedy culture of gay bookstores, was the gateway into the unleashing of his desires for sexual violence.

From the perspective of our legal and political system, pornography, particularly violent pornography, has been determined to place America at risk. The Final Report of the Attorney

General's Commission on Pornography stated: "The available evidence strongly supports the hypothesis that substantial exposure to sexually violent material as described here bears a causal relationship to antisocial acts of sexual violence and, for some subgroups, to unlawful acts of sexual violence."[5] This was the language of the behavioral sciences, which is accurate enough given the scope of the Attorney General's Commission mandate, but understated.

But here is the language of Jefferey Dahmer, after years of exposure to pornography and sexual perversion, coupled with an emotionally troubled past:

> It's hard for me to believe that a human being could of done what I done, but I know that I did it. I want you to understand that my questions regarding satan and the devil were not to defuse guilt from me and blame the devil for what I've done, because I realized what I've done is my guilt, but I have to question whether or not there is an evil force in the world and whether or not I have been influenced by it."[6]

Christians can answer Dahmer's question. There is an evil force in the world, and he influenced Dahmer, and that evil force used pornography as one of his tools. Reliable sources indicate that Jeffrey Dahmer trusted Christ as his Savior and found release from his torment during his short imprisonment. However, within a few short months, he was murdered by another inmate. The curse of pornography not only led Dahmer to kill others, it led directly to his own death.

One of the great sleight-of-hand magic acts in the last 50 years has been the public-relations transformation of pornography. Not too many years ago it was considered forbidden and loathsome. In 1950, Henry Miller's *Tropic of Cancer* was prohibited from distribution in the United States. Now, just a few decades later, the vilest kind of indecency is heralded as an art form. Sexual perversion is justified by the likes of the ACLU as having great social utility: It vindicates the very First Amendment itself.

In fact, the ACLU has gone on record to state that while it does object to the making of child pornography in principle, once that child pornography is printed, filmed, or photographed, it should receive the highest form of protection the First Amendment has to offer. In other words, unless we actually catch the child pornographers in the act of making their films, they should be free to continue reaping their obscene profits by victimizing America's children.

Pornography, formerly found in the darkest corners of society, has exploded onto the screens of hometown theaters. It has invaded the American home through cable television and is reaching out with its tendrils through the computer web of the Internet, connecting men, women, and children to the worst that sexual immorality has to offer.

Larry Flynt, the owner and publisher of *Hustler* magazine, a sex magazine that has prided itself on setting new records for the grossest portrayal of sexuality, has been portrayed as an American hero by Hollywood. In the film *The People vs. Larry Flynt* the pornographer is shown as the defender of the Constitution. His penchant for perversion is passed off as the eccentricity of a free spirit. But the truth about pornography is that it kills families, marriages, and sometimes people. Its effects on children ought to bring a cry of righteous indignation from every Christian in America.

Regulating Indecency

The technology of the Internet will probably be the single most important gateway for the influx of obscene materials into the American family in the next century. We have already seen how pornography has worked itself into the "bloodstream" of computer networks like a malignant cancer. While the Internet has vast opportunities for communication, information, and even Christian evangelism, it is already being coopted by the corrupting influence of sexually explicit websites.

The history of the Internet is amazing. As a phenomenon of the computer age, it is less than 40 years old. In the 1960s, the United States Department of Defense created the first computer Internet system for strategic communications purposes. It was not long, however, before computer experts developed the system as a link between researchers and scholars in various universities and colleges. This computer-linking system exploded into commercial and consumer use, and in the early 1990s the entire world went "on line" with the World Wide Web.

Like any other technology, the Internet is neither inherently good nor inherently evil. The danger lies in the purposes for which it is used. If the history of the world has told us anything, it is this: God is good, and what He creates is good. But that which God creates as good can, and often has been, twisted, corrupted, and perverted by the evil one. What began as a means of defense for our nation's safety, and later as a means of academic cooperation among scholars, has now become awash with "cyber-porn."

"Adult" sites on the Internet are now a billion-dollar-a-year business. The *Playboy* website has received more than four million "hits" by computer browsers in a single week, and sexually explicit information, including graphic child pornography, on the Internet is now the third largest source of cyber sales.

One threat to families is the ease by which a child can intentionally (or sometimes accidentally) enter a pornographic website with a few simple strokes of the keyboard. But there is an additional danger—an increasing incidence of sexual predators who pose as children on the other end of an Internet "chat room," gaining access to dangerous information about a child, his family, his address, and when he might be most vulnerable. The problem is so widespread that the FBI has created a special undercover operation to track down computer child molesters. Through 1997 more than 80 criminal convictions have resulted nationally.

Of course it would be logical to assume that if our computer technology can create this problem, it can also solve the problem through good old-fashioned human ingenuity. And certainly there has been progress made to create child-proofing systems to keep kids from encountering pornography online. There are "monitors" that can prevent private information from being divulged by a child. Blocking and filtering software can be purchased that minimizes inappropriate communications based on the use of identification of certain key words involved in computer porn, and passwords can keep children who do not know the code from accessing the Internet altogether.

But the new technology of sexual filth in the new millennium is not going to be solved as a mere matter of innovation or technical gadgetry. That is because it is a problem involving the deepest depravity of the human heart, coupled with the impotence of the very institutions that should be protecting us. Clever safeguards are always capable of being bested by more clever criminals.

Congress wanted to protect America's children from obscene communications on the Internet when it passed the Communications Decency Act of 1996. The pertinent part of the law prohibited transmissions over the Internet "which is obscene or indecent, knowing that the recipient of the communication is under 18 years of age." Not surprisingly, the ACLU sued to strike down the Act. To its shame, the U.S. Supreme Court declared the law unconstitutional in *Reno v. American Civil Liberties Union.* The primary thrust of the Court's reasoning went like this: We have allowed extensive regulation of the content of what goes out over the television and radio through the rules of the Federal Communications Commission (including "indecent" programming). But the Internet is fundamentally different than television or radio. The Internet is a "vast democratic" forum with interactive elements. Further, the Internet does not "invade" the homes of families the way that television and radio does. Thus, the Court found, relative to the Internet, that there were none of the factors that would otherwise support a restriction of the freedom of speech for users of cyberspace.

Rather than starting with the need to screen obscenity out of a network that has the capacity of reaching into millions of homes and families, the Court started with the assumption that the cost of free speech is the indecent sewage that will flow in through the computer. Yet interpreting sexually graphic pictures that are displayed by one source via computer to someone known to be under 18 years of age is hardly protected "speech."

The professional criminal who communicates plans to commit theft by electronic means is never protected merely because he used computer "speech" to relay his illegal plans. Nor is the criminal protected simply because he uses the technology of the Internet. It is absurd to pretend that the unimaginable sexual depictions used in pornography that now saturate the Internet were what the Founding Fathers had in mind in 1787 when they framed the Constitution.

Again, the Supreme Court has vaunted the First Amendment and has aided and abetted the pornographers who hide behind it. Our judicial branch has ignored the presumptions of decency and common sense that were the foundation of the Constitution when it was ratified. Former federal judge and unsuccessful Supreme Court nominee Robert Bork has both the legal insight and the courage to tell us what is going on here:

> Most people think of the Court as a legal institution because its pronouncements have the force of law. But the perception is flawed. The Court is also a cultural institution, one whose pronouncements are significantly guided not by the historical meaning of the Constitution but by the values of the class that is dominant in our culture. In our day, that means the cultural elite: academics, clergy, journalists, entertainers....The First Amendment is central to the concerns of such folk because they are chatterers by profession, and their attitudes are relativistic and permissive. The mention of censorship, even of the most worth-

less and harmful materials, causes apoplexy in the members of that class."[7]

Lower courts, not surprisingly, have followed the Supreme Court's lead in Internet indecency cases. A federal judge in Alexandria, Virginia, has struck down Internet restrictions placed on a public library's computer. The restrictions were intended to inhibit computer users from accessing pornography on the public library's computer equipment. In January 1999, a federal judge in Philadelphia imposed an injunction blocking enforcement of the Child Online Protection Act. The Act was passed in order to restrict material harmful to minors on Internet websites, but it was challenged in court by the ACLU. The judge based his decision on the First Amendment, which he ruled would be jeopardized if the child protections of the Act were enforced.

What we can expect in the decades to come is the continuing war between the money-hungry entrepreneurs of sex armed with the newest communications technology and our public institutions which seek to restrain them. But those institutions, chief among them being the courts, are increasingly powerless to enforce even the most basic norms of common decency. With judges having divorced the Constitution from the moral and religious underpinnings that framed it, Lady Justice is no longer just blindfolded when it comes to high-tech pornography—she is bound and gagged as well.

The history of the Supreme Court over the last half century indicates that even conservative appointments to that tribunal are not always the answer. The majority of sitting justices now on the high court were appointed by Republican presidents. Stated simply, the Court is not likely to get any better, and it may get a whole lot worse in the next millennium. We can also count on the fact that, absent a powerful restraining response from the Church, the evils of obscenity—its sexual violence, its degradation of women, and its addictive hold on some of our citizens is likely not only to continue, but to escalate.

Drug and Alcohol Abuse

America's love affair with substance abuse will be one of the sad ironies of history. Our nation is the most blessed and prosperous in the history of the world. Yet in the last half of this century, an increasing number of us gave our minds, bodies, and souls over to artificial highs (stimulants, including cocaine, heroin, and PCP), artificial lows (depressants, including alcohol and valium), and hallucinogens (including LSD).

Drugs have infiltrated every strata of our society. Recently major drug busts were even announced among the youth of an Amish community in Pennsylvania. It is not a "ghetto" problem, nor a "poverty" problem, and it is not an "urban" problem. Kids in Christian homes are increasingly involved in this plague. Our hearts break when folks in Christian schools tell us of the availability of drugs even in the best and godliest schools.

Despite the "war on drugs" and numerous social programs instituted in the public schools, drug use continues to rise. In a report released in February 1999, the American Bar Association determined that illegal drug use in America had increased by 7 percent from the year 1996 to 1997. As a result, some 14 million Americans are now involved in the illicit use of drugs.

Illegal or unethical drug use is becoming a crisis in the sports world, too. The Olympics and other international competitions have been marred by a long list of sports heroes who have been accused of trying to get that extra edge from performance drugs. Ben Johnson, a Canadian sprinter, lost his claim to world records and was banned from the Olympics when he tested positive for steroids. Drugs were found in the hotel rooms of the Dutch cycling team in 1998. Uta Pippig, the Boston Marathon champion, was suspended by Germany's track-and-field officials when she tested positive for synthetic testosterone. Zhang Yi, a Chinese swimmer, was ousted from the 1998 World Championships for testing positive for the use of diuretics. In 1998, Randy Barnes, an Olympic shot-putter, was banned for life from USA Track and Field for taking androstenedione, an anabolic steroid.

In one important sense, the problem with unethical drug use for sports is similar to the illegal use of street drugs. In both cases the user is prizing the experiential result above all else, whether it is a synthetic high or a gold medal. The continued influence of drugs in our culture shows a massive failure of will and a loss of personal values and meaning. At its most basic level, the drug problem is a spiritual battle. It reflects the desire to accept the fast, feel-good solution over the things that last. It also shows how we can be tricked by the deceiver into the kind of bad trade that Esau made with Jacob—a bowl of hot soup in exchange for a valuable inheritance, a quick, short-lived moment of pleasure for a loss of self-control. We are trading off our integrity, our health, and our self-respect for the instant gratification of appetites. That is not an educational problem—that is a soul problem.

As we look to the future of America, we pray for the teens and young adults who are being swept into the drug net; we do not pray for increased educational programs to educate our youth. We pray, instead, for a revival of the American soul.

A number of years ago we were at an event in Washington where William Bennett was speaking. He was America's "Drug Czar" back then, and he recounted an event that happened when he had been Secretary of Education for President Reagan. One day the police chief for the District of Columbia showed Mr. Bennett the "homework" project of a teenager. It was a notebook, and inside were a series of expertly drawn maps and diagrams of streets and locations in the city. There were lists of names, addresses, and telephone numbers carefully arranged. One section contained math computations with amounts of money properly added and subtracted with perfect accuracy. Bill Bennett said he would have given it an "A," except for one small problem. The content of the notebook showed a fatal lack of morals. The note-book was the journal of a teenage drug-dealer, and the information in it related to his criminal transactions on the streets of the District of Columbia.

To rid ourselves of this scourge in the coming decades will require more than just good political and social ideas. It will require more than building better jails, and beefing-up our police forces. All those things may be worthwhile in the short run, but in the long run the Christian Church has to share a powerful vision of what life is like with Christ. We have to articulate the kind of fulfillment that comes from walking with the living God. That experience can never be matched by an artificial experience with chemicals.

Of course, that, in turn, requires that we have a deep and ful-filling relationship with the Lord. If we do not have it, we cannot share it. If we cannot share it, we will have nothing to offer the empty souls that will turn to quick-fix drug encounters to try to fill the void.

CHAPTER FIFTEEN

Doctrines of Death

O ne of the more subtle but important lessons we can learn from disasters like the sinking of the *Titanic*, is the "dynamic" or interplay between several different factors that produced the ultimate tragedy. Accident experts and design engineers will usually tell you that disasters are rarely produced from a single, catastrophic failure. Rather, they are usually the result of a convergence of multiple mistakes, faults, and failures, all operating together at the same time and place. And, in the final analysis, human flaws are almost always a major factor.

Roe v. Wade did not happen in 1973 just because of a singular failure of the legal system. That case was America's moral *Titanic* sinking by the convergence of several deadly forces.

The medical profession must carry much of the responsibility for this abortion atrocity. Doctors, after all, are the profiteers of this industry of death. When *Roe v. Wade* was being argued, the American Association of Gynecologists and Obstetricians filed an *Amicus* brief with the Supreme Court, urging the justices to strike down state laws outlawing abortion. The Hippocratic Oath, apparently neglected or forgotten, has instructed physicians for 2000 years not to intentionally do harm to any patient. When an OB/GYN doctor delivers a baby for the mother, the hospital maintains two separate medical records—one for the mother and one for the baby. There are *two* patients; there are *two* human lives. Yet somehow the doctors conveniently forgot one of those lives.

Our judicial system must also bear some of the moral responsibility for *Roe*. From the very start, that decision was decried as an outlandish exercise of court-made law disguised as constitutional interpretation. At the very core of that decision is the concept that a woman's interest in bodily "privacy" can be found in the Constitution. No such right was intended by the founders, and it cannot be found anywhere in the text of the Bill of Rights in any context analogous to abortion.

There is a kind of privacy concept in the Fourth Amendment which forbids the government from entering your house without a warrant and searching through your papers and effects, and seizing either you or your property or both without a legal basis. Likewise the Fifth and Fourteenth Amendments require "due process" be given to you as part of such a search or seizure of you or your house. But no reasonable person would suggest that because you may have some privacy right to your house you have the right to kill your child there and be left alone in order to accomplish it. While a woman may have a right not to be wrongly arrested or maliciously strip-searched by the government because of some concept of privacy of her body, that simply does not translate into the right to kill her preborn baby merely because it happens to reside there.

But the Court was not focusing on the moral life-claims of the baby in *Roe v. Wade*. Instead, through inventive legal reasoning, it catered to the political demands of modern women to be free from state laws restricting their access to abortion. Like the shameful decision by the Supreme Court in *Dred Scott v. Sandford* in 1857, in which a fugitive slave who claimed his freedom in a nonslave state was told he was more property than person, the Court in *Roe* deprived the preborn of their personhood under the Fourteenth Amendment. The Court had been swept away in the dangerous tidewaters of moral relativism and legal rationalization.

Abortion and the Courts

The illegitimacy of the *Roe* decision, and the cases that followed it, have understandably earned well-deserved criticism from other Supreme Court justices. In one dissenting opinion, Justices Scalia, Rehnquist, Thomas, and White pronounced that the abortion decisions have turned the Supreme Court from a constitutional branch of government into a dangerous "imperial judiciary," and they have plainly indicated that *Roe v. Wade* should be overturned. Yet despite the internal combustion within the Court on the abortion issue, the majority of justices have permitted our nation to labor under the plague of prenatal murder. The decisions that have followed *Roe* have expanded, rather than substantially restricted, the rights to an abortion.

A woman cannot legally be required to receive truthful, pro-life information about fetal development and the abortion procedure if the information is intended to influence her choice, under the ruling in the *Thornburgh* case. Requiring that such information be provided only by doctors is unconstitutional under the *Akron* case. The consent of parents cannot be universally required as a prerequisite to a minor having an abortion unless the child has access to a judge to get an exemption from this condition according to the Supreme Court in the *Bellotti*, *Hodgson*, and *Ohio* cases.

Some of these rulings were softened slightly in 1992 by the Supreme Court in the case of *Planned Parenthood v. Casey*, but sadly, at the same time the Court reaffirmed *Roe v. Wade* and refused to overturn it. Just as tragically, the Court struck down the provisions of the state law that required a married woman to notify her husband in advance of having an abortion. The logic of the law seemed simple enough—the father is a joint biological parent of the preborn baby. Shouldn't he be informed so he can try to persuade the mother not to kill his child? The Supreme Court's answer to that is a chilling and disturbing view about marriage and family. The Court stated in the *Casey* case that:

> The marital couple is not an independent entity with a mind and heart of its own, but an association of two individuals each with a separate intellectual and emotional makeup. If the right of privacy means anything, it is the right of the individual, married or single, to be free from unwarranted governmental intrusion.

While noting that in a 1961 case it had been previously said that "woman is still regarded as the center of home and family life," the Supreme Court, in *Casey*, noted that "these views...are no longer consistent with our understanding of the family, the individual, or the Constitution."

Casey was the last time the Supreme Court was willing to face, head-on, the legality of restrictions on abortion. That case represented an end to the first phase of the abortion battle—the struggle over the basic constitutional and moral evil of the *Roe* decision. Unfortunately, from 1973 to 1992 the battle over abortion in the courts failed to make any substantial dent in the most basic core of the decision: a woman has the right under the Constitution, certainly at least up to that time when the "viability" of the baby makes it possible to survive outside the womb, to have an abortion for any reason, or no reason at all, and the state can do little to prevent or hinder it.

This battle over the legitimacy of *Roe* was the first phase of the cultural war over abortion. At the same time, there was a second, related phase in the abortion struggle that was developing. As pro-lifers (many of them coming from a Christian worldview) sought to oppose the wholesale slaughter of America's unborn children and articulate their moral objections, they found that the First Amendment gave them spare shelter indeed. The Supreme Court ruled that public sidewalks (traditionally held to be a primary place where free speech should be permitted) were off-limits to pro-life picketers in residential neighborhoods. The Court went on to rule that a protective "bubble zone" could exist around the entrances of abortion clinics, even on public property, and pro-lifers could be prevented from handing out literature there.

In one case, where Craig represented a pro-life Catholic theologian named Monica Migliorino Miller, the Supreme Court even ruled that federal racketeering laws ("RICO") could be used against pro-lifers though the laws were originally intended to prosecute members of organized crime. Church-going Americans who dared to voice their moral outrage at the murder of preborn life were now America's newest "racketeers." While Craig was thankful to ultimately obtain the dismissal of his client's case on First Amendment grounds, other codefendants like Joe Scheidler and his Pro-Life Action League were taken to trial on this absurd theory. The National Organization for Women (NOW) obtained a substantial money damage award against Scheidler and others on this RICO claim in a jury trial in Chicago.

Congress, motivated by random acts of arson and shootings at a few abortion clinics, hastily passed the Freedom of Access to Clinics Act, which gave harsh criminal penalties to pro-lifers who engage in passive "rescue" efforts by sitting peacefully in front of abortion clinic doors. Meanwhile animal activists, environmental protestors, antinuclear radicals, and gay-rights agitators were suffering few serious legal consequences for attacks on medical laboratories, lumber-cutting teams, whale fishing boats, nuclear plants, and even (in the case of homosexual agitators) attacks on churches during worship services.

Attorney Janet Reno authorized an unprecedented grand jury just outside Washington, D.C., to be convened in order to determine whether there was some kind of nationwide conspiracy of pro-life activists in the works. Typical of their heavy-handed techniques, the Justice Department subpoenaed one poor Christian lady from the Midwest who had merely spoken on one occasion to someone on their hit list of "pro-life terrorists." Craig represented her before the grand jury. Of course, the grand jury discovered nothing about any illegal conspiracy from her, or from anyone else who was forced to appear and testify about their pro-life activities. The drag-net inquiry of the Department of Justice proved little except that the supporters of abortion would leave no stone unturned in their quest to silence pro-lifers.

In this second phase, the Courts and the legislative branch have focused on restricting the methods by which the pro-life community can express its position and oppose legalized baby killing. At the same time, the first phase, with its focus on the rightness or wrongness of the abortion procedure itself, has waned.

The Future of Abortion

As we enter the new millennium we may see a third, even more sinister, phase. With the advent of RU 486 and similar "abortifacients" we see the realistic probability that the death of preborn babies may leave the clinic and enter the home. The pro-abortionists know that by privatizing the act of abortion through self-administered medications, and by sending abortion into the silence of the home, they can avoid state restriction, therefore bypassing the voices of pro-life objectors.

Harvard Law Professor Lawrence Tribe, a long-time advocate of abortion rights, maintains that this new kind of technology is actually a wonderful solution to the social controversy surrounding the abortion debate. By legalizing RU 486 we could, he says, "transform the abortion debate by making abortion a truly private decision."[1]

Of course, Professor Tribe's position begs the very question that the abortion debate raises: Is the act of abortion the killing of a human being? Making it more private does not make it any more moral, any more than Hitler would have been kinder and gentler by simply making his "ovens" more private and discreet. If Stalin's labor camps were more hidden from view, would that "transform the debate" about whether he was really such a brutal despot after all? Technology will most likely continue to be the best friend of sin. We can expect abortion to become ultimately more available to the average woman through technology (coupled with the profit motive of pharmaceutical companies). And when this happens, how will the Church respond?

But what about the flipside of the coin? What happens when, in the name of life, people commit violence? If RU 486 is legalized, will the corner pharmacy become the newest anti-abortion target for bombing and arson "in the name of life?" If so (and we must pray and act against it), we cannot permit these murderous, fringe elements to define the debate for us. We must have grave concern over those who claim to bring righteousness though the barrel of a gun or the percussion of a bomb. We have no doubt that these are wolves in sheep's clothing. There is no way to reconcile the belief that life is sacred because it comes from God with an assassin's dedication to murder abortionists. Christ came to give life, not destroy it. He came to redeem and transform, not to mangle and maim.

Yet the mainstream media fills its headlines with each act of violence against abortionists. On October 23, 1998, a sniper's bullet smashed through a window and killed Dr. Barnett Slepian, an abortionist who lived in upper New York State. The news monopolized CNN, the three major television networks, and every newspaper. Pro-lifers were forced to denounce an assassination that had nothing to do with the legitimate pro-life movement, and furthered the view of anti-abortionists as fanatical. At the same time, these senseless acts of violence are, in part, responsible for reducing the number of doctors willing to do abortions.

In response, pro-abortionists are demanding that abortion procedures become a mainstay of medical training. It won't be long before such organizations as NOW and Planned Parenthood will demand government subsidy and funding to ensure that enough doctors will be available to carry out the constitutional right of women to obtain abortions. Will Congress have the courage to refuse this kind of proposal, particularly in light of the murders of abortionists? To date, there have not been enough votes in Congress even to override President Clinton's veto of the congressional ban on the horrendous late-term abortion procedure known as "partial-birth abortion." The failure of a supposedly conservative Congress to strike down a practice that repels almost everyone is not a good sign. If there is a liberal sweep of the Senate or the House of Representatives, we can expect proposals of this kind of affirmative-action for abortionists. As the political winds blow, so goes Congress.

A Culture of Death

The demographics experts seem to agree that there is an interesting phenomenon going on in America. Some have called it the "graying of America." As life spans have increased, and with the corresponding decrease in child-birth rates among young couples, we are heading for a future with an increased proportion of older Americans making up our population. This will present an interesting and troubling dilemma. In a society where the young and middle-age dominate, the economics work out because they are the wage-earners and can support those who are older, or infirm, or both. But if those proportions are reversed, just the opposite occurs. There is more and more pressure, through increased taxes among other things, for the decreasing, income-producing younger citizens to support an increasingly older population.

This presents the uncomfortable question: Will the movement toward euthanasia and assisted suicide, coupled with an older population, create the kind of moral climate where the aged and the infirm will increasingly come under pressure to take a planned exit?

During the oral arguments before the U.S. Supreme Court in the Nancy Cruzan case, this type of question arose. The precise issue presented before the high Court involved the constitutionality of the procedure by which the State of Missouri required proof of the wishes of the patient to have food and water discontinued. Yet just under the surface there were lingering social questions. Do we have the right to interfere with someone's desire to "die with dignity"? Is there such a thing as a constitutional "right to die"? Is it wise policy, from a population or economics standpoint, to continue life support for America's patients who are in the nether world of "vegetative states" regarding brain activity?

The movement to legalize doctor-assisted suicide has been persistent. Many states have had to grapple with this issue, and Oregon has voter-approved assisted suicide. Yet there is no better picture of the immorality and empty barbarism of this idea than by looking at the practice in nations that have allowed it.

Hebert Hendin is a psychiatrist and executive director of the American Suicide Foundation, which researches suicide prevention. He started traveling in 1993 to the Netherlands, where physician-assisted suicide was legal, in an effort to study the Dutch experience. What he found there appalled him. Here are two examples:

> A depressed 50-year-old woman, a former social worker, otherwise healthy, asked to be put to death two months after she had lost her son to cancer. She also had been abused by her husband. She was seeing a psychiatrist regularly, and when, two months later, she again asked that psychiatrist to help her die—the request thus qualifying under Dutch law as a persistent request—her wish was granted. A man with a

chronic disease, whose wife had grown tired of caring for him, offered him the alternative of a nursing home or euthanasia. He chose the latter.[2]

Dr. Hendin also discovered that—

> [the] more I studied the Dutch cases, I could see this was not an extension of personal rights—in many instances, it became a doctor's decision, not a patient's. And for hospice and palliative care for those who want to die naturally, they are relatively low priorities in the Netherlands. After all, with assisted suicide available, who needs them? It was almost as if you are a poor sport for not choosing it.[3]

Not surprisingly, the U.S. Supreme Court has given neither definitive legal nor lucid moral guidance on this issue. In *Washington v. Glucksberg* and *Vaco v. Quill*, the Supreme Court heard appeals from the Ninth and Second Circuit Courts of Appeal. The Court refused to outlaw the idea of physician-assisted suicide, ultimately making it a legislative battle within the individual states. Yet evangelical Christians have been warning the American culture for almost three decades of the slippery slope that comes with our devaluation of life. We have warned our society of the dangers of our willingness to dilute the belief embedded in the Declaration of Independence: "We hold these truths to be self-evident, that all men are created equal, that they are endowed by their creator with certain unalienable rights, that among these are *life*, liberty and the pursuit of happiness." The message is true, but it has been largely ignored.

In the waning years of the 20th century we see America's dance with death becoming a grisly embrace. In the fall of 1998, in an address to the Counsel for National Policy, Dr. James Dobson gave an impassioned speech on the state of our national moral decline on the life issue. Speaking from his own individual perspective, and as a Christian psychologist, he stated:

You probably are aware of the article in the *New York Times* by Dr. Steven Pinker, an evolutionary psychologist, so to speak, who wrote...about the rationale for mothers killing their newborns.

...Francis Schaeffer told us in 1970 that abortion and infanticide and euthanasia were all connected. You allow one, and you'll have all three, because they all deal with the sanctity of life.

Who made life? If God is eliminated, and therefore you can eliminate the unborn child, you will soon be eliminating not only infants you don't want, and older people you don't want, but all "undesirables."

Francis Schaeffer told us this was coming, and here it comes.[4]

We should not be surprised when we see the degradation of life in music, drama, and art. When alternative-rock icon Marilyn Manson exploits and flaunts death themes in his perverse cross-dressing performances, exemplifying the worst of current pop culture, Christians wince and wail and wonder at the decline of decency and the ruination of art. Yet this is not just about the decline of art, nor just about the standards of decency. Art reflects life. In the life of America, our obsession with death has begun to swallow up the sanctity of life. Our culture has, in effect, mimicked the famous words of Robert J. Oppenheimer on seeing the detonation of the first atom bomb: "We have become death—the destroyer of worlds."

Our challenge is to live and speak the revolutionary truth that Christ died so that He could destroy death and overcome Satan, the actual destroyer of worlds, and rob the grave of its victory. Our culture dances with the "prince of death" because it does not know the "Prince of Peace." People need to know now, more than ever before in the history of our nation, that, as Jesus said in John 10:10, "The thief comes only to steal, and kill, and destroy; I came that they might have life, and might have it abundantly."

CHAPTER SIXTEEN

‿━━‿

Being Holy in a
Wholly Fallen World

Much has been written about the "culture war" raging in America, particularly over the last half of the 20th century. Even Christians seem conflicted about the mission of the Church in the midst of our perverse and wayward society. Those within and without the Church have articulated a variety of ways to find a truce in the battle over moral and social values.

One suggestion is what could be called the "common ground common dialogue" approach. In this view there is hope that through discussion there might be a more peaceful coexistence between competing value systems in a nation that is increasingly more diverse. By seeking those things upon which we agree, rather than by emphasizing the things that divide us, we are told our society can resolve at least some of the border skirmishes between religious conservatives and liberals, between the "religious right" and the "humanist left."

Along these lines, some have pointed to the Williamsburg Charter as an example of common ground among competing groups. This charter, drafted in 1988, was a statement of generalized principles about the importance of the role of religion in American public life. The drafters included some Christian evangelicals, along with more traditional secularists. The following is an excerpt from the charter's introduction:

> Keenly aware of the high national purpose of commemorating the bicentennial of the United States Constitution, we who sign this Charter...call for a bold reaffirmation and reappraisal of its vision and guiding principles. In particular, we call for a fresh consideration of religious liberty in our time....
>
> The Charter is a call to a vision of public life that will allow conflict to lead to consensus, religious commitment to reinforce political civility. In this way, diversity is not a point of weakness but a source of strength.

The problem with statements of common purpose among polar opposite groups is that they are destined to seek "fringe" agreements regarding moral, spiritual, and social values, while there will be little agreement on the essentials. The end result is a process of majoring on the minors, ignoring the major belief differences. Within just a few years of the Williamsburg Charter, the purpose of which was to remind us of the importance of religious profession in the public square, the Supreme Court decided *Lee v. Weisman*. In that case the Court banned the short (and quite innocuous) high school graduation prayer offered by a Jewish Rabbi whose presence was sponsored by a school district.

It is easy to look at the charter as substantially irrelevant in light of the "separation of Church and State" steamroller with which the courts are leveling the cultural landscape. We have not seen a decrease in the hostility toward Bible-believing Christians in our public institutions as a result of either the Williamsburg Charter or any of the other half dozen attempts at "common ground."

One solution offered to Christians is to suggest that we have placed too much emphasis on politics and not enough on practical Christian truth. One Christian pastor surmises: "It is hard for us to face the fact that we as a church might be veering off track, losing sight of our most important goal. It is difficult to admit that we just might have mistaken the American dream for God's dream."[1]

It would seem, however, that the answer lies not in vague agreements of common ground, nor in total retreat of Christians from influencing American public policy. Instead, we must realize that within the political and social reality of the culture war that rages in our nation there is a greater and more important war—a moral war. The responsibility of the Christian in that moral war is radically different from our post-Christian/post-modern culture because our spiritual identity is radically different. We cannot expect the non-church to act like the Church of Jesus Christ. But we can—and must—demand that those of us within the Church live like the Church should.

Jesus did not pray to the Father to take His disciples out of the world, but to "keep them from the evil one" (John 17:15). Our task is to penetrate and influence a fallen world without falling into its practices. Peter instructed the early church: "As obedient children, do not be conformed to the former lusts which were yours in your ignorance, but like the Holy One who called you, be holy yourselves also in all your behavior; because it is written 'YOU SHALL BE HOLY, FOR I AM HOLY'" (1 Peter 1:14-16).

"Holy" is one of those scary words. We are all sinners, so how can we possibly be "holy" in the way that He is holy? Besides, that word has received some consistently bad press. It has been attached to such negative and derisive terms as "holier than thou" and "holy roller." Yet Scripture has given us a clear command: live in a wholly unholy world. How can we do that?

What we need to do first is to identify the three *real* enemies of the Church. Second, we need to know the three approaches of sin so we can avoid them. And third, we should follow the three paths of practical Christian living.

The Real Enemies of the Church

The position and identity of the ultimate enemies of the Church of Jesus Christ have been determined. It is not Bill Clinton and the Democratic Party. Nor is it the secular humanists or the Humanist Manifesto. It is not the communists, the atheists, the ACLU, the practitioners of witchcraft, or even the crystal-bedecked followers of the New Age. To be sure, some (or even all) of these have articulated agendas that have been hostile to the conservative evangelical Church, but that list could also include the Republican Party, church-goers, and numerous "conservative" causes of every variety and stripe.

There are three ultimate enemies of the Church, and everyone else is merely part of the sympathetic civilian population of these spiritually armed foes. Those enemies are the world, the flesh, and the devil. Such a notion has been around for a long time. However, it is time to deploy this spiritual truth so that we can be victorious in the trenches of our current spiritual warfare. Christian Theologian Lewis Sperry Chaeffer wrote, in his eight volume work on Systematic Theology:

> It is generally and properly taught that the Christian's conflict is three-fold, namely, (a) against the world, (b) against the flesh, and (c) against the devil. By this it is asserted that the Christian's solicitation to evil will arise from any or all of these three sources. It is of supreme importance, then, that the child of God be intelligently aware of the scope and power of each of these mighty influences.[2]

Back in the early 1970s, evangelical editor Harold Lindsell wrote a book on the subject of the Christian's relationship with the world, entitling it simply, *The World, the Flesh, and the Devil.*

What is the "world"? It is something other than simply the non-Christian population of the world. In fact, it really does not refer to any group of people at all. It has to do with the New Testament Greek word *cosmos*. It means the world "system," or world "order." The "world is an order or system, but in every instance—and there are many—where a moral feature of the world is in view, this *cosmos* world is said to be opposed to God."[3]

Many people in the Church struggle with the implications of this concept, perhaps because it is such a radical idea. We expect admiration for the gospel of Christ, and for His precepts within a world system that is, by its design and history, aligned against God. We do not want to really practice the truth that there is an invisible system that controls the world because if we are *for* it, then we must be *against* God. Yet if we do not live out the truth of this irrefutable Christian concept, we will become immersed in the system of the world—its values, its forms of entertainment, its lusts, its ungodly goals, and its fallen way of thinking. John Bunyan did not call his work *Pilgrim at Home in the World.* Instead, and quite appropriately, he called his tale of every believer's earthly journey *Pilgrim's Progress.* The life of the Christian is a process of traveling through a foreign land.

This doesn't mean we won't have great times of fellowship, fun, and personal satisfaction, along with good meals, loving relationships, and warm memories. We can enjoy a good cup of coffee, a beautiful hike in the mountains, and a great symphony. In the end, however, these are but pleasant pit stops on the road to the Celestial City. We all know examples of dour Christians who do not seem capable of enjoying the good things God has given us in this life, and that is equally wrong. The majesty of a great ocean fish at the end of a fishing pole, the matchless baseball ballet of a triple-play, the beauty of nature; these can be celebrated by the Christian as well as the non-Christian. The difference is that we know these are fleeting things, temporal things in the eternal scheme of things.

The second enemy of the Church is the "flesh." This means more than just sexual sin. It means we must remember that the sin nature still operates within our bodies and our minds, even though we, as Christians, have been forgiven and our spiritual selves have been reborn with the regenerating work of the Holy Spirit. The Apostle Paul recognized this when he cried out that, though he had been saved by God's grace, nevertheless, "I know that nothing good dwells in me, that is, in my flesh; for the wishing is present in me, but the doing of the good is not" (Romans 7:18).

How do we handle the reality of this sin nature? Chuck Swindoll suggests a realistic but powerful approach:

> We learn to live by short accounts. We refuse to let the filth of our life stack up. We don't ignore even the little things that have broken our fellowship with God or with others. We are to live, in the words of the New Testament, with "a conscience void of offense." That's how we can dress in white for [Christ's] coming, as a bride prepares for her groom. Perhaps all of that is included in our judging ourselves so that we may not be judged.[4]

The third enemy of the Christian is the most obvious: the devil. C.S. Lewis noted that there are two opposite extremes that Christians bring to this issue—both of which are equally wrong. One is to have an unhealthy overemphasis on the power and nature of Satan, the other is to live in ignorance of his strategies.

We are warned that "your adversary, the devil, prowls about like a roaring lion, seeking someone to devour" (1 Peter 5:8). There is good news and bad news here. The bad news is that he seeks to devour the believer in Christ. Yet knowing this, there is the good news that if we recognize his ways, we can hear him coming. There will be escape and safety for the Christian who obeys the first part of this verse: "Be on the alert."

The Three Attacks of Sin

The sins of the world system that constantly attack us are basically simple, though they will come in myriad forms. John put it this way: "For all that is in the world, the lust of the flesh and the lust of the eyes and the boastful pride of life, is not from the Father, but is from the world" (1 John 2:16). In those words, John describes how Satan attacks us. They usually arrive through the lust for physical pleasure and the preoccupation with gratifying our desires, the craving for accumulating more material possessions, and obsessive pride in our status and importance.

When the serpent tempted Eve in the Garden of Eden, he used those three areas. When the devil tempted Jesus in the wilderness, those were also his three areas of attack. The strategies of the devil are highly effective, but they are boringly predictable. They appeal to what our bodies and our fleshly minds crave. This is why pornographers and drug dealers prosper. Sometimes Satan's attacks appeal to the things that are outside of our bodies—things which we do not have, but which we long to possess or control. That is why materialism has become the official value system of American foreign policy. It is why President Clinton's clear commission of perjury did not result in removal from office during a time of strong economic growth.

The evil one also appeals to the ugly power of pride—the selfishness or arrogance that seeks to exalt us over them. This is why the cry of the feminist movement, and its obsession with the right to destroy preborn life, has centered on *my* right to control *my* body."

We live in a sin-weary world. It is sin-ridden because it is a world system opposed to the Creator of the universe. It is a kingdom in rebellion against its King, and it is weary because it is has no real solutions to the problem of evil.

The good news is that we worship a God who specializes in solutions to seemingly insoluble problems.

The Three Solutions for Living in a Fallen World

When we receive Jesus Christ as our Savior, and join God's heavenly family, we obtain three resources for successful living during our earthly pilgrimage: the Word of God, the indwelling of the Holy Spirit, and the intercession of Jesus Christ.

Jesus, in his high priestly prayer to the Father just before His arrest in the garden, asked God to "sanctify them in the truth; Thy word is truth" (John 17:17). God's Word is not only something that communicates propositional truth to us, it is also a Word of truth that can sanctify us in our service to Him. When we hide His Word in our hearts, it will guard us from sin.

As believers, we also have the indwelling power of the Holy Spirit. When Paul recognized his dilemma in wanting to live a holy life while being trapped in his natural body with its tendencies toward sin, he recognized that the practical solution lay in the power of the Holy Spirit. Paul cries out: "Wretched man that I am! Who will set me free from the body of this death?" (Romans 7:24). A few verses later we see the answer:

> For the mind set on the flesh is death, but the mind set on the Spirit is life and peace, because the mind set on the flesh is hostile toward God; for it does not subject itself to the law of God, for it is not even able to do so; and those who are in the flesh cannot please God. However, you are not in the flesh but in the Spirit, if indeed the Spirit of God dwells in you. But if anyone does not have the Spirit of Christ, he does not belong to Him. (Romans 8:6-9)

Believers in Christ already have the resource of this indwelling work of the Holy Spirit. (The remaining verses of Romans 8 explain the miraculous work of the Holy Spirit in the life of the Christian.) As Francis Schaeffer explained, there is also a role we must play in voluntarily and willingly choosing to walk in the Holy Spirit:

> We have seen over and over again that the Bible does not deal with us as machines. We have significance. We have choice. We must have the indwelling of the Holy Spirit. But having the indwelling of the Holy Spirit does not make it automatic. There is a conscious side to sanctification. We are indwelt by the Holy Spirit. That is wonderful. But now the call is to walk according to the Spirit.[5]

The third resource we have is the intercessory work of Jesus Christ. The Bible says that Christ, the Son of God who sits at the right hand of God, continues to make intercession for us. "Intercession" is one of those deep theological terms that has profound practical application. According to Hebrews 7, Christ "always lives to make intercession" for the believer. He is our High Priest, ensuring that we are made acceptable in God's sight and have full access to Him.

Christ is also our advocate. In Romans 8:33, Paul asks: "Who will bring a charge against God's elect?" The question is a rhetorical one because the answer is apparent: Christ "is at the right hand of God, who also intercedes for us" (v. 34). In a court of law, even if the law favors a party before the bar, it is important to have a legal advocate to make sure the law is properly applied and the benefits of the law are received. Satan is the great accuser of the Church, but Jesus Christ is the great attorney for believers. He pleads our innocence before the throne of God based on His shed blood at the cross and our having obtained the benefits of that sacrifice through faith. And He has never lost a case.

It is critical we not underestimate the saving work of Christ. It is easy to do exactly that as we read the headlines that spell disaster, sin, and perversion. But our Savior has targeted this world system, which has accelerated toward degradation and its devolution into a culture of death, for victory. He declared in John 16:33 that

"In the world you have tribulation, but take courage; I have overcome the world."

We have to claim this victory. This is not a victory in the sense of our establishing God's kingdom by the work of the Church here on earth. This is not a false "reconstructionist" view of settling the kingship of Christ by political means. Rather, the victory of Christ over the world means that no sin is stronger than His power to grant forgiveness and turn a sin-sick life around. It means that we can truly live out the life of Christ in the midst of a fallen world.

The victory of Christ over the world also means that His truth transcends culture. Mahatma Gandhi was a leader in the struggle for the independence of India from Great Britain, but because India was a predominantly Hindu nation, even the celebrated atheist and critic of Christianity Bertrand Russell had to admit the possibility that the influence of the Christian gospel in India paved the way for the success of Gandhi's nonviolent methods. Today, Russell's quote to that effect greets visitors to Gandhi's hometown.

When we live lives that reflect the holiness and power of Christ, we will present the most articulate and persuasive argument for the truth of Christ. When our lives are lived in complete contradiction to the custom and experience of the world, there is no limit to the territory that can be won for the Savior.

❦

CHAPTER SEVENTEEN

Post-Christian America

Jonathan Maxcy, an evangelist and preacher, lived during the American Revolution. An influential voice in society and the president of four prestigious colleges, Maxcy issued a warning that we must not forget: "No government except absolute despotism can support itself over a people destitute of religion....The American people therefore, have no way to secure their liberty but by securing their religion."

In the next century, will the religious freedoms of Christians be secure in America? John Adams, an American patriot who was on the drafting committee for the Declaration of Independence, helped spearhead the fight for freedom from England, and served as our second president, worried over the fading influence of faith. In the years after he retired from public life, Adams engaged in a running correspondence with Thomas Jefferson. In a letter penned on June 28, 1813, Adams wrote:

> The *general Principles*, on which the [Founding] Fathers Achieved Independence were the only Principles in which the beautiful Assembly of young gentlemen could Unite.... And what were these *general principles*? I answer, the general Principles of Christianity, in which all those Sects were United; And the *general Principles* of English and American liberty, in which all those young Men United, and which had United all Parties in America, in Majorities sufficient to assert and maintain her Independence.[1]

Elsewhere in the letter, Adams lists more than a dozen Christian denominations that were represented in the "army of fine young fellows" that fought and died for American liberty. There were even some (though "very few") diests and atheists and "Protestants who believe nothing" among them. Yet as Adams noted, all of them were "educated in the *general Principles* of Christianity." A biblical worldview, a core of spiritual understanding of basic rights and responsibilities and of right and wrong, and the governing existence of a Supreme God—these were the cords that banded our nation together.

In 1995, Samuel B. Kent, a federal judge in the United States District Court, sat behind his judicial bench in his Galveston, Texas, courtroom and issued a ruling. Judge Kent gave a verbal "bench" decision in a lawsuit challenging graduation prayers and baccalaureate services in the Santa Fe Independent School District. Among other comments made on the record, here is what Judge Kent said:

> The Court will allow that prayer to be a typical nondenominational prayer, which can refer to God or the Almighty or that sort of thing. The prayer must not refer to a

specific deity by name, whether it be Jesus, Buddha, Mohammed, the Great God Sheba or anyone else.

And make no mistake, the Court is going to have a United States Marshall in attendance at the graduation. If any student offends this Court, that student will be summarily arrested and will face up to six months incarceration in the Galveston County Jail for Contempt of Court. Anyone who thinks I'm kidding about this order better think again.

...Anyone who thinks that this Court is expressing any weakness or lack of resolve in that spirit of compromise would better think again. Anybody who violates these orders, no kidding, is going to wish that he or she had died as a child when this Court gets through with it.[2]

Liberals are quick to point out that this incredible ruling was appealed and overturned by a Federal Court of Appeals. But that is very much beside the point. In the 182 years since John Adams's letter, we have become a culture where too many of our government institutions operate on a presumption of outright hostility toward any expression of Christian belief in the public square. In Alabama another federal judge, concerned about the possibility of separation of church and state violations occurring in public school, took the astounding step of appointing a federal "monitor" to roam the halls and classrooms of the local school district. The job of this nonelected, judge-appointed monitor was to spot and report any illegal prayers or improper religious activities occurring in the school district.

This rising hostility against public expression of Christianity has not been a slow evolution. To the contrary, it has boiled over only in the last quarter of our nation's life. Prior to that time, America had accommodated a spirit of partnership between our public institutions and religion in general (and Christianity in particular). As an example:

- George Washington's speeches, public addresses, and personal correspondence are replete with references to Christ, the Bible, and spiritual themes. As a young man, he kept a prayer and devotional journal. Today it would be illegal to have students read that journal in a public school history class.

- Andrew Jackson once quipped that the Bible was the rock upon which our republic was built. Yet in Horsehead, New York, a high school student was told by his teacher he could only bring his Bible into class if he covered it with brown paper, as if it were pornography.

- One of the most famous Revolutionary War paintings of George Washington shows him, as commander of the American Army, kneeling and praying during the siege of Valley Forge. A few years ago an officer at West Point was reprimanded for using Bible references in his computer e-mail.

- Almost every American president has issued proclamations calling upon citizens to set aside a day of prayer and thanksgiving to God for the blessings of freedom. James Madison, chief architect of the Constitution and the Bill of Rights, was among them. In a public elementary school in Wisconsin, however, a third grader was instructed to remove a reference in her valentine, made in art class, that said simply, "Jesus is what love is all about."

- Thomas Jefferson, founder of the University of Virginia, authorized public and official prayer at its earliest recorded graduation ceremonies. Today, graduation prayers sponsored by school officials are illegal across the nation.

All of these modern religious-freedom atrocities occurred because of a tortured and mistaken view of the relationship between religion and our government institutions. They are but a few examples of actual cases, and they are not unusual.

The Assault on Religious Freedom

If we take a realistic view of where America has come in the last 50 years, we can come to only one conclusion: At the current rate of disintegration of religious liberties, our freedoms will be substantially eradicated well before the next half century. Our children, and their children, will face an officially secular state, where the exercise of faith will be at the behest and licensure of the government.

The official assault on religious liberty began quietly in 1947. In that year, the Supreme Court decided *Board of Education vs. Everson*. Latching onto a phrase that appeared in a letter, written by President Thomas Jefferson to the Danbury Baptist Association in Connecticut, the Court stated that the First Amendment contains a "wall of separation of Church and State." To make matters worse, that wall, declared the Court, must be "high and impregnable."

As most of us know, that phrase appears nowhere in the text of the First Amendment, which provides only that "Congress shall make no law respecting the establishment of religion, nor prohibiting the free exercise thereof...." The Supreme Court, however, had fixed its attention on the first phrase, the "establishment of religion." In the *Everson* case the Court painted over it with the Justices' own critically mistaken view of this "wall of separation." It is strange that the Court should rely so heavily on Jefferson, since he in fact played no part in the Constitutional Convention or the drafting of the First Amendment itself. Even further, his famous letter to the Danbury Baptists was taken out of context. The "wall of separation" mentioned by Jefferson was for *the protection of the Church from the State*, not the State from the Church.

A view of the history of the First Amendment points out how flawed this "wall of separation" really is. James Madison, the chief drafter of the First Amendment, had originally penned an amendment that provided:

> The Civil Rights of none shall be abridged on account of
> religious belief or worship, nor shall any *national religion* be
> established, nor shall the full and equal rights of conscience
> be in any manner, or on any pretext, infringed.[3]

It is clear that his intent was to prevent only the establishment of a *national* religion. However, Representative Elbridge
Gerry of Massachusetts objected to the use of the word "national."
That word was a politically charged phrase back then, and those
who had opposed the idea of a new federal constitution (the
"Anti-federalists") had already been successful in eliminating the
word "national" from the Constitution. It was a word that, for
them, created the fearful image of centralized national power.
Reluctantly, Madison permitted his use of "national religion" to
be replaced simply with "establishment of religion."[4]

Having built a foundation in the Everson case that was made
of inaccurate history, the Supreme Court continued to build, layer
by layer and case by case, a kind of Berlin Wall of hostility separating religious expression and practice from more and more
aspects of American life. From 1962 to the present, the High
Court has had a dismal record regarding religious liberty. In the
last 36 years it has:

- Outlawed prayer in public schools

- Outlawed Bible reading in public schools

- Banned the posting of the 10 commandments in public
  schools

- Banned a silent moment of prayer in public schools

- Banned the use of religious clergy to teach even *optional*
  religious instruction in public schools

- Banned a Christmas nativity scene in a public building

- Banned school-sponsored prayer at graduation ceremonies

Post-Christian America

- Banned a special school district created to accommodate the particular needs of Orthodox Jewish children

- Struck down the Religious Freedom Restoration Act

A valiant attempt by some members of the 105th Congress to amend the First Amendment and reverse the Supreme Court's dangerous trend failed in the spring of 1998. Craig was involved with Congressman Ernest Istook and a coalition of conservatives and supporters of religious liberty in drafting language that would restore the original intent behind the phrases "establishment of religion" and "free exercise" of religion. While picking up a major-ity of votes in the House of Representatives, the constitutional amendment failed to gather the necessary two-thirds vote for approval. Given the past inability of Congress to remedy this sit-uation, the prospect for a future constitutional amendment to pro-tect religious freedom is an open question.

What we must remember is that even brilliantly devised polit-ical documents like our Bill of Rights can, over time, be corrupted through neglect or misinterpretation. We should never forget that in the Constitution of the Soviet Union, the people of Russia had been promised rights that look strangely familiar: "SECTION 3. Every citizen may profess any religion or none at all.... The Church is separated from the State." By the deliberate interpretation of the communist government, the separation of Church from State became the club to bludgeon the rights of citizens to profess their religion. In China, the communist constitution promises "normal religious activity." Yet through a manipulative interpretation of what "normal" religious practices are, the government regime has made a mockery of the idea of religious liberty. Similarly, the mis-interpretation of our First Amendment, though well-meaning, poses a threat to the religious freedom of the Christian Church in the next century. And it has created a society that is consistently being told, by the highest court in the land, that it must be secu-lar in order to be free. This court-enforced secularization of

233

America has trickled down into all areas of our society. Meanwhile, during Gay Pride week in Washington, D.C., federal employees in the Transportation Department had to endure non-stop pro-gay advertisements and announcements on the overhead television sets that normally were reserved for official Department of Transportation announcements.

As we enter the 21st century, the prognosis is grim. Token acknowledgments to the evangelical Christian Church by both political parties cannot hide the fact that none of the current three branches of government are poised to return biblical values to the American way of life. In fact, just the opposite seems to be true—conservative Christians who take evil seriously and believe that government and its laws should reflect the values they hold dear will probably be more and more marginalized.

Exploding the Myth

Not long ago, I heard someone in church say, "Christians need to get out of politics and public policy issues and get back to church, where they can win souls for Christ—which is the only way this nation can be saved." How would you have responded?

It may sound spiritual, since saving souls is the mission of the Church. Politics has always seemed a dirty game, whereas the work of the Church is clean and biblical. But the statement is a dangerous myth. First, it is built on a misunderstanding about the terms we use. "Politics" comes from the Latin word *polis*, which means the city or state. From it we get such words as police, policy, and political. The *polis* is the governing community in which we live, so in a democratic republic that governs by the consent and participation of the governed, the ruling system is not "them," it is "us."

Second, it is a myth to think that we can somehow get out of politics, even if we wanted to. We are in the *polis*, whether we like it or not. The Christians in the first-century church were part of the *polis*, though their community was occupied by a ruthless

Roman government while ruled, in a limited way, by King Herod. If you live in an area and have some say in the government, you are already part of the political system.

Third, Jesus was quite clear that He did not want us to think of ourselves as entirely outside the community or government in which we live. In John 17, Jesus prayed, "I do not ask Thee to take them out of the world, but to keep them from the evil one.... Sanctify them in the truth; Thy word is truth. As Thou didst send Me into the world, I also have sent them into the world" (vv. 15,17,18). In other words, we are to be *in* the world but at the same time we are not to be *of* the world. This is a crucial distinction.

As Bible scholar Colin Brown points out, in this verse "doing the will of God is also doing the truth." Our Savior did not want us separated from the world in a physical sense, except for those activities that are sin in themselves. He wanted us separated from the world system, from its ideas and methods, by His Word of Truth. Christ sends us into the world to be set apart in the way we wage war against evil. But on top of that, we are to be different from the world in *doing His Truth*, penetrating the world in a way that is based on the principles in His revealed Word.

There is no biblical command to get out of politics in the sense that we are to be physically separated from our system of government. In fact, the Bible contains positive commands for us to become involved and make a difference by living the truth of God in a godless society.

Romans 13 states clearly that a Christian is to be in subjection to the governing authorities. Why? Because, according to verse 1, governments are established by God. He is the one who sets up the government, and the purpose of government is to restrain evil and promote good. That means our democratic and participatory system of government is the work of God. It is His design that our national system of politics restrains evil and promotes good. Those two activities cannot be accomplished if church members retreat to the church basement for potluck suppers and complain in our exclusively Christian circles about the fall of America.

Our duty in our daily lives, according to verses 8 and 10, is to love our neighbors. In the first few centuries of the Church, while living in the culture of the Roman Empire with its decadence and paganism and idolatry, that meant being pro-life. It meant opposing an evil and murderous Roman practice called "exposing" infants—tossing unwanted babies along the roadways to die. It meant speaking out against the persecution of Christians. Today, it means involving ourselves in the debate over the evils of abortion, pornography, drug abuse, violence, and the disintegration of the family.

We are also commanded to engage in good deeds such as volunteering at crisis pregnancy centers, where the true work of the pro-life movement is taking place with almost no publicity or fanfare, or working for policies that make it easier—rather than harder—for families to adopt children into loving homes. When God's people have no active presence, catastrophe follows. We are told that in Sodom and Gomorrah, Lot "was *oppressed* by the sensual conduct of unprincipled men." Do we think our Christian families and children will escape unscathed from the oppression of a pagan and evil age if we fail to stop the spread of destruction, evil, and darkness when we have the chance?

Like the Old Testament children of Israel, we find ourselves in a culture hostile to the things of God. But we can learn from their situation. When the Israelites were occupied by the forces of Babylon, they were commanded to build their finances, build their families, and "seek the welfare of the city where I have sent you into exile, and pray to the LORD on its behalf; for in its welfare you will have welfare" (Jeremiah 29:7). In the welfare of America lies the welfare of the Church in America and elsewhere. The responsibility and the privilege we have as Christians is to exert godly influence toward that goal.

God has given us our constitutional form of government as a kind of stewardship. As we fight for that which is good, true, and right for the State, so it shall be a blessing for the Church. At the same time, we must have the courage to proclaim a prophetic message to a heathen, post-Christian nation. We must be like Isaiah, declaring "woe" unto legislators who "enact evil statutes," and "to those [judges] who constantly record unjust decisions, so as to deprive the needy of justice..." (Isaiah 10:1-2). At the same time, we must be working in a positive way to bless the communities in which we live. We must exert effort to elect godly officials, knowing that, as Proverbs 29:2 says, "When the righteous increase, the people rejoice, but when a wicked man rules, people groan."

Above all, we must act with the knowledge that righteousness exalts a nation, but sin is its disgrace before God. Our dual citizenship in both an earthly nation and a heavenly kingdom means that we walk not by sight, but by faith. As we are godly citizens who serve Him above all else, we not only seek the welfare of the city, but we also serve the invisible kingdom to which we are drawn by faith. We do not have the option of serving one kingdom or the other. God has not given us that kind of choice.

Things are going to get rough for Christian conservatives. Even some people in our own ranks have signaled the need for a retreat from the political sphere. One of the architects of the conservative revolution of the 1980s, a leading proponent of Judeo-Christian activism, has called for Christians to pull back. To him, the failed attempt by the U.S. Senate to convict President Clinton marked a new low. The failure of the American people to demand that the Senate reflect norms of moral and constitutional common sense seemed to indicate that the Church and the American public are at an irreconcilable impasse. This is nothing new. But the history of our nation shows us that being outnumbered and overwhelmed can be an opportunity for greatness.

On March 23, 1775, Edmund Burke was in London's House of
Lords urging reconciliation between Britain and the American
colonies. He was offering appeasement on behalf of the tyranny of
King George as a means of keeping the peace. Meanwhile, on that
very day, a meeting was taking place at St. John's Church in
Richmond, Virginia. What a contrast! In attendance were
Thomas Jefferson and Richard Henry Lee, among other Virginia
delegates. The purpose was to address the issue of American
Independence. At that meeting, a young, born-again Christian, a
38-year-old, self-taught lawyer by the name of Patrick Henry
stood to address the 122 delegates. Historians tell us that
American independence was born in Philadelphia on July 4,
1776. If that is true, then that tree of liberty was birthed only
because the seed was planted by Patrick Henry in Richmond in
1775. Listen to what he had to say:

> They tell us sir, that we are weak—unable to cope with
> so formidable an adversary. But when shall we be stronger?
> Will it be the next week, or the next year? Shall we acquire
> the means of effectual resistance by lying supinely on our
> backs?
>
> Sir, we are not weak, if we make a proper use of the
> means which the God of nature hath placed in our power.
> Millions of people, armed in the holy cause of liberty, in
> such a country as that we possess, are invincible by any force
> which our enemy can send against us.
>
> Besides, sir, we fight not our battles alone. There is a just
> God who presides over the destinies of nations....

Our battle is no less great; our enemy is no less formidable.
But our God is greater than any force known to this planet. The
question is not whether He has the power to give us victory, but
whether we have the commitment to achieve victory. The question is not whether winning America back to God is feasible, but

whether we are willing to sacrifice ourselves to living lives that stand for truth, regardless of the personal cost. When we can answer that, then, and only then, can we offer hope to a nation that is racing toward hopelessness.

c━━◆━━っ

Serving the State, Upholding the Church

When we look at the work of the Lord throughout history, the relationship between man and God comes into sharper focus. When God moves mightily, and His people believe and act faithfully, revival explodes. But with genuine spiritual revival also comes social, political, and moral reformation. Jesus did not preach a divided gospel. His truth was truth for all spheres of life.

Our Savior did not preach one truth to the fisherman, and another for the soldier, and yet another for the political leader. His truth is equally applicable for the construction worker and the artist. We are the ones who try to segregate the secular and the sacred aspects of life, the things of God from the political sphere in which we live.

We often hear that Jesus did not tell His disciples to get involved in politics. That is true, but He did send His disciples out to "heal the sick, raise the dead, cleanse the lepers, cast out demons" (Matthew 10:8). These acts of public and private good were inseparable from, and an integral part of, their command to preach that "the kingdom of heaven is at hand."

When we go forth into the world, we do so not only to preach His Word, but to live it out in practical situations. When we work and pray toward the goal of spiritual revival, we are working toward the salvation of souls. But the practical effect of revival is the reforming power of the gospel on a decaying culture.

Such a revival broke out in England in the 1700s. Spiritual revival, the "Great Awakening," broke out in America about the same time. In England, William Law had written a pamphlet called *A Serious Call to a Devout and Holy Life* in 1728, calling on Christians to become consecrated in personal holiness, develop personal relationships with Christ, and commit to the work of the "Great Commission." It greatly affected the likes of John and Charles Wesley and George Whitefield. A powerful evangelical movement began sweeping through England. The practical effects of this evangelical revival were enormous. Throughout England the poor were helped, work was distributed to the unemployed, hospitals for the sick were established, schools were created, and literacy was increased.

This revival also caused evangelists to spring up across Great Britain. They would roam through the countryside and villages, spreading the gospel. One villager, James Taylor, was a skeptic. When a Christian preacher came to his village sharing the good news, Taylor's heart was touched and he accepted Christ as Savior. Taylor not only won his new bride to Christ, but he raised a legacy of Christian families that spanned 200 years. James Taylor's great-grandson was Hudson Taylor, who helped open China to the Gospel.

It was at this time that John Wesley, one of the prominent forces in the evangelical revival, was preaching fiercely against one of England's most profitable, yet abominable evils—slavery. A group of Christian activists, "the Clapham Sect," who lived in Clapham, a village just south of London, came together to put their "shoe leather" to the gospel message. Several of the members were involved in establishing the British and Foreign Bible Society and the Church Missionary Society. But perhaps their most dramatic victory was ridding the British Empire of the slave trade.

William Wilberforce, an influential member of Parliament, eventually moved to Clapham. He was converted to Christ in 1784 and became a member of the "Clapham Sect." John Newton, the slave-trader-turned-preacher, was one of Wilberforce's advisors, and he urged him to fight for the good of the nation. By 1787, Wilberforce was convinced that God was directing him to use his political influence to fight against the evils of slavery.

This was a formidable task. England reaped the economic bounty at home as a result of slave trade overseas, particularly in the West Indies. Opponents to abolition argued that some two-thirds of England's economy was tied to slavery. Wilberforce brought his first antislavery bill before Parliament in 1787. But even with the help of his college friend and the new prime minister William Pitt, the power of the proslavery lobby was too strong. His bill was defeated in the 1789 session.

Wilberforce pushed on. From 1787 through 1806, he and other Christian activists who were convinced of the righteousness of their cause continued to force the issue in a hostile Parliament. Wilberforce was ridiculed in the press. He was vilified by opponents. But popular support was growing. A citizen's boycott of plantation-grown sugar caught the attention of politicians. Petitions containing hundreds of thousands of signatures opposing slavery were being circulated throughout England.

Finally, in 1807 both the House of Lords and the House of Commons passed a law outlawing the slave trade on British lands and territories. However, slaves and their children who were working the British plantations in the West Indies were to remain in bondage, so the institution of slavery was still legal.

Though he retired from politics in 1825, William Wilberforce continued to fight for the total and absolute eradication of slavery. His health declined, but he fought on. In 1833, as he approached death, he knew that the Bill for the Abolition of Slavery was moving toward passage in the Parliament. Finally, in August of that year, one month after William Wilberforce died, the House of Commons passed the bill. Slavery was abolished throughout Great Britain, and all slaves within British lands and territories were emancipated.

Christians Can Make a Difference

The legacy of William Wilberforce is not limited merely to the great causes he advanced, though his mark is considerable. Wilberforce bore the irrepressible distinction of lifestyle evangelism. He didn't simply "do Christian politics." Rather, he lived out the truth of the gospel even though embroiled in a controversial battle pitting him against tough (and, many times, ruthless) opponents.

In the heart of London there is no more impressive building than Westminster Abbey. This huge, ancient cathedral contains busts, statutes, and memorials to such luminaries as William Shakespeare, William Wordsworth, and the kings and queens of English history. Among those tributes, these words appear in memory of William Wilberforce: "He added the abiding eloquence of a Christian life." Wilberforce's life reminds us to conduct ourselves so as to illuminate the cause of Christ, who must always be the force behind the public cause.

Slavery was not merely a political issue for Wilberforce. It was simply part and parcel of his calling, as a disciple of Jesus Christ, to do the truth of the gospel within his sphere of influence and with all of his might. It took 46 years for the antislavery position to prevail. The battle outlived the man himself. But in the long term, his Christian faith made a difference. There is a lesson for the Christian Church here.

Two decades ago, evangelicals woke up to the fact that our culture and our system of government had been abandoned, to a great degree, by Bible-believing Christians. Our public schools were enclaves of anti-Christian secularism, our courts had been responding to a parade of ACLU-led lawsuits, and our cultural and social institutions were reflecting a worldview antagonistic to the core values of the Judeo-Christian tradition. But after we have fought these battles for some 20 years, we have grown weary. You can see it and feel it in the churches: Abortion is still legal; pornography is still rampant. The assault on parental and traditional family rights is constant. The wall of "separation of Church and State" is still used to segregate religious expression from much of our public life.

Perhaps we expected that simple Christian involvement would be the "silver bullet," like some quick and easy way to put down America's problems overnight. If that is the case, then we have been ignorant of the history of Christian statesmen. We must be prepared to dedicate a lifetime to the impact of truth on our nation.

America's Christian roots have much to teach us. While England was experiencing its evangelical revival, the "Great Awakening" was spreading through the American colonies. Jonathan Edwards, a brilliant theologian, was also a powerful gospel preacher. He had a profound affect on the spiritual direction of our nation in the decades prior to the American Revolution. While political ties between Great Britain and America became increasingly strained in the years 1740 to 1776, the evangelical and spiritual ties became stronger. George Whitefield, the great preacher from England, migrated to America in 1738 and traveled across the new land spreading the gospel.

In 1767, a delegation from the College of New Jersey sailed from the colonies to Paisley, Scotland. The College of New Jersey (later called Princeton University) was one of America's most prestigious colleges. Its newly selected president was Jonathan Edwards, but Edwards died from smallpox shortly after beginning his duties there. The delegation began looking for a new college president.

The man they were traveling to see in Scotland was John Witherspoon, the evangelical pastor of Laigh Kirk. His church was large, seating some 1300 people, and Witherspoon had been preaching his evangelistic messages to large crowds there for 11 years. The delegation urged him to accept the vacant presidency of their college, and Witherspoon was enthusiastic, but his wife Elizabeth was reluctant to make the move. The group sailed back to America without a president, but during the next year Elizabeth Witherspoon finally consented. In 1768, John Witherspoon began his duties as the president of New Jersey College.

That event would have a profound impact on the future of America. In the following 26 years of his leadership, 478 men graduated. Of those, more than 100 became pastors, 13 became governors, 53 would later serve in either the United States Senate or the House of Representatives, and 3 became Supreme Court justices. Among his students were Aaron Burr, Jr., who would become vice-president, and James Madison, a future U.S. president and the chief architect of the Constitution.

Witherspoon's duties were not merely administrative. He carried a full teaching load on subjects as diverse and timely as Bible, history, and law. John Adams once spent a day listening to him and had praise for his approach to spiritual matters. The duty of the Christian citizen, to John Witherspoon, was clear. Just as national sin makes a nation "ripe for divine judgment," so also the "reformation of manners" therefore [personal conduct—both private and public] becomes the business of the Church.

It is highly significant that Witherspoon called believers to be involved in a "reformation of manners," which was the 18th-century way of referring to matters of social morality and public policy. William Wilberforce had shared this same credo. Wilberforce had once written that God had called him to important goals: "the abolition of the slave trade and the reformation of manners."

John Witherspoon put this philosophy into action. He was selected as a delegate to the Continental Congress leading up to the Declaration of Independence, of which he was a signer. He preached in support of the cause of American independence, and sacrificed two sons who were killed in battles for that cause. His sermon, "Address to the Natives of Scotland Residing in America," argued for the support of Scotsmen in America's fight for national sovereignty.

In a sermon to his college entitled "The Dominion of Providence over the Passions of Men," just two months before he would sign his name to the Declaration of Independence, Witherspoon set forth the theological, moral, and political case for American independence. In so doing, he commented on the relationship between religious liberty and civil liberty. These are words that America should have taken to heart in this last century: "God grant that in America true religion and civil liberty may be inseparable, and that the unjust attempts to destroy the one may in the issue tend to the support and [or] the establishment of the other."[1]

After the Revolutionary War was won, Witherspoon's worldview of Christian citizenship continued to influence America. A full one-sixth of the delegates to the Constitutional Convention in 1787 were his students. The most prominent was James Madison, whose concept of separation of powers, which is the foundation of our system of tripartite government, was learned while a student at the college.

To Witherspoon, the relationship between civil liberties and religious freedom seemed inseparable. He once wrote: "There is not a single instance in history, in which civil liberty was lost, and religious liberty preserved entire." To fight for the freedom to continue preaching the gospel, one must be willing to oppose tyranny and injustice. The rule of law protects not only our earthly interests; it also protects our ability to spread a heavenly message.

John Adams, one of America's most notable Founding Fathers, called John Witherspoon "a true son of liberty." In the end, Witherspoon was simply putting into practice the true freedom of the gospel. His legacy shows us what can happen when that gospel power is unleashed in a life dedicated to the service of his nation, the Church, and his God.

The Future of America

So, where does that bring us 223 years after the signing of the Declaration of Independence? That document proclaimed an oath to the principle of "inalienable rights" which are "endowed by our Creator." The men who signed that document pledged their lives, their fortunes, and their "sacred honor." The question today is whether our nation has strayed so far from these basic concepts that the idea of revival and reformation are unrealistic fantasies.

When we watched the televised proceedings of the Senate impeachment trial of President Clinton, the polls were telling us that the American people did not care, that the vast majority of us simply wanted to put the whole matter behind us. We believe the trial of President Clinton will have an impact on the future of America. It will also have an impact on the Christian Church. If we ignore the implications of what went on in the Senate, and what will be said in the news media and in the college classrooms about this historic event, our influence on this fallen nation may be destroyed. Many Americans have found the whole episode distasteful or confusing, and many have concluded it was a massive waste of time, energy, and public money. But one thing is certain: If we miss the lessons of this event for the coming decades, we will regret it to our last day.

No sooner had Chief Justice William Rehnquist announced the final vote of the Senate, which failed to convict President Clinton on the impeachment charges of obstruction of justice and perjury, than the national media launched into the telltale dia-tribe. The message of all three major networks, National Public Radio, and the liberal pundits everywhere was unified and twofold. First, we were told that America was breathing a collective sigh of relief that this "national nightmare" was over. It had dominated our prime-time television and interfered with our desire for diver-sion and entertainment. Lacking in entertainment value, this late unpleasantness is now happily to be forgotten. Second, the "night-mare" was not really the illegal and immoral conduct of a presi-dent whom even the Democrats condemned. The "nightmare" was the fault of the messengers—and the messengers were the conservatives. Behind the conservatives, we were told, was the Clinton-hating "Christian right" of the Republican Party.

There will be a backlash; and it is heading to an area near you. You can choose to ignore the backlash, but that will require you maintain a position of silence and acquiescence toward the decay and corruption of American culture. You are free to grumble to one another about the state of America at Wednesday-night Bible study or after church service on Sunday, but nothing more. Or you can take a stand for Christ. To put the truth-claims of the Bible into action will put you right into the path of the hurricane that will hit us in the next presidential election. It is bound to hit us with one or two more liberal appointments to the Supreme Court. It is the force of that hurricane that will hit you when you are identified at the next school-board meeting or the next town hall meeting as one of the "Christian right." When you are associated with the cause of our national "nightmare" or are targeted as one of the causes of our American unpleasantness, you'll feel what it's like to be caught in a strong whirlwind.

There is no handy escape route. When you try to live a life that stakes a claim for the truth of the gospel, Satan's power will be unleashed. You may have to fight against the financial warlords of the status quo and be ridiculed like William Wilberforce. You may be called to leave "kith and kin" like John Witherspoon, putting behind you those things that are most familiar and comfortable so your influence can have an impact where it is most needed in the battle for liberty.

The question is not so much where you go, or what you do, or what political party you support in the next millennium. The great question is who you serve and how faithfully you are willing to serve, even if it makes you the target of the slings and arrows of a hostile culture.

EPILOGUE

c═╪═ɔ

Living with
Tough Faith

Throughout this book we have been exploring the possible scenarios of the future and the perils and challenges they may present to the Christian. But now we would like to refocus the camera lens from the wide-angle to the close-up. We would like to take a look at "tough faith" not from the vantage point of the distant and the future, but from the personal and the present.

Although the ground at Calvary is ever level, the paths that lead there are infinite in variety and topography. Some of us come to the Savior as young children, while others wind through the hills and valleys of life before we seek His saving grace. In the same way, while we are told in Ephesians 4:5 that there is "one Lord, one faith, one baptism," nevertheless there are an infinite variety of human stories that pass through this common faith in Christ.

We came to the subject of "tough faith" from two perspectives. The first was a perspective of reluctance. Frankly, we would rather have written about leisure times than tough times. "Comfortable faith" seems a great deal less stressful than "tough faith." But that would ignore what faith is really about. The kind of faith that is real is also muscular; it is active rather than passive. The second perspective we have on "tough faith" involves some personal experience in the classroom of life. You probably know the classroom we are talking about—that same hard, cold place to which the Lord takes us when it's time to grow.

We both went to the same junior high school. Back then there were a number of classrooms in an old annex building that dated back to the turn of the century. The floors were warped and wooden. The chairs were uncomfortable. In the winter the wind blew through the poorly insulated walls. The ceilings were very high, so whatever heat there was must have hovered up there because it never seemed to reach us. Learning in that room always seemed to be a dreaded thing. The interesting thing though, as we type the last few lines of this book, is that we realize we both learned to type on those big, clumsy typewriters in that dreaded room.

One night, not too long ago, we were both fast asleep when a flash of light awakened us, coming from the driveway just outside our bedroom. We looked out and saw a police car parked there, its radio crackling and engine running. It was 3:00 A.M., and immediately our minds started racing. The doorbell rang, and we made our way to the front door, where two sheriff's deputies greeted us. They tipped their hats somberly. Something terrible had happened. We were entering the classroom.

The older of the two deputies stepped inside and asked the kind of question every parent dreads to hear: "Do you have a son by the name of ..." We nodded. He proceeded to explain that our oldest boy, a second-year college student, had just been shot in the head at point-blank range. We were stunned. At the time, the deputy had few facts to tell us. He could not verify whether our son was alive or dead. He could not tell us how, or why it had happened.

We would later discover that he had been visiting a college friend at the other end of the state. The friend decided to show-off the handgun his father had given him. The gun was loaded, and while our son was stretched out on the couch next to him watching television, it accidentally discharged. The bullet entered our son's head just below his right ear, and in one slow motion he fell off the couch and onto the floor, and the blood started pouring out of the bullet hole in his skull. His friend, hysterical, called 911. The ambulance took him to the nearest hospital, where a medivac helicopter flew him, unconscious and nonresponsive, to the bigger regional hospital that housed a head trauma unit.

But we knew none of this at the time. All we knew is that we were staring at the piece of paper the deputy had given us with a telephone number written on it. It was the number for another police department that was in contact with the hospital. As we called, we knew that whatever we heard at the other end of the telephone, good or bad, the miraculous or the unimaginable, would be what the Lord had designed.

The voice at the other end asked us to identify ourselves. We did, and she quickly wanted to reassure us that our precious son was still alive. She transferred our call to the telephone just outside the room where he was about to undergo surgery. We were connected to a nurse who told us that the surgeon was about to start working on our child. We gave her our car phone number and told her that we would start driving to the hospital immediately. We then woke our younger son, tried to break the news to him as gently as possible, threw a few things in the car, and the three of us sped off.

The hospital was 200 miles away. As we drove through the night we were praying and praying and praying. There were long periods of silence when the only sound was the wheels of the car on the road. In the darkness, the little glow of the car phone light reminded us that we were waiting for a call that could change our lives.

And then the phone rang. It was the surgeon. Samuel, our son, would survive. When we finally arrived at the hospital, the surgeon was waiting for us. To our joy, he told us that the bullet had literally done a "U-turn" at impact, exiting at the back of his skull without actually penetrating the brain. It was as if the finger of God had reached down in front of that flying piece of steel and redirected it. God had said, "No. This is not the time. This is not the place."

We thought that the learning was over. We had our son back from the edge of the grave. But the learning was just beginning. After discharge from the hospital he had partial paralysis and could not walk by himself. His equilibrium was off, and every movement was a crazy, carnival-house kind of misstep. One arm and hand were useless. One of his eyes seemed to focus off in the distance. The other eye had a strange and constant tremor. His speech was slurred. But the worst thing was the unremitting head pain. Despite medication, the pain was a constant reality, and it spiked to terrible proportions at night. We took turns sleeping on the floor of our son's bedroom to be with him, feeling helpless while he moaned in pain.

One night he bolted upright, half awake, and asked, "Is Jesus in the room?" When we reassured him, he fell back asleep.

After a while we started testing him at the medical college. It was then that the full range of damage started to become apparent. He had, at least initially, lost much of his sense of taste, smell, hearing, and sight. It was hard to believe that he could ever fully recover, but he never complained. Not once. There was only the determination on his part to become whole again and the willingness to believe that God was truly in control. The child became the teacher. The parents were the students. Tough faith was the course.

Today, after many months of physical rehabilitation, hard work, and prayer, Samuel has made a miraculous recovery; so miraculous that upon meeting him you would find it incredible to believe that the incident had ever happened. The road our family traveled together has toughened our faith, but we would not have chosen it ourselves. The roads that are the most challenging are rarely those we enjoy.

The future of America is coming. The new century will break upon us, with or without our consent. It will undoubtedly hold challenges beyond the ability of anyone to imagine. But two things are clear—our future will be closer to the horrible tests that will come at the end of human history, but also closer to the magnificent and blessed reign of Jesus Christ. With what kind of faith will we greet that future?

John Harper, who preached the gospel on the *Titanic*, faced the last hours of his life with the essence of tough faith. We think about that as we reflect on the little chapel in Glasgow, Scotland, that is named for him. It is a humble redbrick church surrounded by factories and low-rent housing in the industrial section of the city. A great several-stories-high crane, with its steel beams and outstretched mechanical arm, looms in the background.

This chapel, much like its namesake, is a modest little structure, but it is placed in the right part of town. Like Harper, it is located where the real people live and struggle and die. That is how John Harper lived out the last hours of his life—with real people, ministering to their most important need. In his tough faith, he kept an unflinching focus on Jesus Christ, right down to his last breath.

While bobbing in the frigid sea, with no life jacket, clinging onto debris of the ship that littered the surface after the great *Titanic* had sunk, John Harper spotted a man drifting near him, clinging desperately to a board. Harper, himself barely able to stay afloat, yelled out, "Are you saved?"

"No!" the man answered.

Then Harper replied, "Believe on the Lord Jesus Christ and thou shall be saved."

The man drifted into the blackness of the night.

Later, he drifted back again, closer to Harper. Though slowly freezing to death, John once again shouted out, "Are you saved?"

"No!" came the answer again. And again, Harper urged him, "Believe on the Lord Jesus Christ and thou shalt be saved."

Eventually John Harper was unable to hang on any longer. Frozen from the icy waters of the Atlantic, and without the life vest that he had given to another, he slipped under the surface of the dark water. As John Harper entered eternity with the Lord, the other man, still drifting on the surface, relented and placed his faith in the saving power of Christ.

Later that night the S.S. *Carpathia* arrived. It was the ship that had come to pick up the drifting orphans of the lost *Titanic*. The man on the board was one of them. After being rescued, he declared himself to have been "Harper's last convert."

That is the amazing paradox of tough faith—the essence of being as resilient as granite to the terrible storms of life, while at the same time maintaining the tenderness and compassion of Jesus toward a perishing world. It means keeping our eyes focused intensely on why we are here and on Him who has purchased us, forgiven us, sanctified us, and sent us out into this troubled world with the saving message for the ages. When the storms blow, and the waves rage around us, it is this truth to which we cling. It is the simplicity of Jesus Christ that is available to every drowning sinner. And it is our tough faith that will allow Him to use us to pull those poor wretches to safety.

In the end, tough faith means giving away our life jackets in the midst of disaster, and it means being willing to tell the truth when we see the ship sinking. It means taking a stand for Jesus Christ, even in the face of pain and death. Yet when we enter His gates and meet Him face to face, He will say those words that are more precious than gold and more enduring than silver: "Well done thou good and faithful servant."

That's the reward for tough faith.

A Final Word for Those Who Have
Not Begun the Pilgrim's Faith

Do you know what your future holds? We are not talking about the future in the sense of all the small little details in your life...We mean the big picture. How do you see yourself fitting into the big picture of life? The Bible says it is appointed for every one of us to die, and after that comes judgment.

Thinking about "judgment day" is not politically correct today. But correct or not, it is a reality. There are really only two ways of looking at our long-term future. On the one hand we can dread it, worry about it, try to avoid thinking about it altogether, and attempt to fill our lives with the busyness of careers, financial security, the pursuit of pleasure, power, and relationships, in order to pretend our lives will continue forever. Or we can trust God for our futures. The former focuses on just this life. The latter focuses on eternity.

You can know that there is a God who loves you, and who holds your future in His hands. When you choose that way, you can look forward to spending eternity with a Heavenly Father who has prepared a glorious future for you.

But that second path has an obstacle. The Bible tells us that every one of us has fallen short of the moral standard God requires. In order for us to become part of His family and enter into a personal relationship with Him, something has to happen to our sin. While He is an infinitely Loving Lord, He is also an infinitely Holy Lord. We are sinners, but He is perfectly sinless. Therefore we are separated and estranged from Him. We cannot make ourselves acceptable to Him by our own efforts any more than He can make Himself less than Holy by lowering His moral standards. Thus there is a great dilemma, a wide canyon separating us from God. Something in our hearts longs to be on the other side of the canyon with Him, to rid ourselves of the guilt and failures of sin. We have the feeling that if we could connect with Him, it would be like finding our way back home.

The good news is that He is a God of miraculous solutions. The Lord has prepared a secure bridge over that wide canyon— His son, Jesus Christ. The Bible says that He came down to earth as a perfect sacrifice for our sins. He died on the cross and paid the penalty for us, so that we can receive the forgiveness of sins and therefore be made acceptable to a Loving and Holy God. Being both God and Man, Jesus Christ did for us what we could not do for ourselves. He has prepared the path that connects us to God. That path begins with our recognition that we are sinners and we enter onto it when we make a confession of faith in Jesus Christ as the Son of God who died for us. You can pray to Him at this very moment and accept Him as Lord and Savior of your life.

The choice is yours. According to Revelation 3:20, Jesus Christ is saying: "Behold I stand at the door and knock; if anyone hears the sound of My voice and opens the door, I will come in to him, and will dine with him and he with Me." Why not answer the door, and secure your future right now?

NOTES

Introduction

1. *The Life Millennium: The 100 Most Important Events & People of the Past 1,000 Years* (New York: Life Books, 1998), p. 188.
2. *Civil Rights Journal*, Fall 1997, p. 36.

Chapter 1

1. Kitty Ferguson, *The Fire in the Equations: Science, Religion & the Search for God* (Grand Rapids, MI: Wm. B. Eerdmans, 1994), p. 239.
2. Stephen Hawkins, *A Brief History of Time* (New York: Bantam Books, 1996), p. 149.
3. A.E. Wilder Smith, *Man's Origin, Man's Destiny: A Critical Survey of the Principals of Evolution and Christianity* (Wheaton, IL: Harold Shaw Publishers, 1968), pp. 133-34; *Nature*, Nov. 28, 1953, p. 981.
4. Paul Harvey, "A Time to Be Alive," *Imprimis* 27(10):2 (Oct. 1998).
5. Stephen Meyer, *The Wall Street Journal*, Monday, Dec. 6, 1993.
6. *The Washington Times*, April 10, 1998, p. A9.

Chapter 2

1. Francis A. Schaeffer, *The Church at the End of the Twentieth Century* (Downers Grove, IL: InterVarsity Press, 1970), p. 53.

Chapter 3

1. Lisa Miller, "The Age of Divine Disunity," *Wall Street Journal*, Feb. 10, 1999, p. B1.
2. Deepak Chopra and Richard Moss, *What Is Personal Transformation*, Spring (1998), p. 51.
3. Cited in Peter Jones, *Spirit Wars: Pagan Revival in Christian America* (1997), pp. 45-46, quoting a letter of Ferguson's documented in Constance Cumbey's *Hidden Dangers of the Rainbow* (Shreveport, LA: Huntington House, 1983), p. 147.
4. Patricia Elam, "Buddhism Lighted the Way to the Joy Within," *Washington Post*, Oct. 10, 1998, p. B9.

Notes

Chapter 4

1. Michael J. Wilkins and J.P. Moreland, *Jesus Under Fire* (Grand Rapids, MI: Zondervan Publishing House, 1995), p. 1.
2. Robert W. Funk and The Jesus Seminar, *The Acts of Jesus: What Did Jesus Really Do?* (San Francisco, CA: Harper Collins, 1998), p. 5.
3. Robert Goss, *Jesus Acted Up: A Gay and Lesbian Manifesto* (1993), p. 85, cited in Elizabeth Stuart, *Religion Is a Queer Thing* (London: Cassell, 1997), p. 77.
4. Ibid., p. 84.
5. For more on this topic, see Merrill Unger, *Unger's Commentary on the Old Testament*, vol. 1 (Chicago: Moody Press, 1981), p. 66.
6. Enrique T. Rueda, *The Homosexual Network: Private Lives and Public Policy* (Old Greenwich, CN: The Devin Adair Co., 1982), p. 259.
7. Rita Gross, *Feminism & Religion* (Beacon Press, 1996), p. 212.
8. Elisabeth Schussler Fiorenza, *Jesus: Miriam's Child, Sophia's Prophet* (London: SCM Press, 1994), p. 178.
9. Mary Daly, *Pure Lust: Elemental Feminist Philosophy* (London/Boston: Women's Print Ltd., 1984), p. 74.
10. James C. Dobson, "Spooked by the Zietgieist: Don't Give in to the Feminist Pressure to Rewrite the Scriptures," *World*, May 3/10, 1997, p. 30. See also *World*, March 29, 1997, pp. 2-15; April 19, 1997, pp. 14-18; May 31, 1997, p. 16; June 14, 1997, p. 20; June 17, 1997, pp. 3-17.
11. Phil Roberts, "Tempest in a Teapot?"—"Conservatives Question Evangelical-Catholic Pact," *National Liberty Journal*, June 1998, p. 1.
12. Robert A. Sungenis, *Not by Faith Alone* (Santa Barbara, CA: Queenship, 1996), pp. 599-600.

Chapter 6

1. Tal Brooke, *Lord of the Air: Tales of a Modern Antichrist* (Eugene, OR: Harvest House Publishers, 1990), p. 17.
2. Ibid., p. 344.
3. Ibid., p. 351.

Chapter 7

1. Williston Walker, Richard Norris, David Lotz, and Robert Handy, *A History of the Christian Church*, 4th ed. (New York: Scribner and Sons, 1985), p. 71.
2. Jack George Sayer, *C.S. Lewis and His Times* (New York: Harper and Row, 1988), pp. 134-35.

Chapter 8

1. For details on Christian persecution in Sudan, see Cal R. Bombay, *Let My People Go! (The true story of present-day persecution and slavery)* (Sisters, OR: Multnomah Publishers, 1998), p. 21.
2. Mindy Belz, "The Modern Martyrs: The International Crisis of Religious Persecution Takes No Break as Washington Deliberates Its Response," *World*, Nov. 1, 1997, p. 15.
3. Neelesh Misra, "Missionary Mourned in India," Associated Press, January 24, 1999.
4. Charles Colson, *Breakpoint*, May 1998, p. 12.
5. "U.S. Courts China While Anti-Christian Persecution Rages," *The First Freedom*, May 1998, p. 2.

Chapter 10

1. See, for example, Walker, Norris, Lotz, and Handy, *A History of the Christian Church*, p. 80.
2. Debra Evans, *Six Qualities of Women of Character* (Grand Rapids, MI: Zondervan, 1996), p. 98.
3. John Knox, *The History of the Reformation of Religion Within the Realm of Scotland* (Edinburgh: Banner of Truth Trust, Reprinted 1898), pp. 5-6.
4. Ibid. See also J.H. Baxter's *George Wishart: Reformer and Martyr* (St. Andrew's University, 1946), pp. 8-9.

Chapter 11

1. Curt Suplee, "Past Patterns Suggest a Future 'Megadrought,'" *Washington Post*, Dec. 21, 1998, p. A3.

Chapter 12

1. Ben Wattenberg, *Values Matter Most* (Washington, D.C.: Regnery Publishing, 1996), p. 30.
2. Linda Y.C. Lim, "Whose 'Model' Failed? Implications of the Asian Economic Crisis," *The Washington Quarterly*, Summer 1998, p. 33.
3. *The 500 Year Delta: What Happens After What Comes Next* (New York: Harper Business, 1997), pp. 270-73.
4. Hamish McRae, *The World in 2020: Power, Culture and Prosperity* (Boston: Harvard Business School Press, 1996), p. 276.
5. CNN Interactive, June 26, 1998, p. 1.
6. Alvin Toffler, *Power Shift: Knowledge, Wealth, and Violence at the Edge of the 21st Century* (New York: Bantam Books, 1991), p. 418.
7. *The 500 Year Delta*, pp. 237-38.
8. Ibid., p. 254.
9. Alexander Solzhenitsyn, "A World Split Apart," commencement address, Harvard University, June 8, 1978.

10. Alexander Solzhenitsyn, Nobel lecture, 1972, The Nobel Foundation, pp. 24-25.

Chapter 13

1. Jim Bakker, *Prosperity and the Coming Apocalypse* (Nashville: Thomas Nelson Publishers, 1998), p. 23.
2. Ron Blue, *Master Your Money* (Nashville: Thomas Nelson Publishers, 1986), p. 219.
3. Russell Chandler, *Racing Toward 2001* (Grand Rapids, MI: Zondervan Publishers, 1992), p. 136.

Chapter 14

1. *The Starr Report: The Official Report of the Independent Counsel's Investigation of the President* (Rocklin, CA: Forum/Prima Publishing, 1998), p. 53, citing Quinn's statement from CBS's "Face the Nation," as reported by John F. Harris, "In Political Washington, A Confession Consensus," *Washington Post*, Aug. 4, 1998, p. A1, emphasis added.
2. Alexis de Tocqueville, *Democracy in America*, vol. 1, Francis Bowen, ed. (New York: Vintage Books, 1945), p. 315.
3. Riesman and Eichel, *Kinsey, Sex and Fraud* (Lafayette, LA: Huntinghouse Publishers, 1990), p. 3.
4. Patterson & Kim, *The Day America Told the Truth* (New York: Prentice Hall, 1991), p. 94.
5. Final Report of the Attorney General's Commission on Pornography (Nashville: Rutledge Hill Press, 1988), p. 40.
6. Milwaukee Police Department Incident Report #91-51767/M-2472-2482/ Sec. 5, p. 132 (Aug. 8, 1991).
7. Robert Bork, *Slouching Towards Gomorrah: Modern Liberalism and American Decline* (New York: Harper Collins, 1996), p. 149.

Chapter 15

1. Lawrence Tribe, *Abortion: The Clash of Absolutes* (New York: W.W. Norton, 1990), p. 215.
2. *New York Times* magazine, July 21, 1996, section 6.
3. Ibid.
4. James C. Dobson, "Phoenix Address," Council for National Policy, Oct. 1997.

Chapter 16

1. Erwin Lutzer, *Why the Cross Can Do What Politics Can't Do* (Eugene, OR: Harvest House Publishers, 1999), p. 34.
2. Lewis Sperry Chaeffer, *Systematic Theology*, vol. 2 (Dallas: Dallas Seminary Press, 1947), p. 329.
3. Ibid., p. 330.

4. Charles R. Swindoll, *Growing Deep in the Christian Life* (Portland, OR: Multnomah Press, 1986), p. 290.

5. Francis Schaeffer, *The Finished Work of Christ*, Udo Middelmann, ed. (Wheaton, IL: Crossway Books, 1998), p. 193.

Chapter 17

1. Lester J. Cappon, ed., *The Adams-Jefferson Letters* (Chapel Hill, NC: University of North Carolina Press, 1987), pp. 339-40, emphasis added.

2. *Jane Doe Individually and as next of friend for her minor children, Jane and John Doe, Minor Children v. Santa Fe Independent School District, et al.*, U.S. District Court for the Southern District of Texas, Galveston Division, case no. G-95-176, Transcript of Excerpt of Proceedings, pp. 3-4.

3. 1, Annals of Congress, p. 434, June 8, 1789, emphasis added.

4. See Daniel L. Driesbach, *Real Threat and Mere Shadow: Religious Liberty and the First Amendment* (Winchester, IL: Crossway Books, 1987), p. 58.

Chapter 18

1. *Lend Me Your Ears: Great Speeches in History*, William Safire, ed. (New York: W.W. Norton, 1992), p. 430.

Other Good Harvest House Reading

Why the Cross Can Do What Politics Can't
Erwin Lutzer

A powerful and incredibly relevant release from bestselling author Erwin W. Lutzer, *Why the Cross Can Do What Politics Can't* takes a realistic look at our rapidly disintegrating society and asks "How can I, as a Christian, bring about positive change?"

Darwin's Leap of Faith
John Ankerberg & John Weldon

Ankerberg and Weldon present the major arguments against evolution, including fossil and scientific support, provide the facts on the day-age theory, the gap theory, and progressive creationism, and examine the evidence for creationism.

Occult Invasion
Dave Hunt

Channeling, extraterrestrials, mystic religions, and psychology are infiltrating our schools, homes, and churches. Hunt gives signs to look for and practical steps for countering this invasion.